THE IMPACT OF THE CIVIL WAR

A Series Planned By
The Civil War Centennial Commission

The Public Good

THE IMPACT OF THE CIVIL WAR

[THE CIVIL WAR CENTENNIAL COMMISSION SERIES]

Planned by Allan Nevins

Edited by Harold M. Hyman

THE PUBLIC
GOOD

Philanthropy and Welfare
in the Civil War Era

by Robert H. Bremner

New York: Alfred · A · Knopf

1 9 8 0

THIS IS A BORZOI BOOK
PUBLISHED BY ALFRED A. KNOPF, INC.

LIBRARY OF CONGRESS CATALOGING IN PUBLICATION DATA
Bremner, Robert H. (Date)
The public good, philanthropy and welfare
in the Civil War era. (The Impact of the Civil War)
Bibliography: p.   Includes index.
1.   Public welfare—United States—History—19th century.
2.   Charities—United States—History—19th century.
3.   United States—History—Civil War, 1861–1865—War work.
I.   Title.   II.   Series: Impact of the Civil War.
HV91.B684   1980   361'.973   80–7623
ISBN 0–394–51123–9

Manufactured in the United States of America
FIRST EDITION

FOR STUDENTS

PAST AND PRESENT

Contents

Illustrations

The illustrations will be found following page 76
in the order indicated below.

ILLUSTRATIONS

Introduction

In a sermon delivered in 1824 Henry Ware, a Unitarian minister in Boston, cited ten eminent philanthropists whose example, he said, should be kept before the public so that others might be stimulated "*to go and do likewise.*" Ware used the word "philanthropist" to cover "those who have devoted their fortunes, or consecrated their labors, or expended their strength, or hazarded their lives, for the consolation of sufferers, the relief of the poor, the rescue of the exposed, the salvation of the perishing." His list included three wealthy English donors active in the seventeenth and eighteenth centuries, John Kyrle, Edward Colston, and Richard Reynolds; two religious leaders—St. Vincent de Paul and John Wesley—who preached and practiced charity; an American-born scientist, inventor, and administrator, Benjamin Thompson, Count Rumford, who eradicated mendicity while relieving the poor of Bavaria; and four reformers, two remembered for their part in the struggle against slavery and the slave trade (Anthony Benezet, an American, and Thomas Clarkson of England) and two for their efforts to improve conditions in prisons (John Howard and Elizabeth Fry).

Ware had kind words to say about all ten, from Kyrle (1637–1724), who, on a modest income, "accomplished almost prodigies of beneficence," and Colston (1636–1721), a Bristol merchant who bestowed charities "not in tens only, nor in hundreds, but in thousands,—on one occasion in the splendid gift of *twenty thousand* pounds"—to Elizabeth Fry (1780–1845), "the reformer of Newgate . . . who has changed its confusion and filth into order and industry." Appropriately, since his sermon was delivered in observance of the anniversary of the Howard Benevolent Society in Boston, Ware saved his choicest praise for John Howard (1726–1790). For many Americans in the first two-thirds of the nineteenth century, this English country gentleman turned inspector of prisons and hospitals, often referred to simply as "Howard, the philanthropist," was the exemplar and epitome of philanthropy. He never visited the United States, but streets in American cities were named in his honor, and charitable and benevolent societies from Boston to New Orleans adopted his name as theirs. As late as 1872 Henry W. Bellows, who will appear frequently in the following pages, declared that "the name of Howard has become the synonym of philanthropy. It stands for universal mercy, world-wide sympathy, and absolute consecration to human service."[1]

This study follows Ware's example and nineteenth-century practice in adopting a definition of philanthropist broad enough to include both givers and doers, advocates and administrators. Discussion will not be limited to the 10 or even 100 preeminent philanthropists of the Civil War era because long before the middle of the nineteenth century Americans had been conducting their philanthropic affairs not just as individuals but in associations. "We have societies for everything," declared James Walker in 1825. "Scarcely a month passes in which we are not called upon to join, or aid, some benevolent association." Today we would change "scarcely a month" to "scarcely a day" and "some" to "several," but we know what Walker meant, and we can appreciate his examination of the pros and cons of associated giving and his efforts to formulate a "wise and consistent" policy for dealing with "this peculiar mode of charity." Ten years before Alexis de Tocqueville commented on the prevalence of associations in American life, Walker (who became president of Harvard in the 1850s) explained their necessity. Many important objects, he noted, could not be obtained in any other way:

> . . . individuals may do much, undoubtedly, as individuals; but there are many publick objects and humane undertakings, which from their nature or magnitude absolutely

---

[1] Henry Ware, Jr.: "Eminent Philanthropists," *Christian Examiner*, vol. II (1825), pp. 18–25; Henry W. Bellows: "John Howard: His Life, Character and Services," in Edwin Pears, ed.: *Prisons and Reformatories at Home and Abroad, Being the Transactions of the International Penitentiary Congress Held in London, 1872* (London, 1872), p. 739.

require the consent and co-operation of numbers. This holds true especially in a country and under institutions like ours. Such is the distribution of property amongst us, and such the nature of our government, that individuals here can never hope to rival the splendid acts of princely munificence sometimes recorded of the old and immensely rich families of other countries; neither can we expect the same degree of legislative patronage. Much, therefore, of good that is effected elsewhere by private munificence, or royal and legislative patronage, can be effected here only by voluntary associations. It is idle to say of this, that it is not our best resource, for we have no other.[2]

As evidence of the advantages and achievements of associated giving, Walker cited "the Bible Clause": "its agents are in every land; its presses are going in every language; its publications are counted by the millions; and its revenues are such as kings might envy." Of the "Missionary Enterprise," which was supported mainly by members of evangelical churches, Walker, a Unitarian, commented coolly: "When it is stated that between two and three millions are annually collected and expended in the almost hopeless attempt to convert the heathen, all must admit the efficacy of the instrument employed, however they may question the wisdom by which it is directed."[3]

While recognizing the usefulness of associations for benevolent purposes, Walker was aware of and did not hesitate to point out the abuses and pitfalls of associated giving. Some of his ob-

---

[2] James Walker: "Associations for Benevolent Purposes," *Christian Examiner*, vol. II (1825), pp. 241–42; *cf.* Alexis de Tocqueville: *Democracy in America*, ed. by J. P. Mayer and Max Lerner (New York, 1966), p. 485:

Americans of all ages, all stations in life, and all types of disposition are forever forming associations. There are not only commercial and industrial associations in which all take part, but others of a thousand different types—religious, moral, serious, futile, very general and very limited, immensely large and very minute. Americans combine to give fetes, found seminaries, build churches, distribute books, and send missionaries to the antipodes. Hospitals, prisons, and schools take shape in that way. Finally, if they want to proclaim a truth or propagate some feeling by the encouragement of a great example, they form an association. In every case, at the head of any new undertaking, where in France you would find the government or in England some territorial magnate, in the United States you are sure to find an association.

[3] Walker: "Associations for Benevolent Purposes," p. 245.

jections have a familiar ring: the possibility of "interior misman-
agement"; exaggerated, false, or misrepresented claims of success;
encouragement of ostentation (rather than benevolence or sense
of duty) on the part of donors; and temptations to "religious
dissipation"—i.e., "the passion for doing good on a grand scale."

> Who cares for the drudgery of family matters [Walker com-
> plained], who cares for the wants of a few poor neighbors,
> or relations, when he has joined a society that promises to
> open the doors of heaven to forty millions of idolaters, that
> would otherwise perish everlastingly! Men like to be busy
> without being industrious, and the remark applies to women
> also. For this cause many will leave their homes and places
> of business, though ever so much wanted there, and make
> themselves abundantly active for one of these societies;
> when there is no want of candour in suspecting, that they
> think more of the society itself, and the excitements attend-
> ing it, than of its object. . . . He, therefore, who neglects his
> family, and the common and everyday duties of justice
> and humanity, will find it but a poor excuse for his de-
> linquency, that he belongs to a thousand societies, and
> is passing generous with other people's money.[4]

In 1835 ten leading American benevolent societies, founded
for the most part between 1810 and 1820, raised slightly more
than $800,000 for distributing Bibles and tracts, sending mis-
sionaries to the heathen at home and abroad, encouraging Sunday schools, educating poor youth as Protestant clergymen, and
colonizing Negroes in Africa. Modest as the figure seems, it sug-
gests the possibility of competition among the benevolent societies for attention and support of the charitable public. Other
national associations, including prison reform, temperance, and
antislavery societies, as well as a large number and wide variety
of local charitable organizations also solicited for funds. By 1829
Philadelphia had such an abundance of good causes pleading for
support that the economist Mathew Carey tried, unsuccessfully,
to organize a united fund drive.[5]

Philanthropy is far from a bland and placid subject. Benevo-

---

[4] *Ibid.*, p. 247.
[5] "Benevolent Institutions," *The American Almanac and Repository of
Useful Knowledge for the Year 1836* (Boston, 1835), p. 177; Mathew
Carey's proposal for federated financing in Philadelphia is reprinted in
The Social Service Review, vol. XXIX (1955), pp. 302–05.

lent organizations offer as many opportunities for internal differences and struggles for power as other human institutions. Rival programs for doing good in this world are often related to contending schools of thought about saving souls for the next and are almost as productive of discord. Certainly contests among and between philanthropic groups to secure and maintain leadership in public support and recognition can be as intense and rancorous as similar struggles in business and politics. In the following pages I have attempted to pay due attention to major philanthropic contests of the Civil War era without burdening readers with excessive detail about the conflicts.

"Social welfare" in the sense of comprehensive programs for the prevention and alleviation of distress caused by poverty, dependency in old age or childhood, and mental illness, retardation, or physical handicap is a phrase that has come into common use only in the twentieth century. Nineteenth-century terms, not quite synonymous with but roughly equivalent to social welfare, were "public relief," "public charities," "charities and corrections," and "care of the dependent, defective, and delinquent classes."

It is sometimes assumed that there is a basic hostility between public and private activities in the field of welfare. Historically, however, relations, if not always harmonious, have been cooperative and complementary rather than antagonistic. Private philanthropists (including voluntary associations) assisted public authorities by assuming responsibility for certain categories or classes of the needy (e.g., aged widows of Methodist ministers or children of Irish Catholic seafarers); public authorities recognized the usefulness of services performed by private charitable organizations by granting them tax exemptions and subsidies from public funds; and in cases involving wills, American courts generally adopted a permissive rather than restrictive attitude toward bequests for "pious and charitable uses."[6] Traditionally Americans assumed that assistance offered by private charity was

---

[6] For the tradition of exempting charitable organizations from tax under state and local law see John P. Persons et al.: "Criteria for Exemption under Section 501 (c) (3)," *Research Papers Sponsored by the Commission on Private Philanthropy and Public Needs* (5 vols., Washington, D.C., 1977), vol. IV, 1923–24; Arlien Johnson: *Public Policy and Private Charities* (Chicago, 1931), pp. 20–22, 39–51, deals with tax exemption and public aid to voluntary associations; Irvin G. Wyllie: "The Search for an American Law of Charity, 1776–1844," *Mississippi Valley Historical Review*, vol. XLVI (1959–60), pp. 203–21, and Howard S. Miller:

of a better quality and less demeaning in its consequences than public; even the most ardent supporters of voluntary efforts ordinarily recognized, however, that public agencies must bear the heavy burden of caring for unfortunates without family, relatives, or friends. One form of philanthropic activity we shall be concerned with consists of organized efforts to compel public officials to discharge responsibilities of an eleemosynary nature in a conscientious and efficient way.

In nineteenth-century America some charitable uses such as providing dowries for poor girls and buying apprenticeships for orphan boys—both practiced by the beloved John Kyrle, who "scattered happiness with a lavish hand"—went out of fashion. Both Stephen Girard (1750–1831) and John McDonogh (1779–1850) bequeathed large sums for educating the poor, a favorite employment of surplus wealth for many centuries, but by midcentury, in the Northern and Western states, provision of common schools for normal children had become accepted as a public obligation rather than as a charitable prerogative. Rightly or wrongly, Southerners looked upon the free school system as a peculiarly and objectionably Northern institution. "We have got to hating everything with the prefix free," a Southern newspaper acknowledged in 1857, "from free Negroes down and up through the whole catalogue—free farms, free labor, free society, free will, free thinking, free children and free school. . . . But the worst of all abominations is the modern system of free schools . . . ."[7]

In practice, during the 1850s and 1860s, many public schools were not free. The story of the advocacy of and opposition to free, public, tax-supported education has been told so often that I have decided not to repeat it here. Yet even after the battle for free public schools had been won, charitable societies in cities like New York maintained industrial schools for children too poor, ragged, and irregular in habits to be accepted in the public schools, as well as foreign-language schools and night schools for working children. Substantial parts of Chapters 6 and 7 deal with philanthropic efforts—and rivalries—in the establishment of

---

The Legal Foundations of Philanthropy, 1776–1844 (Madison, Wis., 1961), trace the development of American legal policy toward charitable trusts and institutions.

[7] Arthur C. Cole: *The Irrepressible Conflict, 1850–1865* (New York, 1934), p. 51, quoting *Richmond Examiner*, cited in *Belleville Advocate*, November 6, 1857.

schools for freedmen during and after the war. Throughout the Civil War era, especially in the postwar years, higher education was a major object of philanthropy. To some extent in the 1850s, more often in the 1870s and after, philanthropists contributed to popular education and cultural enrichment through endowments or gifts to libraries, lecture series, institutes for adult study, and museums of art and science.

"He is too good, *too much* merchant prince and liberal Christian, and glorified donor to charitable uses. Fatuous and fat-headed, I think, and puffed up, I fear." The writer who confided these comments to his diary in 1854, George Templeton Strong, was a conservative, conventionally religious Wall Street lawyer; the subject was Robert B. Minturn (1805–1866), a New York merchant and shipowner who ranked as one of the "eminent philanthropists" of his day. Five years later, after attending the funeral of Mary Johnson, a less conspicuous philanthropist who happened to be a relative, Strong wrote:

> Many poor persons attended the service, followed her all
> the way to Trinity Churchyard, and cried a great deal. . . .
> She gave most of her income and far the larger portion of
> her time to the charities or to the church; was abundant
> in labor and self-denial, visiting, relieving, and tending the
> sick, destitute, and ignorant—energetically doing good by
> systematic personal effort.[8]

Attitudes toward philanthropy and philanthropists sometimes tell as much about the observer as the object. It is or should be possible to adopt a questioning attitude toward professions of benevolence and assertions of beneficence without doubting that altruism is a part of human nature. "We see no reason why men's principles should be suspected in their charities, any more than in their other actions," wrote James Walker. He was willing to grant "that men are often actuated in their benevolent undertakings by poorer principles than we could wish, or than they avow; still," he concluded, "it is certainly better, that these principles, poor as they may be, should be exerted in doing good,

[8] George Templeton Strong: *Diary*, ed. by Allan Nevins and Milton Halsey Thomas (4 vols., New York, 1952), vol. II, pp. 149, 438.

rather than in doing evil. It is better for the persons themselves. It is better for society."[9]

Some readers will interpret and perhaps deplore many of the activities dealt with in this book as examples of social controls imposed by the upper and middle classes on the poor. My feeling is that elements of social control enter every aspect of organized human activity, from teaching a Sunday school class to governing a dictatorship. The question is not whether dominant groups will seek to control the behavior of others, but how the control is exercised and to what ends it is directed. Men and women like Samuel Gridley Howe and Josephine Shaw Lowell certainly hoped and intended that the reforms they initiated and policies they advocated would influence people's conduct in ways beneficial to society and advantageous to individuals. Perhaps they were presumptuous in thinking they knew what was good for others, but that fault is not peculiar to them or their class. However harsh they sometimes sounded, the ultimate control they sought to impose on people was self-discipline; instead of subjecting the poor to rigid authority, they proposed to put them on the path to self-help and independence.

The dominant message of Americans concerned with philanthropy and welfare in the mid- and late-nineteenth century was the necessity for disciplining the charitable impulse so that goodwill and benevolent intentions would be enlightened and directed by intelligence. The reformers' advice was not always consistent, was not always heeded, and, when followed, did not inevitably produce the promised results. In the great test of the Civil War, philanthropists of many kinds found opportunities to prove the value of their plans or methods of benevolence. Most of them emerged from the war with a feeling that the war had vindicated their particular approach. The frustrations as well as the successes experienced during the war stimulated a number of philanthropists and reformers to postwar efforts to realize the unsatisfied ideal of rational, systematic, orderly conduct of both public and private charities.

[9] Walker: "Associations for Benevolent Purposes," p. 245.

Part One

THE 1850s AND
THE WAR YEARS

Prologue

Trouble Before the Storm

T he seventy-fifth anniversary of the Declaration of Independence, celebrated in states and territories from the Atlantic to the Pacific, found the United States emerging from the most serious of the sectional controversies that had periodically threatened the nation's existence since birth. The constitutional union of slave and free states was in some respects as peculiar and irksome as the cartilaginous connection joining the Siamese twins, Chang and Eng, in stormy but profitable brotherhood. On July 4, 1851, however, the bonds of union, although strained, were still intact. Throughout the country, newspaper editorials called on North and South to forget animosities and contemplate the advantages derived from brotherly feeling between sections. "We are a great people," declared Cincinnati's *Daily Enquirer*; "we have grown and strengthened without parallel in the history of the world; and there is nothing to stop our rapid progress . . . should mutual forbearance, concession, and respect for each other's rights control our actions toward each other as they did in the earlier days of the Republic."[1]

In Washington, at the laying of the cornerstone for the expansion of the Capitol, Daniel Webster delivered his last major oration on the permanence of the Union and the glory of the

---

[1] *Cincinnati Daily Enquirer*, July 4, 1851. Chang and Eng (1811–1874), brought to America in 1829, invested earnings from their exhibitions in a farm and slaves in North Carolina. They differed in temperament, often quarreled, and desired separation, but medical authorities held that severance of the cord connecting them would be fatal to both. *American Annual Cyclopaedia*, vol. XIV (1874), p. 105.

Constitution. Baltimore celebrated the occasion by releasing all debtors from jail, firing guns in their honor, and treating them to a grand torchlight parade. A crowd estimated at 50,000 gathered in Philadelphia to watch a fireworks display, which by some mischance fizzled. At West Point on the Hudson a vacationing attorney, George Templeton Strong, gave more thought to Charles Kingsley's novels *Yeast* and *Alton Locke* than to a cadet's bombastic Fourth of July address. Strong, pondering the message of Kingsley's books, noted in his diary that poverty, vice, crime, and disease were not yet as serious problems in New York as in London or Manchester. "Yet we have our Five Points," he observed, "our emigrant quarters, our swarms of seamstresses to whom their utmost toil in monotonous daily drudgery gives only a bare subsistence, a life barren of hope and enjoyment; our hordes of dock thieves, of children who live in the streets and by them. . . . Meantime," Strong continued, "philanthropists are scolding about the fugitive slave law, or shedding tears over the wretched niggers of the Carolinas . . . , or agitating because the unhanged scoundrels in the City Prison occupy cells imperfectly ventilated."[2]

Judged by almost any standard, the United States made prodigious advances in the ten years after 1851. Population growth, volume of immigration, expanding output of mines, forests, fields, and factories, miles of railway track laid and telegraph wire strung—even quantities of oysters consumed —measured material progress. The record was as impressive qualitatively as quantitatively. In the mid-century years, American inventors, explorers, scientists, shipbuilders, businessmen, yachtsmen, and pugilists scored notable, sometimes heroic triumphs. In literature and popular culture the 1850s possessed a range and richness unsurpassed in American experience. Ironically, the diverse achievements of the age and the vigor and confidence of the people imposed new strains on the American Constitution. Recession and depression marred the mid-fifties, but during the greater part of the decade the historic union of states faced the test not of adversity, but of success. Meanwhile, in prosperity as in depression, the social problems Strong noted at the start of the decade became steadily more pressing.

Among the more than 23,000,000 people enumerated in the

[2] George Templeton Strong: *The Diary of George Templeton Strong*, ed. by Allan Nevins and Milton Halsey Thomas (4 vols., New York, 1952), vol. II, pp. 56–57.

United States census of 1850 were men and women who, as children, had been counted in the first census of 1790. In 1850 the country contained almost six times as many people as in 1790, and more than twice as many as in 1820. Between 1850 and 1860 population increased more than 35 percent, reaching nearly 31,500,000 in 1860. The high rate of growth in the 1850s approximated that of the 1840s and was considerably larger than that of any subsequent period of American history. By 1860, although still less populous than France, Austria-Hungary, or Russia, the United States had passed Italy and Great Britain in population. In area, the United States was fifteen times bigger than France and almost as large as all of Continental Europe.

In 1860, 6 out of every 7 Americans were white; 6 out of 7 were native-born; and 4 out of 5 lived in rural areas or towns with fewer than 2,500 inhabitants. In the country as a whole, 9 percent of adult whites were illiterate; all but one (Indiana) of the free states were below the national average; all but one (Maryland) of the slave states were above it. Of the approximately 4,500,000 Negroes, 4,000,000 were slaves, 500,000 free. The foreign-born, predominantly Irish, German, and English, approached the Negroes in numbers but were distributed between North and South in reverse order; 3,600,000 lived in free states, 500,000 in slave states. City dwellers, a sizable portion of whom were foreign-born, remained a distinct minority, but the urban population was growing at more than twice the general rate. Scattered through the country, ranging from county seats to commercial metropolises, were 101 communities with more than 10,000 inhabitants. Nine American cities had populations in excess of 100,000, four had more than 200,000 inhabitants, and two more than 500,000. Modest as the figures seem, they meant that in 1860 the United States boasted or despaired of more large cities than most of the nations of the Old World.[3]

The aspect of the population problem that aroused most concern in the prewar years was the vast number of newcomers swarming into the United States each year from foreign shores. Something like 500,000 immigrants entered the country in the 1830s, 1,500,000 in the 1840s, and 2,500,000 in the 1850s. More immigrants arrived during the 1850s (mainly in the first

[3] Edwin Leigh: "Illiteracy in the United States," in U.S. Bureau of Education: *Report . . . for the Year 1870* (Washington, D.C., 1870), pp. 474–80; U.S. Census Office: *Twelfth Census, Statistical Atlas* (Washington, D.C., 1903), pp. 25–47.

half of the decade) than in the preceding half-century. The coming of hundreds of thousands of foreigners, some of whom were in sorely distressed conditions, magnified health, housing, and relief problems in a country already troubled by political unrest and social disorder. Popular sympathy for the sick and starving of distant lands, abundantly manifested in times such as the Irish famine of the late 1840s, turned to revulsion when the scene of suffering, and responsibility for alleviating it, shifted to the United States. Antagonism toward the immigrant, by no means unknown in earlier decades, mounted in the 1850s as America became, in fact, "an asylum for mankind." Reports, true but exaggerated, that European governments shipped a portion of their unwanted population to the United States, and reiterated exclamations over the cost and consequences of imported pauperism and crime, intensified hostilities based on religious and ethnic prejudices. "It is not only the thriftless poor who come hither . . . to add to the burden of our poor laws," complained Henry Mills Fuller, Whig Congressman from Pennsylvania, "but inmates of the prisons of Europe . . . sent . . . by their governments to prey upon society and to contaminate our people with their vices."[4]

The tide of immigration continued in spite of nativist opposition until stemmed, in the mid-fifties, by war in Europe and depression in the United States. Congress received and issued reports deploring the influx of needy foreigners but, instead of restricting their entry, passed laws in 1847, 1848, and 1855 intended to improve accommodations and alleviate overcrowding on immigrant vessels. In the absence of federal legislation regulating immigration, the states in which the principal ports of entry were located collected commutation fees and indemnity bonds from shipmasters for support of needy immigrants in hospitals, poorhouses, and other charitable institutions. Constructive efforts to meet problems of mass immigration were overshadowed, however, by a series of demonstrations against foreigners. Perhaps the worst of these outbursts occurred in September 1858, when a mob invaded the Quarantine Hospital on Staten

[4] "Foreign Criminals and Paupers," House Report, 34 Cong., 1 Sess., No. 359 (1856), p. 1 (serial 870); see also Benjamin J. Klebaner: "The Myth of Foreign Pauper Dumping," The Social Service Review, vol. XXXV (1961), pp. 302–09, and Maldwyn Allen Jones: American Immigration (Chicago, 1960), pp. 152–53.

Island and, abetted by local firemen, set fire to buildings shelter-
ing helpless victims of yellow fever and smallpox.[5]

Anti-immigrant riots formed only a part of the streak of violence running through the mid-century American style of life.
The divisions of the people were seemingly limitless; occasions
for disagreement, inexhaustible. Twenty-two people were killed
and thirty-six injured, and the Astor Place Opera House in New
York City was almost wrecked, in 1849 during a conflict between
militia and demonstrators seeking to disrupt a performance by
William Macready, an English rival of the American favorite
Edwin Forrest. "Great excitement"—a phrase used by contemporary newspapers to describe brawling—attended elections, enforcement or nonenforcement of laws, court decisions in murder
trials and constitutional cases, the hanging or reprieving of criminals, changing the gauges of railway track, and the settlement of
new territories. The social and political tensions of the times
made for excitability and extremism rather than concession and
moderation. In this atmosphere, both the basest fears and the
noblest ideals justified resort to violence as a method of settling
disputes or resolving frustration.[6]

The violence of the 1850s stands out not as peculiar to the
decade, but as a bad omen for the future. So, too, although every
period has its quota of pestilence, fire, and flood, the disasters of
the prewar years seem to prefigure the greater cataclysm that lay
ahead. Beginning late in 1848 and continuing for the next six
years, cholera ravaged cities, towns, and villages in all sections of
the country. The epidemic moved inland from the seaports, prov-
ing especially deadly in the Mississippi Valley and Great Lakes
Region. After exacting a heavy toll among immigrants and the
resident poor, it unexpectedly attacked the more prosperous and
respectable classes. In 1853, while cholera was still menacing

[5] David M. Schneider: *The History of Public Welfare in New York State, 1609–1866* (Chicago, 1938), p. 302; Strong: *Diary*, vol. II, pp. 412–13; *Harper's Weekly*, vol. II (1858), pp. 578, 581; *Frank Leslie's Illustrated Newspaper*, vol. VI (1858), pp. 232, 236, 238.

[6] Chronologies in the annual volumes of the *American Almanac and Repository of Useful Knowledge* (32 vols., Boston, 1830–1861) record the places and dates of the major riots of the 1850s. At the Astor Place riot, militia fired over the heads of the demonstrators, with the result that most of the casualties were onlookers or passersby rather than participants. David Grimsted: *Melodrama Unveiled, American Theater and Culture* (Chicago, 1968), p. 72.

other cities, New Orleans suffered the worst of its recurring epidemics of yellow fever. Vicksburg, Mississippi, in 1853, Montgomery, Alabama, in 1854, and Norfolk and Portsmouth, Virginia,
in 1855 also experienced devastating sieges of yellow fever.[7]

Disaster, even more than disease, exposed the harsh side of
American life. Philip Schaff, a scholarly young Swiss immigrant,
commented on the tendency of the American spirit of enterprise
to degenerate into foolhardiness and carelessness of life, "fearfully
manifest in the countless conflagrations in cities, and disasters on
steamboats and railroads." From San Francisco to Augusta,
Maine, portions of cities went up in flames, tenement houses
burned, factories collapsed, exploded, and caught fire. A false
alarm of fire at a New York City school in 1851 sent 1,800 children stampeding down the stairs. George Templeton Strong recorded the terrible story in his diary:

> The stair banister gave way, and the children fell into
> the square well round which the stairs wound, where
> the heap of [50] killed and wounded lay for hours before
> help could reach them. The doors opened inwards. The
> bodies were piled up to the top of the doors; they did not
> dare to burst them open and had to cut them slowly away
> with knives.

The worst of the industrial disasters was the fall of the Pem-
berton Mill at Lawrence, Massachusetts, on January 10, 1860,
which took the lives of almost 100 textile workers and seriously
wounded as many more. So many immigrants perished from natural or unnatural causes on westward crossings that Friedrich
Kapp, who had made the voyage, declared: "If crosses and tombs
could be erected on the water . . . the routes of the emigrant
vessels from Europe to America would long since have assumed
the appearance of crowded cemeteries." But immigrants were not
the only passengers who met watery or fiery deaths while jour-
neying to their destinations. The annals of the 1850s abound in
accounts of shipwrecks, railway accidents, riverboat explosions,

---

[7] Charles E. Rosenberg: *The Cholera Years: The United States in 1832,
1849, and 1866* (Chicago, 1962), pp. 101–72; Jo Ann Carrigan: "Yellow
Fever in New Orleans, 1853: Abstractions and Realities," *Journal of
Southern History*, vol. XXV (1959), pp. 337–55; Elizabeth Wisner:
Public Welfare Administration in Louisiana (Chicago, 1930), p. 53;
Robert C. Reinders: *End of an Era: New Orleans, 1850–1860* (New
Orleans, 1964), pp. 95–105.

fires, and collisions on the Great Lakes. The same headline might have been used for all: HEAVY LOSS OF LIFE.[8]

Nature, as if challenged by the example of human reckless-ness, sent killing frosts too early in the autumn and too late in the spring, swept the Atlantic with gales, inundated a Louisiana is-land, buried cities in snow, toppled Table Rock at Niagara Falls, and uprooted Charter Oak at Hartford, Connecticut. In one year or another, earthquakes, tornadoes, floods, and drought visited portions of the country. "From the Atlantic to the Mississippi the sky has bent hot, hard, and hollow over a parching soil," ex-claimed Thomas Starr King in a sermon on the great drought of 1854. "It seems as though the earth was turning on its axis to be roasted by the sun." During the middle and later 1850s hot, dry summers preceded or followed by bitterly cold winters destroyed livestock and ruined crops in parts of the Midwest and South. For people in the poorer, remoter agricultural areas, without money or means to import provisions, crop failures meant virtual starvation. In the wake of the climatic vagaries of 1854 and 1855 a famine Frederick Law Olmsted called "unprecedented in North America" struck northern Georgia and Alabama and western South Carolina. Five years later a succession of rainless months in 1859 and 1860 reduced thousands of Kansas settlers to destitu-tion. Short harvests in 1860 brought near-famine to parts of Ala-bama, Georgia, and Mississippi. On the other hand, Illinois farmers, burdened with a huge corn crop, faced ruin from surplus rather than shortage. Two months after Mississippi had seceded from the Union citizens of Springfield, Illinois, sent 1,000 bushels of corn, which might otherwise have been burned for fuel, to starving Mississippians.[9]

[8] Philip Schaff: *America: A Sketch of Its Political, Social, and Religious Character*, ed. by Perry Miller (Cambridge, Mass., 1961), p. 48 (first published 1855); Strong: *Diary*, vol. I, p. 73; Donald B. Cole: *Immigrant City: Lawrence, Massachusetts, 1845–1921* (Chapel Hill, N.C., 1963), pp. 31–32. For contemporary accounts see *Frank Leslie's Illustrated Newspaper*, vol. IX (1859–60), pp. 113, 119–22, and *Harper's Weekly*, vol. IV (1860), p. 34; Friedrich Kapp: "Immigration," *Journal of Social Science*, vol. II (1870), p. 20.

[9] Thomas Starr King: *Christianity and Humanity* (Boston, 1877), p. 106; Frederick Law Olmsted: *Journeys and Explorations in the Cotton Kingdom* (2 vols., London, 1862), vol. II, pp. 248–50; J. N. Holloway: *History of Kansas* (Lafayette, Ind., 1868), pp. 560–69; Grace A. Browning: *The Development of Poor Relief Legislation in Kansas* (Chicago, 1935), pp. 10–12; H. C. Hubbart: *The Older Middle West, 1840–1880* (New York, 1936), pp. 155–56.

America's economic climate was as disturbed and almost as unpredictable as its weather. In the late 1840s and early 1850s population growth, expanding markets, and inflation stimulated all forms of enterprise to extravagant growth. Recession in 1853 and depression in 1854 interrupted the boom, but 1855, an unusually riotous year in social relations, brought economic recovery, and 1856, a year of natural disasters, found the nation enjoying unprecedented prosperity. In the spring of 1857 the editors of *Harper's Weekly*, after surveying the national economy, concluded that the United States had made more material progress in the short space since 1850 than in any twenty-five years before that date. Then, during the harvest season of 1857, investors, speculators, borrowers, and lenders reaped the fruits of optimism or folly in a financial panic. "Providence has not unsealed the pestilence, nor blighted the harvests, nor spread the desolations of violence over the land," wrote Robert Hartley of the New York Association for Improving the Condition of the Poor, "but in the midst of unparalleled health, overflowing plenty, peace, and prosperity, suddenly as a clap of thunder in a clear sky, commercial confidence has been shaken by an unseen hand, and panic and distress pervade the entire community."[10]

The financial panic subsided in the winter of 1857–58, but reverberations of the collapse of commercial confidence continued for at least a year and a half longer. Although relatively short, the depression brought hardship to people in all layers of society because more Americans than ever before were dependent for livelihood on the production and distribution of consumer goods, professional and service occupations, factory jobs, and construction work. Tragically, but as is customary in such occurrences, those who had benefited least from prosperity and increased productivity—factory operatives, the unskilled, seamstresses, and other poorly paid marginal workers—suffered most during the depression. The city council of Chicago, for example, sought to raise funds for unemployment relief by cutting wages of street cleaners from 75 cents to 50 cents a day.[11]

[10] *Harper's Weekly*, vol. I (1857), p. 338; New York Association for Improving the Condition of the Poor: *Fourteenth Annual Report* (New York, 1857), p. 43.

[11] George W. Van Vleck: *The Panic of 1857, An Analytical Study* (New York, 1943), pp. 75–85; Allan Nevins: *The Emergence of Lincoln* (2 vols., New York, 1950), vol. I, pp. 194–97.

The social response ranged from riots by the unemployed of Philadelphia, Newark, and New York to a religious revival, stimulated by Young Men's Christian Associations, in the East and Midwest. When construction of New York City's Central Park began in autumn 1857, a mob with a banner inscribed "Bread or Blood" surrounded the office of Superintendent Frederick Law Olmsted and demanded jobs for 10,000 men. Nothing came of the demonstrations, and George Templeton Strong, a staunch Episcopalian, expected little more from the religious revival. "People miss their wonted excitement in Wall Street and seek a substitute in the sensations of the prayer meeting," he scoffed. James Shaw, a Methodist minister from England, took the revival more seriously. "From Washington, the capital, to Omaha City in Nebraska territory," he exulted, "wherever a Christian traveller stopped to spend the evening he could find a crowded prayer meeting across the entire breadth of the great republic."[12]

Piety gave way to politics in the congressional campaigns—including the Lincoln-Douglas contest—of 1858. During the next two years, gradually improving economic conditions seem to have intensified, rather than lessened, the heat and rancor of partisan and sectional differences. In midsummer 1859 the French acrobat Charles Blondin diverted the nation with daredevil stunts on a cable strung high over the Niagara gorge. Blondin's feat in pushing a wheelbarrow across the rope symbolized the precarious course of national economic recovery. His subsequent crossing, this time as he carried a man on his back, suggested all too clearly the American political predicament at the end of the 1850s.[13]

For most Americans, the return of prosperity in 1859 and 1860 meant simply a continuation of the always difficult struggle to make ends meet. Rich and poor alike complained of the advancing cost of living, and workers, in unprecedented numbers, struck for higher wages. The most extensive strike in American history before the Civil War began on Washington's Birthday 1860 among shoemakers in Lynn, Massachusetts, and eventually

---

[12] Frederick Law Olmsted to Charles Loring Brace, December 8, 1860, Frederick Law Olmsted Papers, Library of Congress (hereafter cited as LC); Strong: *Diary*, vol. II, pp. 391–92; James Shaw: *Twelve Years in America* (London, 1867), p. 180.

[13] *Frank Leslie's Illustrated Newspaper*, vol. VIII (1859), pp. 98–99, 155; *Harper's Weekly*, vol. III (1859), p. 551, and vol. IV (1859), p. 544.

spread to 20,000 boot and shoe workers in Massachusetts, New Hampshire, and Maine.[14]

At the end of the 1850s, in most parts of the country, the going rate for unskilled and factory labor was around $1 and for skilled labor $1.50 to $2 a day. The bulk of industrial employees probably earned from $250 to $400, and clerks and white-collar workers $300 to $500, per annum. Annual earnings for skilled workmen were in the neighborhood of $600 or $700; farmhands received about $140 a year plus board; overseers on Southern plantations were paid $500 or $600 a year; and the income of professional men was about $1,000 a year in rural districts and $2,000 in cities. In New York City, where extremes of wealth and poverty were most apparent, only 1 percent of the population earned as much as $850 a year. Generalizations about wages and income, however, are subject to innumerable qualifications. Lynn shoemakers were earning only $3 a week when they went on strike in 1860; the wages of women in industry were 25 to 50 percent lower than those paid men; and in the upland South, white farm workers took their pay not in cash, but in corn and bacon.[15]

In 1860 most American workers were better off in real wages than their fathers had been in 1830 or their grandfathers in 1800. Immigrants and foreign travelers regularly reported that standards of living were higher among the laboring classes of the United States than in Europe. In actual numbers, however, the poor and very poor were more numerous in 1860 than a generation earlier. New World poverty rivaled Europe's in intensity, if not in extent. Business journals bemoaned the national inclination toward "inordinate expenditures," a vice allegedly permeating every grade of American society. In fact, the great majority of American families spent nearly all their income on food, clothing, and shelter; yet the surplus left after these elemental needs had been met—estimated at 5 percent of income—exceeded that

---

[14] Joseph G. Rayback: *A History of American Labor* (New York, 1959), p. 106; *Frank Leslie's Illustrated Newspaper*, vol. IX (1859–60), pp. 239–40, 250, 290.

[15] Edgar W. Martin: *The Standard of Living in 1860, American Consumption Levels on the Eve of the Civil War* (Chicago, 1942), pp. 393–94; Chester W. Wright: *Economic History of the United States* (New York and London, 1941), pp. 409–10, 1038; Clement Eaton: *The Growth of Southern Civilization, 1790–1860* (New York, 1961), pp. 171–72; *Hunt's Merchants' Magazine*, vol. XLI (1859), pp. 760–61.

available to people in other countries. Individually small but col-
lectively great, this narrow margin sufficed to give Americans a
reputation for generosity as well as extravagance.[16]

[16] George Rogers Taylor: *The Transportation Revolution, 1815–1860*
(New York, 1951), p. 393; James Silk Buckingham: *America, Historical,
Statistic, and Descriptive* (3 vols., London and Paris, 1841), vol. II,
p. 85; *Hunt's Merchants' Magazine*, vol. XLI (1859), p. 141; Martin:
Standard of Living in 1860, pp. 401–02.

Chapter 1

Private Charity and

Public Relief

In the 1850s foreign observers tempered criticisms of many
aspects of American civilization by praising the benevolent
disposition of the people and the flourishing condition of philanthropy. Philip Schaff, who believed that the United States was
"the country for average intelligence, average morality, and
average piety," concluded in 1854 that Americans, although
acquisitive, made good use of their gains. Materialistic influences,
Schaff thought, were counterbalanced by Christianity, zeal for
education, and liberality in voluntary contributions to benevolent
institutions. P. T. Barnum, a shrewd student of national psy-
chology, was also impressed by the benevolent attributes of the
American character. In promoting Jenny Lind's American concert
tour of 1850–52, Barnum counted on the singer's renown as a
philanthropist to attract people who might be indifferent to her
artistic talent. At the start of the tour, at Barnum's suggestion,
Miss Lind donated a total of $10,000 to ten carefully selected
New York charities, and in the course of her visit she made
additional well-advertised gifts to assorted philanthropic institutions. Barnum, whose first wife's name was Charity, professed to
regard these donations as "purely a business operation, 'bread
cast upon the waters' which would return, perhaps buttered. . . ."
The master showman, as adept at publicizing himself as his
exhibits, boasted in his autobiography that he had pulled his

countrymen's heartstrings preparatory to relaxing their purse-strings.[1]

Even without Barnum's sly assistance, a multitude of religious, charitable, patriotic, and humanitarian causes vied for public sympathy and support. The largest American benevolent organizations were the missionary, tract, Bible, and Sunday school societies of the evangelical Protestant churches. From headquarters in Boston, New York, or Philadelphia, and operating through hundreds of local auxiliaries, the societies appealed to national constituencies for funds to carry out far-flung activities. For a generation before 1850, managers of these societies had been developing systematic methods of tapping the philanthropic resources of the country. With varying degrees of success, similar methods were employed by societies opposing slavery and promoting peace, temperance, prison reform, the moral and social elevation of seamen, the conversion of Jews and Roman Catholics, the colonization of Negroes in Africa, the ministerial education of poor youths, support for superannuated clergymen, and the recruitment and transportation of Protestant women teachers to the West. Territorial and population growth furnished ever-expanding opportunities for stewardship, and fear of Roman Catholicism provided a perennial motive for action. "If you do not assist," cried a correspondent who besought the Board of National Popular Education to send teachers to Oregon, "the 'Sisters of Charity' from Papal Rome will do the work! Oh send us some Sisters of Charity from Protestant New England. . . ."[2]

Incorporation, either by a special act of the state legislature or by general laws providing for chartering nonprofit corporations, gave benevolent societies the right to receive bequests and govern themselves as legal entities. Although the societies vigorously solicited both annual and life members, their constitutions vested control of their affairs in small executive committees

---

[1] Philip Schaff: *America: A Sketch of Its Political, Social and Religious Character*, ed. by Perry Miller (Cambridge, Mass., 1961), pp. 8, 54; P. T. Barnum: *Struggles and Triumphs: or Forty Years' Recollections of P. T. Barnum Written by Himself* (Hartford, Conn., 1869), p. 343; Neil Harris: *Humbug, The Art of P. T. Barnum* (Boston, 1973), pp. 79, 214.

[2] Clifford S. Griffin: *Their Brothers' Keepers: Moral Stewardship in the United States, 1800–1865* (New Brunswick, N.J., 1960), pp. xi, 199–200; P. J. Staudenraus: *The African Colonization Movement, 1816–1865* (New York, 1961), pp. 12–13, 69, 98–99; Board of National Popular Education: *Third Annual Report* (Cleveland, 1850), p. 40.

or boards of managers. The major national societies (American Board of Commissioners for Foreign Missions, American Home Missionary Society, American Tract Society, American Bible Society, and American Sunday School Union) derived their support from membership fees, regular collections in the churches, fund-raising efforts by auxiliaries and field agents, and gifts and bequests from rich donors like Anson Greene Phelps. The Bible, Tract, and Sunday school societies obtained much of their income from the sale of their publications. The Bible Society, for example, sold Bibles at cost to such of its 1,000 auxiliaries as could pay for them; the auxiliaries returned any profit from sales to the parent society, which used the money to provide free Bibles to auxiliaries too poor to purchase them. Contributions to and earnings of the societies reached their prewar peak in the mid-fifties, when annual receipts ranged from more than $200,000 for the Home Missionary Society to approximately $500,000 for the American Bible Society. All the societies were embarrassed in 1857 by the revelation that the secretary of the Sunday School Union had lost $88,000 of its funds through speculation. The ensuing scandal, together with the financial panic of that same year, resulted in decreased revenues during the last years of the decade.[3]

As national organizations the benevolent societies, like religious denominations and the federal government, were caught up in the dispute over the rights and wrongs of slavery and slaveholders. Divisions between factions opposing slavery and those supporting or condoning it widened between 1856 and 1859. The Bible Society and the Board of Foreign Missions, the abolitionist members of which had withdrawn in 1846 to form the American Missionary Association, weathered the storm, but the Tract and Home Missionary societies, already subjected to schisms, lost branches, auxiliaries, and donors as a result of adopting policies deemed, respectively, too soft and too hard on the moral issue of slavery. The separations indicated no lessening of enthusiasm for tract and mission work. After the Home Missionary Society discontinued subsidies to churches admitting slave owners to membership, Northern business leaders like William E. Dodge, who sympathized with the South or were out of sympathy with

[3] Griffin: *Their Brothers' Keepers*, pp. 62, 78–79, 199–200; on the gifts of Anson Greene Phelps and his son see Henry Boynton Smith: *A Memorial of Anson G. Phelps, Jr.* (New York, 1960), pp. 4–5, 90–124.

abolitionists, contributed to a new mission organization, the Southern Aid Society. On the other hand, Northerners who complained that American Tract Society publications condemned every sin except slavery shifted their allegiance to more militant tract societies based in Boston and Cincinnati. Charles F. Hovey, a Boston merchant who died in 1859, left $40,000, one-fourth of his estate, in trust to Wendell Phillips, William Lloyd Garrison, and other leading abolitionists with instructions to spend it "by employing such agents as believe and practice the doctrine of no union with slaveholders, religiously or politically, and by circulating such publications as tend to destroy every pro-slavery institution."[4]

As the slavery controversy became more intense the venerable American Colonization Society, languishing in the 1840s, took on new life. Although the Colonization Society enjoyed only indifferent success in inducing free Negroes to emigrate to Liberia, its efforts won kind words from many admirers. Philip Schaff told a German audience that through the work of the society "the gloom of slavery begins to break into the dawn of the Christianization and civilization of Africa by her own unfortunate children once violently torn from her and now peacefully sent back to the Republic of Liberia." The Colonization Society received several large bequests, including one of $83,000 from John McDonogh of New Orleans, grants from state legislatures, and appropriations from Congress—the latter for returning and resettling Africans taken from illicit slave traders. Annual receipts climbed from $65,000 in 1850 to $160,000 in 1859, and in 1860 the society hopefully opened a new headquarters building in Washington.[5]

Disaster relief, requiring brief but large outbursts of giving and businesslike mobilization and distribution of assistance, was a form of benevolence particularly congenial to the American temperament. Yellow fever epidemics in the South and the tribulations of rival settlements in parched and bleeding Kansas involved the major disaster-relief operations of the prewar years.

---

[4] Smith: *Memorial of Anson G. Phelps, Jr.*, pp. 182–85, 191–97; Louis Filler: *The Crusade Against Slavery, 1830–1860* (New York, 1960), pp. 260–63; Louis Ruchames, ed.: *The Letters of William Lloyd Garrison* (4 vols. to date, Cambridge, Mass., 1971–75), vol. IV (1975), pp. 8, 636.

[5] Schaff: *America*, pp. 7–8; Allan Nevins: *Ordeal of the Union* (2 vols., New York and London, 1947), vol. I, pp. 511–17, cites other testimonials to the Colonization Society; Staudenraus: *African Colonization Movement*, pp. 239–46; *The African Repository*, vol. XXXIII (1857), pp. 66, 124, 377.

Contributions for the succor of victims and survivors of the epidemic of 1853 flowed into New Orleans from the North and South. The heroes of the epidemic, however, were not distant givers, like the abolitionist Gerrit Smith, but members of the Howard Association and other responsible residents of New Orleans who remained at their posts in the stricken city. The Howards, organized in the epidemic of 1837, took their name from John Howard, the eighteenth-century English philanthropist and reformer, who was widely admired in the United States. Members of the association, mainly clerks, sought out and personally cared for the sick, opened dispensaries, recruited physicians and nurses, and established temporary asylums for children whose parents died in the epidemic. Theodore Clapp, pastor of the Unitarian Church of the Messiah in New Orleans, paid tribute to the "miracles of benevolence" wrought by the Howards. Having lived in New Orleans for thirty years before 1853, however, he pointed out that the aftermath of epidemics, when aid had to be found for widows and orphans, was as tragic and trying as the pestilence itself. "When a man is buried," wrote Clapp, "he can trouble you no more; but these survivors of the conflict may follow you to your grave."[6]

Political and sectional rivalries, spurring Northern and Southern partisans to aid emigration to Kansas, also stimulated efforts to assist distressed settlers in the embattled territory. In the trial of philanthropic strength the North gained a clear victory. Kansas was already committed to entering the Union as a free state when famine, following the long droughts of 1859–60, threatened to depopulate parts of the territory. Between October 1860 and April 1861 individual donors, including President James Buchanan, churches, special committees, and the legislatures of New York, Pennsylvania, and Wisconsin sent money, tons of provisions and feed grain, and large quantities of clothing, medicine, and garden seed to relief agents in Kansas. "God foresaw our necessities and provided for them," said Mrs. S. C. Pomeroy, wife of one of the agents. She was referring to the recently completed railroad that carried the bounty of the East to a point across the Missouri River from Atchison. From there

[6] Elizabeth Wisner: *Public Welfare Administration in Louisiana* (Chicago, 1930), pp. 20–21, 53, 190; Robert C. Reinders: *End of an Era: New Orleans, 1850–1860* (New Orleans, 1964), p. 98; Theodore Clapp: *Autobiographical Sketches and Recollections, During a Thirty-five Years' Residence in New Orleans* (Boston, 1857), pp. 201–02, 212–13.

relief supplies were ferried (or hauled, when the river was frozen) to Atchison for distribution to approved applicants and county relief committees. Fifty years later, disgruntled Kansans were still charging favoritism in the distribution of supplies and demanding an accounting of the use made of the $84,000 in cash received by the Relief Commission.[7]

On local levels churches, YMCAs, which reached the United States in 1851, fraternal lodges, benevolent societies of nationality groups, and miscellaneous relief associations ministered to normal and emergency charitable needs. By the mid-fifties towns in the North and South had well-entrenched Female Benevolent Societies assisting select categories of the poor, and in the larger cities there were conscientiously managed charitable societies patterned more or less after the New York Association for Improving the Condition of the Poor. Proliferation of benevolent enterprises and institutions such as hospitals, dispensaries, orphanages, and infirmaries by sectarian and ethnic groups denoted increased ability to give among both immigrant and native Americans. Continuing concern for children and youth was the strongest philanthropic tendency of the decade. It was evinced, in different ways, by the spread of YMCAs, the establishment of orphanages for children left homeless and destitute by cholera and yellow fever epidemics, the founding of nurseries for children of working women and wet nurses—"mothers whose poverty forced them to give enrichment intended for their own infant to the children of the rich"—and the rise of new organizations such as the Children's Aid Society and the New York Juvenile Asylum for helping neglected and vagrant children.[8]

---

[7] George W. Glick: "The Drought of 1860," *Kansas Historical Collections*, vol. IX (1905–06), p. 482; Samuel A. Johnson: *The Battle Cry of Freedom: The New England Emigrant Aid Company in the Kansas Crusade* (Lawrence, Kan., 1954), pp. 54–57 and 265–66, indicates that S. C. Pomeroy was careless in the handling of money.

[8] C. Howard Hopkins: *History of the Y.M.C.A. in North America* (New York, 1951), pp. 29–30. J. D. B. DeBow: *Statistical View of the United States . . . , Being a Compendium of the Seventh Census* (Washington, D.C., 1854), pp. 162–63, gives statistics on relief furnished by the Order of Odd Fellows; Rosenberg: *Cholera Years*, pp. 118–19; John O'Grady: *Catholic Charities in the United States* (Washington, D.C., 1931), pp. 73–74, 80–82; Barbara J. Berg: *The Remembered Gate: Origins of American Feminism, The Woman and the City, 1800–1860* (New York, 1978), p. 235; Henry W. Thurston: *The Dependent Child* (New York, 1930), pp. 66–68, 92–108; Miriam Z. Langsam: *Children West: A History of the Placing-Out System of the Children's Aid Society, 1853–1890* (Madison, Wis., 1964), pp. 1–10.

The "charity months" of winter always intensified efforts for the poor, but the depression winters of 1854–55 and 1857–58, when unemployment swelled and agitated the ranks of the distressed, imposed extraordinary demands on all local charities. Neither public nor private relief agencies were equipped to meet, yet neither could afford to ignore, the exigencies of mass unemployment. Emergency soup kitchens and fuel and clothing depots, hastily adopted relief appropriations, and rudimentary work projects helped stem the tide of misery. Established private associations, suspicious of interlopers in the charitable field, assumed heavier burdens of work and responsibility. Fortunately the crises were of short duration. When they were over, all concerned in organizing and dispensing aid congratulated themselves, if not each other, on the competency and unique value of their labors.[9]

American liberality to philanthropic causes stemmed not only from habits of giving but from the national penchant for spending. In good times and bad, charitable groups sponsored fairs, festivals, balls, and benefit concerts. When economic conditions inhibited giving, as in the panic of 1857, philanthropic pressures induced a spurt of spending at fairs and festivals. Practically every fund-raising device employed during the Civil War was in use in the 1850s. The charity fair, an outgrowth of the church bazaar, was a special favorite. Boston's annual Anti-Slavery Bazaar, organized by Maria Weston Chapman for the support of the Massachusetts Anti-Slavery Society, set the standard for fairs benefiting similar or less controversial causes in other cities. In Philadelphia in 1857 the aging Rebecca Gratz joined younger women in arranging a fair for the Jewish Foster Home and Orphan Asylum; the San Francisco Ladies' Seamen's Friend Society held a fair in 1858 to raise money for a sailors home; and in February 1860 a "Grand Festival" of the Buffalo (New York) Benevolent Association raised $6,000 for the poor of that city.[10]

[9] New York Association for Improving the Condition of the Poor: *Fifteenth Annual Report* (New York, 1858), p. 58; Leah Hannah Feder: *Unemployment Relief in Periods of Depression* (New York, 1936), pp. 18–36; David M. Schneider: *History of Public Welfare in New York State, 1609–1866* (Chicago, 1938), pp. 270–71, 277.

[10] Charlotte L. Forten: *The Journal of Charlotte L. Forten* (New York, 1953), pp. 56, 74–75, 98–99, 215, 223, 228; David Philipson, ed.: *Letters of Rebecca Gratz* (Philadelphia, 1929), p. 407; Ladies' Seamen's Friend Society of San Francisco: *Third Annual Report* (San Francisco, 1859), pp. 5–7; *Frank Leslie's Illustrated Newspaper*, vol. IX (1859–60), pp. 204, 206.

Besides offering socially acceptable occasions for frivolity, the constant round of charitable entertainments provided outlets for the energies of upper- and middle-class women and gave them opportunities to display or develop entrepreneurial talents. In 1856 George Templeton Strong said of Mrs. Cornelius Du Bois, founder of the New York nursery for children of wet nurses:

> Had that lady ordinary health and vigor instead of being, as she is, a mere embodiment of "Neurology," a bundle of active diseases and morbid changes of structure, unable to speak but in a whisper, and paralyzed suddenly at intervals by disease of the heart, she'd found a dynasty and die Imperatrix of The United States with a secured succession to her issue, therein probably beating Louis Napoleon. I look with absolute awe on her.

Another ailing but awesome woman, Ann Pamela Cunningham, founded the Mount Vernon Ladies' Association in 1853 for the purpose of acquiring and preserving Washington's home and tomb as a national shrine. A semi-invalided South Carolinian, Cunningham originally directed her appeal to "Ladies of the South." By December 1859, when the purchase of Mount Vernon was completed, she had marshaled a national corps of vice-regents—selected with meticulous regard for "personal, family and social qualifications"—to direct the association's fund drives in their respective states. The Mount Vernon Fund received gifts from Washington Irving, the proceeds of numerous balls and entertainments, and about $70,000 from Edward Everett's orations and writings. Male canvassers for the Washington National Monument Association were less successful than Cunningham's ladies. In 1859, at the National Masonic Convention, the wives, sisters, and daughters of members of the order resolved to organize themselves into a Ladies' Washington Monument Society to raise money for completing the monument.[11]

Children participated in as well as benefited from philanthropy. Young residents of the Newsboys' Lodging House in New

[11] George Templeton Strong: *Diary*, ed. by Allan Nevins and Milton Halsey Thomas (4 vols., New York, 1952), vol. II, p. 264; Grace King: *Mount Vernon on the Potomac, History of the Mount Vernon Ladies' Association of the Union* (New York, 1929), pp. 19, 41, 71–75; Edward Everett: *The Mount Vernon Papers* (New York, 1860), pp. iii–iv, 2, 9–10; *Harper's Weekly*, vol. IV (1860), p. 130.

York contributed to the Mount Vernon Fund, Kansas relief, and sufferers from tenement house fires in Manhattan. Boys and girls in more fortunate circumstances sent their gifts into benevolent channels through church and Sunday school collections. Children in Boston supported the Children's Mission to the Children of the Destitute, a child-placing agency. In 1855 sixteen-year-old John D. Rockefeller, who probably thought himself an adult, began his recorded philanthropies with a donation of 15 cents to the "Mission Cause." In 1856, 100,000 children in the United States and the Hawaiian Islands responded to an appeal from the American Board of Commissioners for Foreign Missions for $12,000 to build a packet ship to serve mission stations in Micronesia. An offering of 10 cents or more gave the donor a share of stock in the clipper *Morning Star*, which sailed from Boston in December 1856. By the following spring, when the *Morning Star* reached Honolulu, the children's contributions were sufficient to allow construction of a sister ship.[12]

Without the importance of women's and children's philanthropic activities being slighted, it remained true that when large sums were needed for ambitious projects, nothing took the place of big gifts from rich men. William Augustus Muhlenberg, rector of the Episcopalian Church of the Holy Communion in New York City, proved unusually successful in interesting wealthy men like Robert Minturn, John D. Wolfe, William B. Astor, and, later, J. P. Morgan in St. Luke's Hospital and the other charities he promoted. George Templeton Strong, who was on the committee charged with raising funds for the hospital, noted with approval Astor's unsolicited increase in his pledge, making him the largest donor to the project. "If he and [Stephen] Whitney and the other twenty or thirty millionaires in the city would do so a little oftener," mused Strong, "they would never feel the difference and in ten years could control the course of things in New York by the public confidence and gratitude they would gain." After giving the subject further thought, Strong added: "Property is the ruling element in our society. Wealthy men are meant

[12] Children's Aid Society, *Eighth Annual Report* (New York, 1861); Allan Nevins: *Study in Power: John D. Rockefeller, Industrialist and Philanthropist* (2 vols., New York, 1953), vol. I, pp. 16–17; *The Missionary Herald*, vol. LII (1856), p. 284, 380; William E. Strong: *The Story of the American Board: An Account of the First Hundred Years of the American Board of Commissioners for Foreign Missions* (Boston, 1910), p. 236.

to have supreme influence in the long run; they do not possess it because they will not use the power wealth gives them."[13]

No reliable estimates of the annual aggregate of private gifts and bequests to religious, charitable, and benevolent causes are available for the 1850s. If voluntary contributions for such purposes averaged $1 per free person per year, the total for 1860 would have been $27,500,000. That figure, although conjectural, may help put estimates of public expenditures for relief and welfare into perspective. The census of 1860 reported that for the country as a whole the cost of supporting public paupers was $5,400,000. If divided on a per capita basis, that sum would have entailed a charge of about 20 cents on each free inhabitant of the United States.[14]

The four states reporting the largest expenditures for relief of paupers in 1860 were:

STATE	POPULATION	ANNUAL COST	APPROXIMATE PER CAPITA COST
New York	3,880,735	$1,440,904	38 cents
Pennsylvania	2,906,115	665,398	23 cents
Massachusetts	1,231,066	579,397	48 cents
Ohio	2,339,502	311,109	13 cents

The total cost of relieving paupers in these four states—roughly $3,000,000—was approximately the same as the total for all states in 1850. Except in Louisiana, New Hampshire, Rhode Island, and Vermont, where the figures for 1860 were lower than or about the same as those for 1850, the annual cost of supporting public paupers rose sharply between 1850 and 1860. The nationwide total in 1860 was 45 percent higher than in 1850. Neither the 1850 nor the 1860 census returns on numbers of paupers can be relied on, but the figures given (135,000 in 1850, 322,000 in

[13] Alvin Skardon: *Church Leader in the Cities, William Augustus Muhlenberg* (Philadelphia, 1971), pp. 1, 21–22; Strong: *Diary*, vol. II, p. 92.

[14] U.S. Bureau of the Census: *The Eighth Census, 1860, Mortality and Miscellaneous Statistics* (Washington, 1866), p. 512.

1860) indicate that during the decade the number of persons relieved advanced 60 percent.[15]

Despite increases in both the means and the objects of public bounty, American taxpayers do not seem to have overburdened themselves to assist the needy and afflicted poor. In 1860 states, counties, and towns raised an estimated $94,000,000 through general property taxes, the principal source of revenue for state and local governments. Taxes for the poor accounted for only $2,700,000, or less than 3 percent of the total. In addition to special levies, however, counties and towns devoted a portion of regular tax receipts to poor relief, and state legislatures appropriated funds for institutions for the insane, blind, and deaf, for relief of "state paupers" and "transient poor," and for occasional or regular subsidies to private charities. Besides direct taxation of real and personal property, and sometimes in preference to it, public authorities applied to poor relief moneys received from licenses for theaters, taverns, and grogshops; court fines for offenses such as drunkenness, disorderly conduct, and gambling; and a variety of other fees, penalties, and forfeitures. Commutation fees or head taxes on immigrants provided at least a part of the oft-lamented sums spent for the support of "imported foreign pauperism."[16]

Decentralization of responsibility for poor relief to towns in New England, counties in the South, and a mixed township-county system in the Midwest resulted in differences in care for the destitute not only in different sections of the country but also within the same state or even within the same county. Since local governments accepted responsibility only for the needy who could claim legal settlement in their jurisdictions—ordinarily one

[15] De Bow: *Statistical View of the United States*, p. 163; for comment and criticism of the 1850 and 1860 census returns on pauperism, see Francis A. Walker: "Remarks on the Statistics of Pauperism and Crime," in U.S. Bureau of the Census: *The Ninth Census, 1870* (3 vols., Washington, D.C., 1872), vol. I, pp. 563–67.

[16] U.S. Bureau of the Census: *The Eighth Census, 1860, Mortality and Miscellaneous Statistics*, pp. 511–12; Robert Kelso: *The History of Public Poor Relief in Massachusetts, 1620–1920* (Boston and New York, 1922), pp. 136, 141; Wisner: *Public Welfare Administration in Louisiana*, pp. 28–29, 46–49; Schneider: *History of Public Welfare in New York State*, pp. 240–51; Guion Griffis Johnson: *Ante-Bellum North Carolina, A Social History* (Chapel Hill, N.C., 1937), p. 531; Peter J. Coleman: *The Transformation of Rhode Island, 1790–1860* (Providence, 1963), p. 251.

year's residence without receipt of public charity—special provision had to be made for the "unsettled" and immigrant poor.
Every effort was made to remove persons without settlement or,
when that was not possible, to pass the cost of their support to
higher authorities. In the 1850s Massachusetts established state
almshouses for some of the "state paupers," including immigrants, and reimbursed towns for the care of the rest. After 1847
the Board of Commissioners of Emigration, an agency of the
state of New York, developed a comprehensive program for assisting immigrants entering the United States, as the bulk of
them did, through the port of New York. The board, established as
a result of the joint efforts of members of immigrant societies and
the Whig politician Thurlow Weed, operated the Quarantine
Hospital on Staten Island, built a refuge for destitute and sick
foreigners of the New York City area, and reimbursed supervisors
of the poor for the care of recent immigrants in other counties of
the state. In 1855 the commissioners obtained the use of Castle
Garden, where Jenny Lind had made her American debut, as a
central depot at which incoming aliens could be registered,
shielded from fraud, and helped toward independence.[17]

Town and country methods of relieving the native and settled poor were not very different from those of a half century
earlier—or fifty years later. Although jealous of the principle of
local authority, public officials did not hesitate to delegate responsibility for care of paupers to private individuals and charitable institutions. Where possible, orphan children were bound
out as apprentices or, in cities, sent to orphanages. The most
extreme examples of the delegation of public responsibility were
the practices—often disparaged but in common use—of auction-
ing paupers to the lowest bidder or of farming out groups of
paupers to contractors who agreed to keep them for a stipulated
period at so much per day, week, or year. On a visit to North
Carolina in 1848 Dorothea Dix found the poor of one county
being bid off for 8 cents a day, a decade later trustees of an Ohio

---

[17] Kapp: "Immigration," pp. 20–21; Schneider: *Public Welfare in New
York State*, pp. 306–15; Robert Ernst: *Immigrant Life in New York City,
1825–1863* (New York, 1949), pp. 29–32; Thurlow Weed Barnes: *Memoir
of Thurlow Weed* (Boston, 1884), pp. 138–43; New York (State)
Commissioners of Emigration: *Annual Report for the Year Ending
December 31, 1864* (New York, 1865), describes miscellaneous services for
immigrants developed during the agency's first seventeen years.

township discovered a "responsible bidder" who was willing to keep a pauper for 99 cents a week, and in 1859 the sheriff of Barry County, Missouri, reported the successful sale of a poor man for $15 a year.[18]

Well before 1860, sale of the maintenance of paupers by auction or contract, although sanctioned by law and usage, had fallen into disrepute. On the other hand, relief to the poor in their own homes, the simplest and most prevalent form of public assistance, was opposed by reformers as productive of pauperism. After about 1820 reformers advocated and secured wider adoption of the almshouse or county poor farm system. Economic as well as humanitarian considerations figured in arguments for the poor farm. In 1857 the youthful educator Andrew Dixon White told citizens of Syracuse, New York, that good management could make poor farms not only self-sustaining but profit-making. Citing the financial achievements of the New Haven, Connecticut, poorhouse as an example, White declared: "The success of this reform is triumphant." Unfortunately, in the absence of good management and in consequence of public disinterest and official neglect, poor farms proved anything but humane and efficient social instruments. A committee of the New York State Senate reported in 1857 that the fifty-five county almshouses in the state were "badly constructed, ill-arranged, ill-warmed, and ill-ventilated." Almost worse than bad conditions in the institutions, declared the committee, was the indifference toward them of people living in the immediate neighborhood. Despairingly the committee recommended return to the system of outdoor relief. Thomas Hazard, whose survey of almshouses in Rhode Island revealed that keepers treated inmates like criminals, also favored return to outdoor relief for the poor who had homes or friends with whom they might live. If such a course exposed the public to imposition, said Hazard, "other plans subject the *poor* to impositions which they are quite as unable to bear as the public."[19]

---

[18] Johnson: *Ante-Bellum North Carolina*, p. 697; Fern Boan: *A History of Poor Relief Legislation and Administration in Missouri* (Chicago, 1941), p. 195; for a contemporary survey of poor relief practice see *Eighty Years' Progress of the United States from the Revolution to the Great Republic* (New York, 1864), pp. 445–48; and for criticism of the contract and auction systems see Samuel H. Elliot: *New England's Chattels; or Life in the Northern Poor-House* (New York, 1858), pp. 34–36.

[19] David J. Rothman: *The Discovery of the Asylum, Social Order and Disorder in the New Republic* (Boston, Toronto, 1971), pp. 287–95; Elliot: *New England's Chattels*, pp. 456, 479; New York (State) Legislature:

While the great majority of paupers remained on and in the hands of local officials, state legislatures and the national Congress (acting for the District of Columbia) established institutions for at least some of the indigent deaf, blind, and insane. As of 1860, there were in the United States about fifty tax-supported or tax-assisted asylums for the insane, and thirty-eight schools for the deaf and blind. Some of the schools and asylums, following a familiar American pattern, were chartered as private corporations but received substantial grants or payments from public treasuries. Others, including most of those founded after 1840, were owned, constructed, and operated by the states. At the end of the 1850s, while officials of state hospitals in Ohio and Wisconsin were complaining of inadequate support by legislatures, the Pennsylvania Hospital for the Insane, a chartered institution, proudly opened a new building for 250 patients erected entirely by voluntary contributions.[20]

Much of the credit for expanded facilities for the insane belongs to Dorothea Dix, a New England spinster whose patient investigations, genteel agitation, and skillful lobbying prodded state after state into building or enlarging hospitals for the insane. Like a migratory bird, Dix moved south in the winter and advanced northward with the spring. Contemporaries, praising her benevolent and beneficent labors, boasted of the munificent liberality with which state governments endowed institutions for the children of affliction. Yet as Dix repeatedly pointed out, the new institutions, excellent as they were, accommodated only a small proportion of the insane. The rest were still in poorhouses, jails, or private homes partly because town or county officials found it cheaper to leave them there than to send them to state hospitals and partly because there was no room for them in overcrowded state institutions. As early as 1848, Dix concluded that states could not or would not provide for all the indigent insane without the assistance of the federal government. For the next six

---

Report of the Select Senate Committee to Visit Charitable and Penal Institutions, 1857, in New York (State) Board of Charities: *Thirty-seventh Annual Report* (3 vols., Albany, 1904), vol. I, pp. 797, 799, 805; Hazard is quoted in Margaret Creech: *Three Centuries of Poor Law Administration* (Chicago, 1936), p. 205.

20 Joseph C. G. Kennedy: *Preliminary Report on the Eighth Census* (Washington, 1862), pp. 32–36, 43–47, 50–53; Gerald N. Grob: *Mental Institutions in America, Social Policy to 1875* (New York, 1973), pp. 343–68; "Reports of American Asylums," *American Journal of Insanity*, vol. XVII (1860–61), pp. 77–78.

years, while continuing to promote hospital building in Southern and Western states, she sought congressional approval for a grant of lands from the public domain which would serve as the basis of a fund for the care of indigent insane and deaf-mutes. In 1854 both houses of Congress approved the bill, but Dix and her friends were unable to muster enough votes to override President Franklin Pierce's states' rights veto. Rebuffed at home, Dix temporarily transferred her activities to Europe. By the end of the 1850s she was back in the United States, visiting hospitals and corresponding with superintendents, not—as some of her admirers assumed—as a ministering angel, but as a friendly adviser on matters like drainage, roofing, ventilation, and appropriations.[21]

In the 1850s state prisons held about the same number of inmates as state asylums for the insane. Reformers, who in 1859 organized the American Society for Improvement of Penal and Reformatory Institutions, continued to debate the merits and defects of the rival Auburn and Pennsylvania systems of prison discipline. Prison administrators, however, tended to subordinate theories of reformation to the practical object of making their institutions self-supporting or, if possible, profitable. By 1860 the prevailing practice was to sell the labor of prisoners to contractors who employed them in prison workshops. In 1859, for example, the Ohio Penitentiary earned a profit of $20,000 by bartering the labor of convicts to contractors for 35 cents to 48 cents per day. In much the same way that local communities farmed out paupers, eight states—including Kentucky, Alabama, Illinois, and Louisiana—surrendered control of both prison and prisoners to lessees. Ordinarily the lessees assumed responsibility for maintaining prisoners and paid the state a nominal annual sum for the privilege of using convict labor; in Arkansas, however, the state paid the contractor 35 cents a day for each prisoner. As late as 1860 North and South Carolina, Delaware, and Florida avoided the expense and trouble of building penitentiaries by using county and district jails for the confinement of state prisoners. In this practice the backward states were like the national govern-

---

[21] Grob: *Mental Institutions in America*, pp. 103–08, 200–01; Seaton W. Manning: "The Tragedy of the Ten-Million-Acre Bill," *The Social Service Review*, vol. XXXVI (March 1962), pp. 44–50; fairly typical of letters from superintendents to Dorothea Dix is one from George Poindexter of the Western Kentucky Lunatic Asylum, March 21, 1861, in Dix Papers, Houghton Library, Harvard University.

ment, which, maintaining no penal institutions except those in the District of Columbia, boarded federal prisoners in state prisons and county jails.[22]

For a generation before 1860, evidence accumulated that local jails, whether in the North or the South, in booming cities or forlorn rural communities, were unsuited for either the confinement or the correction of their occupants. Yet at the end of the 1850s, poorly arranged and indifferently managed jails continued to hold—usually in idleness and often in loose association —convicted criminals, people awaiting trial in civil or criminal cases, persons detained as witnesses, a residue of the insane, and a heterogeneous collection of the unfortunate of all ages and every degree of waywardness. In 1859, in the Guilford County (North Carolina) jail, the Reverend Daniel Worth suffered frozen feet while awaiting trial for the crime of circulating Hinton R. Helper's *Impending Crisis*. In 1860, New York City newspapers reported instances of intoxicated men being eaten by rats in jails in the metropolis and its environs. All observers agreed that American jails, with very few exceptions, were a disgrace to an enlightened and humane people. But on this issue the public conscience was hard to rouse. The only advance in local penal institutions for adults was the establishment in scattered Northern cities of workhouses for drunks, vagrants, and other short-term offenders.[23]

Despite failure to accomplish much in the way of ameliorating prison conditions and although sharply divided over proper systems of prison discipline, reformers scored some modest successes in saving minor offenders from incarceration and in helping discharged prisoners. John Augustus (1785–1859), a shoemaker in Boston, took it upon himself to befriend, act as counsel, and furnish bail for juveniles and petty offenders hauled before the municipal court. Augustus was not a rich man (he worked at night to make up time spent in court), represented no sect or society, and received only meager financial assistance from admirers of his work, but between 1842 and 1858 he bailed out nearly 2,000 persons and made himself liable for almost

[22] *The American Almanac and Repository of Useful Knowledge for the Year 1861* (Boston, 1861), pp. 253, 342; Blake McKelvey: *American Prisons, A History of Good Intentions* (Montclair, N.J., 1977), pp. 54–62.

[23] Johnson: *Ante-Bellum North Carolina*, pp. 580, 680–82; *The New York Illustrated News*, vol. II (1860), pp. 2, 355; *Eighty Years' Progress*, p. 437.

$250,000. The Prison Association of New York, founded in 1844, was authorized by law to visit and inspect both state prisons and county jails. From the start, however, the association gave much attention to the plight of discharged convicts who, for want of employment, were "reduced to great distress and sore temptations." "To starve or to steal," warned Judge John W. Edmonds, one of the principal founders, "is too often the only alternative granted to them." Finding work for men and women lacking in skill and experience was difficult, but the association asserted that the success of its agents exceeded expectations and warranted continuance. Abigail Hopper Gibbons (1801–1893), daughter of one of the organizers of the Prison Association, took a leading part in the women's department and its successor (1853), the Women's Prison Association, which maintained a shelter for women released from jail.[24]

Advocates touted reform schools for delinquent youth as the most progressive mid-century development in corrections. By 1860, one-third of the states and about twenty cities had founded, or were in the process of building, special institutions for juvenile offenders. At the state schools the official daily program called for four hours in the classroom and six hours of labor in farm, workshop, or domestic duties. Massachusetts, the leader in the reform school movement, maintained the Westborough Reformatory for 600 boys, an industrial school for delinquent girls, and a training ship manned by sixty reform school boys. In 1856, Ohio founded a farm school for boys that supposedly incorporated the most advanced European reformatory theory and practice. The boys lodged, not in a huge barracks, but in log-cabin "cottages," each under the supervision of an "elder brother." In 1859, when a fire set by one of the inmates destroyed the main building at Westborough, the Massachusetts legislature voted funds to rebuild the institution on the cottage or family plan.[25]

[24] Harrison E. Starr: "Augustus, John," *Dictionary of American Biography* (26 vols. to date, 1928–1980), vol. I (1928), p. 429; Edmonds's statement is reprinted in Prison Association of New York: *Annual Report for the Year 1874* (Albany, 1875), p. 16; Merton L. Dillon: "Gibbons, Abigail Hopper," *Notable American Women 1607–1950*, ed. by Edward T. James (3 vols., Cambridge, Mass., 1971), vol. II, pp. 28–29.

[25] *American Almanac and Repository of Useful Knowledge, 1861*, p. 302; E. C. Wines: *The State of Prisons and of Child-Saving Institutions in the Civilized World* (Cambridge, Mass., 1880), pp. 80–81, 125–26; Robert H. Bremner, ed.: *Children and Youth in America, A Documentary History* (3 vols., Cambridge, Mass., 1970–74), vol. I (1970), pp. 705–09.

Privately managed but tax-supported reformatories, including Houses of Refuge in Boston, New York, and Philadelphia, supplemented and antedated the state reform schools. In addition, as noted above, a number of organizations founded in the 1850s attempted to forestall delinquency by engaging in "child-saving" work. The most aggressive of the new agencies was the Children's Aid Society of New York (1853), which gathered poor boys and girls into industrial schools, operated cheap lodging houses for newsboys, and sent companies of children from New York City to foster homes in Western states. Among the trustees of the society were men of the stature of Abram Hewitt, Cyrus W. Field, and Archibald Russell; its secretary was Charles Loring Brace, whose long and vigorous leadership of the society made him the country's foremost advocate of home placement, as opposed to institutional care, for dependent children. In an appeal for funds in 1859, Brace argued, in characteristic vein, that the organization deserved the support of the city, the state legislature, and private citizens because its emigration program reduced the cost of supporting pauper children in expensive public institutions. The Children's Aid Society, he said, was rescuing children who, if neglected, would sink in vice and poverty, and "by sending them out, we are supplying the greatest and sorest need in American families, a permanent labor force, educated in the habits of the house."[26]

For the most part, expansion rather than innovation characterized private charities and public welfare in the 1850s. As in earlier decades some social problems were evaded; others, if not solved, were at least attacked. American resources were still not sufficient to satisfy all demands on public and private bounty. The apportionment of attention and aid among competing claims indicated indifference to some sorry but mundane needs, sympathy for victims of specialized conditions or combinations of distress, conscientious support of religious and moral causes, generosity in disaster relief, and lively interest in child welfare.

Contemporary spokesmen, impressed by what they deemed unprecedented efforts to help the unfortunate, tended to exaggerate the extent and efficacy of those efforts. Thus, in 1855, the

[26] Charles Loring Brace: *The Best Method of Disposing of Our Pauper and Vagrant Children* (New York, 1859), pp. 12–13, 17.

National Intelligencer reported: "Thanks to the active benevolence that has exhibited itself during the past few years, . . . charitable institutions of all kinds have multiplied and there is relief and assistance ever ready for those who require it." Although such pronouncements were oversanguine, benevolent activities were widening in scope and responding to the influence of what Charles Loring Brace called "a more practical piety." Volunteer service in charitable enterprises was becoming a recognized form of social diversion and a mark of high social status. "It has become fashionable," George Templeton Strong observed in 1855, "and creditable and not unusual for people to busy themselves in personal labors for the very poor and in personal intercourse with them."[27]

As early as 1840, founders of the National Institute (later called the National Gallery of Art) objected that the pursuit of material success, with consequent neglect of the arts and general culture, was making the sons of the Founding Fathers less intelligent and less enlightened than their sires. In the 1850s, Peter Cooper and George Peabody set examples for later millionaires by breaking out of the rut of gifts for exclusively religious and charitable purposes, and endowing cultural institutions for the benefit of all classes: Cooper Union (1859) "for the advancement of science and art" in New York City, and the Peabody Institute (1857) in Baltimore. The former offered free classes in general science, engineering, and art, a reading room, library, and free lectures; the latter, in addition to a library and lecture series, contained an art museum and academy of music. As if in anticipation of such gifts, Henry Ward Beecher declared in 1855: "There never can be too many libraries, . . . too many galleries of art. . . . The power of the mind at the top of society will determine the ease and rapidity of the ascent at the bottom."[28]

In the thirty years before 1860, American reformers and philanthropists had formulated, or borrowed from English and Con

[27] *National Intelligencer*, June 5, 1855; Charles Loring Brace: "The Formation of the News Boys' Lodging House," in *Short Sermons to News Boys* (New York, 1866), p. 7; Strong: *Diary*, vol. II, p. 209.

[28] Daniel M. Fox: *Engines of Culture, Philanthropy and Art Museums* (Madison, Wis., 1963), pp. 10–11; Helen Lefkowitz Horowitz: *Culture and the City* (Lexington, Ky., 1976), pp. 21–22, quoting Beecher: *Star Papers* (New York, 1855), p. 296.

tinental writers, a comprehensive body of charitable theory. The cardinal tenet of their creed was that charity should prevent rather than merely relieve need. One of America's earliest paid social workers, Abigail Alcott—wife of Bronson and mother of Louisa May Alcott—wrote in 1850 that the only efficient charity was that which helped relieve the causes of poverty. Mrs. Alcott and other charity workers still attributed the causes of poverty mainly to the personal idiosyncrasies of sufferers and believed that many bad traits of the poor could be corrected by making assistance hard to get. In 1852 Horatio Wood, minister at large in Lowell, Massachusetts, advised those for whom he served as almoner:

> Necessity seems a hard mother, but she trains up smart, vigorous children, and we do not want to take them from her, and make them feeble and puny for this world and the next. There is an obligation upon us, with our overflowing mercy, not to forget the real kindness of a resolute no.

Denunciations of "thoughtless alms giving" and "indiscriminate liberality," however, were regularly accompanied by pleas for generous contributions to "wise" and "efficient" charities. "There never was a time when riches regularly bestowed seemed to do more good than at present," declared *Hunt's Merchants' Magazine* in September 1859. "Nor was the cry from perishing men ever louder than now."[29]

As in other aspects of American life, acrimony and extremism, self-righteousness and intolerance, left their marks on prewar efforts to do good. "Extremes meet," said the Reverend William Greenleaf Eliot of St. Louis, "and the great cause of social reform goes on, if at all, in spite of its advocates." Another clergyman, Henry W. Bellows of New York, told a young friend: "Our reformers generally lose their feet, through the lightness of their heads." Yet far from relying on sentiment or impulse, Charles Loring Brace, Dorothea Dix, Horace Mann, Horace Greeley, and Samuel Gridley Howe tirelessly advanced economic arguments, or appealed to "sound public policy," in support of

---

[29] Abigail M. Alcott: Mss. Reports to Boston Women's Societies, 1849–52, Houghton Library, Harvard University (hereafter cited as HLHU), *passim*; Lowell Missionary Society: *Eighth Annual Report of the Minister at Large* (Lowell, Mass., 1852), p. 15; *Hunt's Merchants' Magazine*, vol. XLI (1859), p. 398.

humanitarian objectives. Their common theme was the necessity of applying the principle of prevention to all social ailments.[30]

Practically every social and educational reform advocated in the generation before the Civil War was presented as a preventive measure, usually as a specific against pauperism. Sanitary reformers championed improvements in public hygiene as a means of reducing dependency caused by unnecessary sickness and premature death of breadwinners. The recommendations of Lemuel Shattuck's *Report of the Sanitary Commission of Massachusetts* (1850), a survey of factors affecting public health in Massachusetts, received little attention from Commonwealth legislators. But Shattuck's findings, cogently set forth in the *Report*, alerted reformers throughout the country to preventable "social murders and suicides."[31] As the decade wore on, sanitary reform gained prestige as the newest and most scientific of reform causes, as the prerequisite for other attempts to elevate the poor, and as the precursor of a general campaign for "social sanitation." The coming of war gave this lifesaving movement new meaning and urgency.

[30] William G. Eliot: *Social Reform* (St. Louis, 1857), p. 5; Henry W. Bellows to Marvin H. Bovee, July 27, 1860, Bovee Collection, Huntington Library.

[31] Lemuel Shattuck: *Report of the Sanitary Commission of Massachusetts, 1850* (Cambridge, Mass., 1850), pp. 30, 264–66; "Sanitary Reform," *North American Review*, vol. LXXIII (1851), pp. 117–35.

Chapter 2

Organizing Military Relief
in North and South

T he span of a single lifetime separated the secession con-
ventions of 1860–61 from the Constitutional Convention
of 1787. In 1860 it was still possible for Americans to speak of
the Founding Fathers in a literal sense because, in both North
and South, sons and grandsons of the Revolutionary generation
occupied positions of leadership in politics, business, and the
professions. A few veterans of the Revolution were alive at the
start and even at the end of the Civil War, and widows of Revolutionary soldiers survived until after the turn of the twentieth
century. At the time of Lincoln's inauguration, older citizens of
the Republic remembered the deaths of George Washington and
Benjamin Franklin. The outgoing President, James Buchanan,
had been born during Washington's first administration; General
Winfield Scott, ranking officer of the army, was older than the
Constitution, and Chief Justice Roger Taney, born in 1777, was
almost as old as the United States. In populous communities in
Illinois, Indiana, and Ohio—possibly within earshot of the special
train that carried Lincoln from Springfield to Washington—lived
men whose axes had felled the first trees in their settlements and
women who had seen the unbroken forests, as one of them
recalled, "with not a stick amiss."[1]

Living ties to the past and a sense of continuing the work of
earlier generations strengthened the will of both North and
South. "This is no time for timid counsels," wrote a Yankee intel-

[1] William Tallack: *Friendly Sketches in America* (London, 1861), p. 67.

lectual in December 1860. "Safety no less than honor demands of us to take a firm stand, and to shrink from none of the consequences of the resolute maintenance of our principles, the principles of justice and liberty."[2] At the same time Southern moderates—to say nothing of extremists—were declaring that peace and union could be purchased "by no less price than a thorough recognition of our right to regulate our own domestic affairs and full constitutional guarantees for the maintenance of our rights for all time to come."[3] Henry W. Bellows, a Unitarian minister in New York City, returned from a trip to the South early in 1860 with the conviction "We are *two* peoples in civilization, religion, temperament, tastes, climate." Devotion to duty, loyalty to principles, and obedience to conscience were as strongly felt in one section as the other. According to Bellows, the difference that counted was drastic divergence in moral and social sentiments. "We are not talking about the same thing when we talk about duty, principle, conscience, interest," said Bellows, "and we are the more bewildered and deceived because we think we *are* talking with a *common denominator* under our numerators."[4] Frederick Law Olmsted came closest to expressing the temper of the times when he told his friend Charles Loring Brace: "My mind is made up for a fight. The sooner we get used to the idea, the better, I think."[5]

Both North and South likened the Civil War to a second War of Independence. Each interpreted the struggle as being as much a test of righteousness as a trial of strength. Resort to arms fired the people of both sections to an intense pitch of patriotic ardor and made men, women, and children eager to contribute to the success of the cause they supported. For noncombatants the most practical method of expressing hatred for the enemy was to shower their own fighting men with loving attention. Since neither Union nor Confederate government was prepared for war, opportunities for voluntary efforts to supply the armies with comforts and necessities were virtually unlimited. British, Rus-

[2] Charles Eliot Norton to George William Curtis, December 17, 1860, Norton Papers, HLHU.

[3] W. L. Chipley, superintendent of the Eastern Lunatic Asylum, Lexington, Kentucky, to Dorothea L. Dix, December 19, 1860, Dix Papers, HLHU.

[4] Henry W. Bellows to an unidentified correspondent, January 24, 1860, Bellows Papers, Massachusetts Historical Society (hereafter cited as MHS).

[5] Olmsted to Brace, December 8, 1860, Olmsted Papers, LC.

sian, and French civilians had contributed to the relief of troops in hospitals and on battlefields during the Crimean and Austro-French wars. Americans, although appreciative of civilian efforts abroad, characteristically thought their soldiers entitled to higher standards of living and care than those prevailing in European armies.[6]

In the spring of 1861, while young men volunteered and older ones joined drill companies, women met in churches, schools, and homes to cut and sew garments, make flags, and scrape lint. Circles and associations of women multiplied like rings in the water, observed Katharine Prescott Wormeley of Providence, Rhode Island, their members working busily without knowing what to make or where to send.[7] Just a month after the firing on Fort Sumter, a New Jersey housewife, whose grandmother had sewed for soldiers of Washington's army, hazarded the guess that shirts, drawers, and hospital gowns sufficient to clothe armies of both North and South had already been made.[8] Southern women were similarly active and hardly less confused. In Richmond, where "socks for the soldiers" was the cry, Mary Boykin Chesnut rarely saw a woman without knitting in her hands. "One poor man," Mrs. Chesnut noted in her diary, "said he had dozens of socks and just one shirt. He preferred more shirts and fewer stockings."[9]

The war was barely under way when Northern clergymen and physicians began to try to put civilian aid to soldiers on a systematic basis. Among the leaders of this movement was Henry W. Bellows. In April 1861 he was approaching his forty-seventh birthday and beginning his twenty-third year as minister of the Church of All Souls in New York City. His congregation included Peter Cooper, William Cullen Bryant, and other rich and distinguished men, but to evangelical Protestants Bellows's rational

[6] Henry W. Bellows: "The Sanitary Commission," *North American Review*, vol. XCVIII (1864), p. 415; George Templeton Strong: *Diary*, ed. by Allan Nevins and Milton Halsey Thomas (4 vols., New York, 1952), vol. III, p. 604.

[7] Katharine Prescott Wormeley: *The United States Sanitary Commission, A Sketch of Its Purposes and Its Work* (Boston, 1863), p. 2.

[8] Mary Bache Walker to Alexander Dallas Bache, May 12, 1861, Bache Collection, Huntington Library; Mrs. Walker's grandmother was Sally Franklin Bache, daughter of Benjamin Franklin.

[9] Mary Boykin Chesnut: *A Diary from Dixie*, ed. by Ben Ames Williams (Boston, 1949), p. 121; Mary Elizabeth Massey: *Bonnet Brigades* (New York, 1966), pp. 25–42 *et passim*, provides the best and fullest treatment of women's role in the war, North and South.

Unitarian faith was as repugnant as the Italianate architecture of the new edifice—nicknamed "The Church of the Holy Zebra"— in which he preached. In 1857 he had outraged the pious by delivering an address in defense of the theater in which he criticized the moral confusion of people who attacked "the recreations rather than the sins of society." On most issues, however, Bellows avoided radicalism. "I think one kind of extravagance no excuse for another," he advised an ardent young reformer in 1860. "I long to see sobriety, moderation, candor in the treatment of all social & political & religious questions."[10] As a result of studying the works of the English sanitary reformers Edwin Chadwick and Thomas Southwood Smith, Bellows had become convinced that most social ills, including poverty and crime, were preventable. He believed that in the United States, poverty was a symptom of "spiritual disorder," the proper remedy for which was not "practical relief" but doses of "moral tonics." His program for preventing poverty included equal enforcement of law, secular and religious education for all, encouragement of self-respect and self-reliance at every level of society, and, not least, "withholding of careless relief."[11]

Naturally enough, Bellows viewed the outpouring of war-inspired generosity with mixed feelings. He appreciated and shared the universal desire to aid volunteers, but feared that "spontaneous beneficence," exercised without plan or direction, would be wasteful and possibly harmful in its results. Toward the end of April 1861 he joined like-minded men and women of New York City in organizing the Women's Central Association of Relief as a coordinating body for soldiers' aid societies in the metropolitan area. In May, Bellows and Dr. Elisha Harris, representing the Women's Central, went to Washington with Drs. W. H. Van Buren and Jacob Harsen, emissaries of two hospital and medical societies, to learn how the several associations could best serve the government. During a thirteen-hour train journey the four

[10] Henry W. Bellows: *The Relations of Public Amusements to Public Morality* (New York, 1857); Bellows to Marvin H. Bovee, July 27, 1860, Bovee Collection, Huntington Library.

[11] Bellows presented his social views in "The Treatment of Social Diseases," the Lowell Institute Lectures delivered in Boston in 1857; he summarized the principal points of these lectures in a letter to Charles J. Stillé, November 15, 1865, Bellows Papers, MHS; George M. Fredrickson comments on Bellows's hostility to perfectionist and millennialist strains in American reform in *The Inner Civil War: Northern Intellectuals and the Crisis of the Union* (New York, 1965), pp. 26–27, 100.

men discussed British and French experiences in the Crimean War. Out of their conversation emerged the idea of an American sanitary commission.[12] On arriving in Washington, Bellows and his friends gave rather than solicited advice. They requested Secretary of War Simon Cameron to appoint a commission composed of military officers, medical men, and "civilians distinguished for their philanthropic experience and acquaintance with sanitary matters," whose duties would be (1) to investigate "the best means of methodizing and reducing to practical service the already active but undirected benevolence of the people toward the army," and (2) to study and suggest ways of preventing sickness and unnecessary suffering among soldiers. Citing the experience of the Crimean and Indian sanitary commissions, the petitioners declared: "We wish to prevent the evils that England and France could only investigate and deplore. The war ought to be waged in a spirit of the highest intelligence, humanity, and tenderness for the health, comfort and safety of our brave troops."[13]

After an exasperating interlude, which Bellows termed "a month's struggle with the apathy, preoccupation, or suspicions of the government," Secretary of War Cameron issued an order establishing "A Commission of Inquiry and Advice in Respect to the Sanitary interests of the United States Forces." The five civilians and three army officers named to the commission began work on June 12, 1861, a day before President Lincoln, who thought such an agency might prove "a fifth wheel to the coach," gave unenthusiastic approval to the order.[14] Concern for the morale and welfare of the volunteers, who were believed to represent a higher social class than, and to present different problems from those of regular troops, was an important factor in inducing the government to accept the offer of advice from a voluntary body. Surgeon General Clement A. Finley consented to the formation of the commission only after stipulating that it confine its attention to volunteers.

As if to make up for previous delays the commission or-

[12] Bellows to Stillé, November 15, 1865, Bellows Papers, MHS.

[13] Bellows et al.: "An Address to the Secretary of War," May 18, 1861, United States Sanitary Commission: *Documents* (2 vols., New York, 1866), vol. I, document I.

[14] Bellows: "The Sanitary Commission," p. 167; William Quentin Maxwell: *Lincoln's Fifth Wheel: The Sanitary Commission* (New York, 1956), p. 8.

ganized rapidly, choosing Bellows as president, Alexander Dallas Bache vice-president, and George Templeton Strong treasurer. The commissioners appointed or elected in the summer of 1861 included the assistant Surgeon General, the head of a government scientific bureau, two clergymen, two lawyers, and six physicians or physician-scientists. As a group the civilian members represented the professions rather than business, and the Eastern seaboard, especially New York City, rather than the West. The addition of new members from Illinois, Ohio, and Kentucky soon gave the commission broader geographical representation, and through appointment of several hundred associate members, it sought to promote the organization of regional branches and local auxiliaries. The most eminent, although not the most active, commissioners were Samuel Gridley Howe and Alexander Dallas Bache. Howe, who had first won fame for directing relief operations in Greece during the 1820s, was even better known for his work for the education of the blind and mentally retarded: Bache, superintendent of the United States Coast Survey, regent of the Smithsonian Institution, and great-grandson of Benjamin Franklin, had official, social, and family ties to the two worlds of science and politics. Bellows, Strong, Van Buren, Wolcott Gibbs, and Cornelius Agnew, all New Yorkers, made up the executive committee. John Strong Newberry, an Ohio geologist and the only one of the original commissioners with a Western background, accepted responsibility for directing the commission's operations in the Mississippi Valley.

Allan Nevins wrote of the Sanitary Commission: "Nothing quite like it, in its combination of specialized skill, sturdy common sense, and consecrated devotion to a great aim, had previously been known in American annals; and its success was to show that a new era of national organization was opening." Members of the commission certainly deserved high marks for their willingness to give unstinted time and labor to the organization. At frequent intervals, sometimes monthly or every six weeks, they traveled to Washington for meetings that might last four or five days; between sessions Bellows and the executive or standing committee held almost daily (or nightly) meetings in New York. Mark Skinner of Chicago and Horace Binney, Jr., of Philadelphia proved valuable additions to the commission, not only in its internal deliberations and decisions but by organizing strong branches in their respective cities. Not all the 400 dignitaries tapped as associate members in the summer of 1861 accepted the invitation—none of the four men originally nominated in Chicago, for example, was able or willing to serve—but those who joined gave the Sanitary Commission recognition in professional and business circles. Some of the associate members aided its technical work by writing medical manuals; others, as in New York City, helped raise funds; and, no less important, many of their wives and daughters became faithful supporters of the Sanitary cause.[15]

At an early meeting the commissioners appointed Frederick Law Olmsted general secretary, or executive officer, of the organization. Olmsted, nearing forty at the time of his appointment, was in the process of condensing his earlier accounts of journeys through different parts of the South into *The Cotton Kingdom* (1861). For several years before joining the commission he had been architect and superintendent of construction for Central Park in New York City. The skill he displayed in planning and realizing this great project was his chief recommendation for the position of general secretary.[16]

By his own admission, Olmsted was a "growler." Restless, anxious, irritable, and fault-finding, he began the assignment with misgiving, warning his father that the duties he had assumed would be "ungrateful" and advising his wife, "I do not get on very well; do not accomplish much and shall not I fear." Although Olmsted was irregular in personal habits—Strong said he stayed up until 4 A.M., slept in his clothes, and breakfasted on pickles and strong coffee—he had a passion for order and efficiency. In *The Cotton Kingdom*, Olmsted condemned slavery not only because it was inhumane but because it was wasteful and inefficient, and he declared that white Southerners were poor because they worked little and badly.[17] In the Sanitary Commis-

---

[15] Allan Nevins: *War for the Union* (4 vols., New York, 1959–71), vol. I, p. 416; Sarah Edwards Henshaw: *Our Branch and Its Tributaries, Being a History of the Northwestern Sanitary Commission and Its Auxiliaries During the War of the Rebellion* (Chicago, 1868), pp. 24–26.

[16] "Frederick Law Olmsted, His Life and Work," in Charles Capen McLaughlin, ed.:*The Papers of Frederick Law Olmsted* (1 vol. to date, Baltimore and London, 1977–), vol. I, p. 24; Olmsted's career is treated in full in Laura Wood Roper: *FLO, A Biography of Frederick Law Olmsted* (Baltimore and London, 1973).

[17] Frederick Law Olmsted to John Olmsted, June 26, 1861, and to Mrs. F. L. Olmsted, July 2, 1861, Olmsted Papers, LC; Strong: *Diary*, vol. III, p. 291; Olmsted: *The Cotton Kingdom, A Traveller's Observations on Cotton and Slavery in the American Slave States*, ed. by Arthur M. Schlesinger (New York, 1953), p. 12.

sion's first comprehensive report Olmsted informed the Secretary of War: "Slovenliness is our most characteristic vice." Wartime Washington abounded in examples of the "national vice," not only in "the unmitigated shabbiness and filth of unsewered, unpaved, unpoliced streets" but also in the conduct of officers of the army and officials of the administration. "Men with great responsibilities are careless about them," Olmsted complained to Charles Loring Brace, "will not take the trouble—apparently cannot study carefully and thoroughly how they can be executed, but *get along somehow and guess it will do*. Damn them."[18]

Guesswork was not Olmsted's style. Bellows said he had never known a more painstaking organizer. Strong, who shared many of Olmsted's characteristics, acknowledged the general secretary's talent and energy but eventually came to believe he suffered from "monomania for system" and an insatiable appetite for power. "He is a lay-Hildebrand," Strong exclaimed after two and a half years of close association with him. Olmsted's faults were accentuations of his merits. His perfectionism was the more remarkable because he recognized that the strength of the Union cause lay in endurance, cheerful or sullen. "In stupid British, blind, lumbering momentum," he said, "we beat the British themselves."[19] A less demanding man could not have made the officially powerless Sanitary Commission an effective instrument of benevolence.

Bellows, Olmsted, and the other leaders of the commission maintained that its principal object was to reduce the toll of preventable deaths in the army. They knew that in the recent past armies had lost four, seven, or ten times as many men from disease as from injuries in battle and that for every man who died from disease, scores suffered illnesses that reduced the strength and efficiency of the fighting forces. The commission's first general appeal for funds, dated June 22, 1861, declared that the successful conduct of the war depended more on the health of the troops than on all other conditions combined. Strong, who drafted the circular, declared: "We cannot afford to waste

[18] U.S. Sanitary Commission: *A Report to the Secretary of War of the Operations of the Sanitary Commission, and upon the Sanitary Condition of the Volunteer Army, December 1861* (Washington, 1861), p. 27; Olmsted to Brace, August 25, 1862, Olmsted Papers, LC.

[19] Strong: *Diary*, vol. III, pp. 304–05; Olmsted to Brace, August 25, 1862, Olmsted Papers, LC.

life."[20] Preliminary inspection of assembly points revealed such ignorance of hygiene and neglect of sanitary precautions that members of the commission, mindful of the epidemics of the 1850s, feared one-half the volunteers might succumb to cholera, fevers, or dysentery before October. "Soap! Soap! Soap!" cried Samuel Gridley Howe during an inspection of Massachusetts troops. The army took better care of horses than of soldiers, Howe reported, and needed health officers and washerwomen more than chaplains or nurses.[21]

As a board of inquiry and advice the commission was particularly concerned about the scarcity, unsuitability, and lackadaisical management of military hospitals. Within a few weeks of being organized, it protested against the practice of converting houses, stores, warehouses, hotels, and schools into hospitals and urged erection of "a sufficient number of wooden shanties or pavilions," each to accommodate thirty to sixty patients, and set far enough apart "not to poison each other." Drs. Agnew, Gibbs, and Van Buren, medical members of the commission, prepared plans for model hospitals which, after slight modification, were approved by the government in October 1861. Inexpensive and commodious pavilion hospitals of the type recommended by the commission eventually proved to be among the major lifesaving advances of the war. Concurrent with the agitation for hospital improvement, members and associate members of the commission prepared medical and surgical monographs for distribution among army and navy surgeons. The monographs or sanitary tracts brought together the latest views on prevention and treatment of diseases prevalent in camps.[22]

To inquire into and promote the health of the army, the commission recruited a staff of physicians—fourteen by the end of 1861—who conducted minute inspections of the sanitary condition of camps or posts. Following a schedule prepared by members of the commission, the sanitary inspectors investigated and reported on a long list of matters relating to the health, morale,

---

[20] U.S. Sanitary Commission Circular, June 22, 1861, reprinted in Wormeley: *Sanitary Commission*, p. 266; Strong: *Diary*, vol. III, p. 162.

[21] Laura E. Richards: *Letters and Journals of Samuel Gridley Howe* (2 vols., Boston, 1906–09), vol. II, pp. 481, 494–95.

[22] U.S. Sanitary Commission: *Report of the Secretary of War . . . December 1861*, pp. 88–89; Charles J. Stillé: *History of the United States Sanitary Commission* (Philadelphia, 1866), pp. 110–11, 553.

or efficiency of the troops: healthfulness and drainage of the campsite, administration of the hospital, adequacy of hospital supplies, quality of water and rations, methods of camp cooking, ventilation of tents or quarters, clothing and cleanliness of the men, condition of privies, and disposition of offal. On the basis of their investigations, inspectors called circumstances detrimental to health to the attention of responsible officers and offered advice on methods of remedying them. Pampering of volunteers was not the commission's objective; on the contrary, it advocated stricter discipline and closer adherence to army regulations as the first and essential step toward sanitary improvements. In the soul-searching that followed the debacle of Bull Run, Olmsted privately remarked: "There is but one sanitary measure to be thought of now, and that is discipline."[23]

Prevention rather than relief was the watchword of the Sanitary Commission. From the beginning, however, inspectors discovered and sought to alleviate critical shortages of supplies in hospitals and camps. As early as August 1861 Bellows lamented that the press of work for the cure and comfort of soldiers impaired the commission's ability to fulfill its more important duties as a board of prevention; as late as February 1862, Howe expressed concern lest lavish gifts of "extras" and comfort articles to troops might accustom the nation to "*a system of alms-giving and alms-taking.*"[24] Supervising the flow of relief supplies to volunteers, although one of the original objectives of Bellows and his associates, was not among the functions assigned the Sanitary Commission by the Secretary of War. During the summer of 1861, as inspectors' reports showed some regiments neglected and others overindulged by friends at home, the need for a central agency to superintend the collection and distribution of voluntary contributions became too urgent to ignore. Olmsted in Washington and Newberry in the West undertook the formation of a network of branches and auxiliaries linking local soldiers' aid societies with the Sanitary organization. In the autumn of 1861 the commission sent out circulars urging local societies to forward relief supplies to depots it had established in Boston, New York, Baltimore, Washington, Wheeling, and Cin-

---

23 Olmsted to Mrs. F. L. Olmsted, July 29, 1861, Olmsted Papers, LC.
24 Bellows to Charles Eliot Norton, August 21, 1861, Norton Papers, HLHU; Richards, ed.: *Letters and Journals of Howe*, vol. II, p. 498.

cinnati. Not content to remain simply a body of inquiry and advice, the commission sought to make itself the agent and channel of all friends of the Union army.[25]

Expansion into the field of supply—justified as necessary to prevent waste and duplication of effort—involved the Sanitary Commission in conflicts with other would-be almoners. The first skirmish was with Dorothea Dix, whom Strong impatiently called "that philanthropic lunatic." Dix, although approaching sixty years of age, had volunteered her services to the army on April 19, 1861, the day Massachusetts troops were attacked by a secessionist mob while passing through Baltimore. Appointed Superintendent of Female Nurses, she held a commission from the Secretary of War authorizing her "to receive, control, and disburse special supplies bestowed by individuals or associations for the comfort of . . . the citizen soldiers from all parts of the United States."[26] Not unreasonably, Dix resented the Sanitary Commission's efforts to create a nationwide system for collecting supplies as an encroachment on her authority. The initial disagreements were smoothed over, but relations between Dix and the Sanitary organization remained less than cordial.[27] After the war, Bellows commented: "She never seemed . . . able to accept our plans and methods or to cooperate much with us, or we with her." According to Strong, Dix belonged "to the class of comets, and [could] be subdued into relations with no system whatever."[28]

In attempting to direct the springs of patriotic philanthropy into one "national, complete, unsectional" channel, the Sanitary Commission struggled against forces of state pride, local sentiment, and personal ambition. Desire to help "our own boys" or "our regiment," present in all communities, was especially strong in the Midwest. The commission made little headway in Indiana

[25] U.S. Sanitary Commission: *Report to the Secretary of War . . . December 1861*, pp. 75–78; J. S. Newberry: *The U.S. Sanitary Commission in the Valley of the Mississippi, During the War of the Rebellion, 1861–1866* (Cleveland, 1871), pp. 17–20.

[26] Strong: *Diary*, vol. III, p. 165; commission dated 23 April 1861, signed by Simon Cameron, Secretary of War, Dix Papers, HLHU; on Miss Dix's work as superintendent of nurses see Helen E. Marshall: *Dorothea Dix, Forgotten Samaritan* (Chapel Hill, N.C., 1937), pp. 201–37.

[27] Olmsted to Dix, October 24, 1861, U.S. Sanitary Commission Papers, New York Public Library (hereafter cited as NYPL).

[28] Bellows to Stillé, November 15, 1865, Bellows Papers, MHS; Strong: *Diary*, vol. III, pp. 173–74.

and Iowa, and it suffered defeat in Missouri, where a rival body, with headquarters in St. Louis, was set up in September 1861. William Greenleaf Eliot (like Bellows, a Unitarian clergyman), disregarding the original commission's St. Louis representative, obtained an order from General John C. Frémont establishing an independent Western Sanitary Commission to serve troops quartered or on duty west of the Mississippi. Bellows tried in vain to persuade Secretary Cameron to rescind Frémont's order; efforts to induce the St. Louis group to accept branch status in the United States Sanitary Commission proved fruitless.[29]

Both Eliot and James Yeatman, president of the Western Sanitary Commission, were strong Unionists who believed that circumstances in St. Louis and Missouri necessitated an autonomous organization. Moreover, as long-time leaders of religious, educational, civic, and philanthropic affairs in St. Louis they were unwilling to accept subordinate roles in the larger commission. Strong pronounced the Western Sanitary Commission schismatic; Bellows denounced it as secessionist—"an example of state and local insubordination." Eliot responded that no excellence of organization could take the place of independence and individuality of action.[30] The quarrel worsened in 1862, when the Western Sanitary Commission began to solicit and to receive large contributions of goods and money from Boston and New England. Sniping between the rival commissions continued throughout the war, bearing out Eliot's contention that "The most hateful of all jealousies and controversies are those among philanthropic or charitable associations."[31]

[29] Maxwell: *Lincoln's Fifth Wheel*, pp. 97–106; James Yeatman to Major General Henry W. Halleck, January 3, 1862, in U.S. War Department: *The War of the Rebellion: A Compilation of the Official Records of the Union and Confederate Armies* (70 vols., Washington, D.C., 1880–1901), Series 1, vol. VIII (1883), pp. 484–87 (hereafter cited as *Official Records*); William Greenleaf Eliot, *The Story of Archer Alexander* (Boston, 1885), p. 121.

[30] Strong: *Diary*, vol. III, p. 188; Bellows to C. E. Norton, February 16, 1864, Norton Papers, HLHU; Eliot: "Loyal Work in Missouri," *The North American Review*, vol. XCVIII (1864), pp. 524, 529.

[31] Charlotte C. Eliot: *William Greenleaf Eliot, Minister, Educator, Philanthropist* (Boston and New York, 1904), p. 236; J. G. Forman: *The Western Sanitary Commission* (St. Louis, 1864), p. 119; Eliot: *Story of Archer Alexander*, p. 119; Eliot stated in 1864 that the $500,000 contributed to the Western Sanitary Commission by residents of New England constituted one-third of its total receipts; Eliot: *A Statement Relating to the Endowment of Washington University* (Boston, 1864), pp. 12–13.

*   *   *

In zeal to assist fighting men, Southern civilians yielded nothing to noncombatants in the North. Soldiers' aid societies in cities, towns, and hamlets made or collected clothing, hospital stores, blankets, and other supplies the Confederate government could not furnish its troops. Like many similar groups in the North, these local societies preferred to have their contributions go to men from their own communities—to husbands, sons, brothers, cousins, friends, and neighbors. Sentiments of this kind were not peculiar to the South, but in the Confederacy the forces counteracting particularism were weak, and those fostering it overpowering. Newspapers and citizens groups launched wide-ranging fund drives for specific objectives such as shoes for General Lee's army, and the Richmond YMCA canvassed distant parts of the South for support of its work in the Confederate capital.[32] Neither sentiment nor circumstances, however, favored organization of military relief on a Confederacy-wide basis. The states' rights philosophy justified particularistic tendencies in charities as in nearly everything else. Shortages of supplies, transportation difficulties, financial disorder, and the disruptive effects of military operations made cooperation on a national scale virtually impossible. After the war, in a characteristic mixture of pride and sorrow, a Confederate veteran explained: "We had no Sanitary Commission in the South. . . . We were too poor; we had no line of rich and populous cities closely connected by rail, all combined in the good work of collecting and forwarding supplies and maintaining costly and thoroughly equipped charities. With us, every house was a hospital. . . ."[33]

In the summer of 1861 the Confederate Congress directed the Secretary of War to make arrangements for receiving and allocating gifts for able-bodied soldiers and to appoint a clerk to take charge of voluntary contributions for the sick and wounded. From time to time Confederate officials issued special appeals for blankets and drugs. Medical purveyors, who were responsible for procuring hospital supplies, frequently called on local aid soci-

[32] E. Merton Coulter: *The Confederate States of America, 1861–65* (Baton Rouge, La., 1950), p. 529; Mary Elizabeth Massey: *Ersatz in the Confederacy* (Columbia, S.C., 1952), pp. 22–23; C. Howard Hopkins: *History of the Y.M.C.A. in North America* (New York, 1951), pp. 94–96.

[33] Alexander Hunter: *Johnny Reb and Billy Yank* (New York and Washington, 1905), p. 347.

eties to help stock depots serving military installations in the surrounding area. In Alabama, Georgia, Louisiana, and South Carolina private citizens formed statewide associations for the benefit of their troops. The Georgia Relief and Hospital Association and the Central Association for the Relief of South Carolina Soldiers, the best known of these organizations, coordinated the efforts of local societies within the borders of their respective states and undertook vigorous programs to aid Georgia or South Carolina volunteers in hospitals or camps in other parts of the Confederacy. Both these associations received, and in large measure depended on, subsidies from public funds.[34]

Officials in other states, bypassing voluntary associations, established tax-supported agencies to look out for the welfare of their men in the Confederate forces. North Carolina, too poor in peacetime to care for its dependent classes, found the means to provide more generously for its soldiers than any other Confederate state. The Southern practice of designating hospitals for the reception of men from particular states made it easier for official agencies and voluntary associations to assist the sick and wounded for whom they felt responsible. But state-oriented and state-supported military relief programs, whatever their justification, inevitably resulted in unequal treatment of men supposedly enlisted in a common cause.[35]

Partly by necessity and partly because of state and local pressures, Confederate war charities were alleviative rather than preventive in character. The closest approximation to a national organization was an association for maimed soldiers that, with the assistance of the Confederate government, sought to supply artificial limbs to amputees.[36] The Southern ideal of hospitality found institutional expression in wayside homes or rests established by local associations to provide meals and lodgings for sick

[34] H. H. Cunningham: *Doctors in Gray, The Confederate Medical Service* (Baton Rouge, La., 1958), pp. 139–43; E. B. Coddington: "Soldiers' Relief in the Seaboard States of the Southern Confederacy," *Mississippi Valley Historical Review*, vol. XXXVII (1950), pp. 20–31; Charles W. Ramsdell: *Behind the Lines in the Southern Confederacy* (Baton Rouge, La., 1944), p. 15.

[35] Cunningham: *Doctors in Gray*, pp. 38, 143–44; Coddington: "Soldiers' Relief," pp. 32–34; Phoebe Yates Pember: *A Southern Woman's Story, Life in Confederate Richmond*, ed. by Bell Irvin Wiley (New York, 1959), p. 58; Frank Lawrence Owsley: *State Rights in the Confederacy* (Chicago, 1925), pp. 120, 126–27.

[36] Cunningham: *Doctors in Gray*, pp. 144–45; Coulter: *Confederate States*, p. 450.

and wounded troops passing through their communities. The first of these shelters was founded in Columbia, South Carolina, in March 1862. Thereafter women's societies set up similar hostels at railway junctions throughout the South. As transportation of goods over long distances became increasingly difficult, maintenance of wayside homes took precedence over the other work of aid societies. Although ordinarily supported by local resources, some of the wayside homes, like the one in Charleston, South Carolina, were assisted by appropriations from state funds. The most celebrated and possibly the most characteristic charitable feat during the war was a dinner the people of Virginia prepared for Robert E. Lee's troops on New Year's Day 1865. At a time when the outlook was gloomy and food was desperately scarce, Cabinet officers, state legislators, clerks, society women, shopkeepers, churches, the Richmond YMCA, and the Southern Express Company joined forces to "set a table twenty miles long" to serve what was proudly declared to be "the biggest barbecue ever gotten up on this continent."[37]

Philanthropic agencies are remembered as much for what they attempt as for what they accomplish. Nothing the U.S. Sanitary Commission attempted was more difficult to achieve than reform of the War Department's Medical Bureau. Far from wishing to usurp official authority, the commission urged that the bureau be entrusted with broader powers and heavier responsibilities. The first barrier to reform was the incumbent Surgeon General, Clement A. Finley, whose qualifications for the post rested principally on seniority, and who was unwilling to acknowledge deficiencies in the medical services. Beginning in September 1861, while Sanitary agents inspected camps, prepared medical monographs, distributed supplies, and urged construction of model hospitals, Bellows and his associates agitated for Finley's removal and lobbied for passage of a bill reorganizing the Medical Bureau. The struggle occurred during a period when the commission's treasury was almost exhausted, and at one point the

[37] Francis B. Simkins and James W. Patton: *The Women of the Confederacy* (Richmond, Va., 1936), p. 95; Coddington: "Soldiers' Relief," pp. 35–36; Chesnut: *Diary from Dixie*, pp. 270, 430, 435, 449; James W. Patton, ed.: *Minutes of the Greenville Ladies Association* (Durham, N.C., 1937), pp. 40–41, 111–14; Coulter: *Confederate States*, pp. 452–529.

commissioners considered disbanding. Strong declared it was useless to appeal to the public to support an advisory body whose advice was neither wanted by the army nor heeded by the administration. "Funds are running low," Wolcott Gibbs wrote to Bache in February 1862, "and our existence as a commission draws nigh its ending. Let us die game and fight red tape to the last."[38]

Just when the outlook was bleakest, the new Secretary of War, Edwin M. Stanton, an enthusiast for system, order, and efficiency, quarreled with Surgeon General Finley and gave his support to the movement for remodeling the Medical Bureau. On April 16, 1862, a year and a day after the first call for volunteers, President Lincoln signed the Medical Reorganization Act. The measure was not a clear victory for reform, but it included some of the features the commission had proposed, notably provision for commissioning sanitary inspectors and for appointing the Surgeon General and his chief assistants on the basis of merit rather than seniority. Shortly afterward the commission's candidate, William A. Hammond, was appointed Surgeon General. Strong, who a few weeks earlier had thought the commission would have to go out of business, exulted: "The Sanitary Commission is treated with profound respect by all Washington officials. Our relations with the government are now [April 1862] more intimate than they have ever been."[39]

The honeymoon lasted scarcely a month. Having secured the appointment of a friendly Surgeon General, the commission found itself at odds with a Secretary of War who, in the opinion of Bellows, Strong, and Olmsted, impeded efforts to carry through the reorganization of the Medical Bureau. Stanton, on the other hand, was affronted by what he deemed the commission's meddling in the affairs of the War Department.[40] He regarded Surgeon General Hammond as a creature of the Sanitary Commission and ultimately secured his dismissal from the

[38] Stillé: *History of the United States Sanitary Commission*, pp. 100–125; Strong: *Diary*, vol. III, p. 207; Gibbs to Bache, February 19, 1862, Bache Collection, Huntington Library.

[39] For the Medical Reorganization Act see *Official Records*, Series 3, vol. II (Washington, 1899), pp. 22–23; Strong: *Diary*, vol. III, p. 218.

[40] Bellows to W. H. Van Buren, May 13, 1862, Bellows Papers, MHS; Strong: *Diary*, vol. III, p. 227: Benjamin P. Thomas and Harold M. Hyman: *Stanton: The Life and Times of Lincoln's Secretary of War* (New York, 1962), pp. 366–68.

army.[41] Bellows and Strong accused Stanton of duplicity and questioned his sanity; Olmsted declared the greatest service the commission could render would be to "help hang Stanton."[42] According to rumor, Stanton never mentioned the commission without a curse; he did not attack it directly but showed his opposition in petty ways and by granting recognition to the Western Sanitary Commission.[43]

Cordiality between officialdom and a fault-finding voluntary agency was too much to expect. After the war, recalling that the Sanitary Commission began and ended its work in an atmosphere of official "suspicion, jealousy, and check," Bellows concluded that the tension had had the beneficial effect of keeping it alert and critical.[44] Its agents and officials continued to maintain "comprehensive watchfulness" over the health of volunteers and to press for improvements in medical service. Inspectors scrutinized conditions in camps and hospitals; their reports, tabulated and classified by the commission's statistical bureau, indicated that although the Union army was one of the healthiest on record, the rate of sickness among its members was three to five times as high as among civilians of comparable age.[45] The commissioners asserted that lax medical examination of recruits burdened the army with men unfit for duty. Bellows and the executive committee neglected no opportunity to remind government and people that fever and dysentery were deadlier than rebel bullets, and that debility, immaturity, and disease took heavier tolls of soldiers' lives than the bloodiest battles. On the first anniversary of Bull Run, Bellows advised President Lincoln that nine out of every ten deaths in the army during the previous year might have been prevented.[46]

Fortunately, the Sanitary Commission was able to do more

[41] Allan Nevins: "The United States Sanitary Commission and Secretary Stanton," Massachusetts Historical Society *Proceedings*, vol. LXVII (1941–1944), pp. 402–19; George W. Adams: *Doctors in Blue, The Medical History of the Union Army in the Civil War* (New York, 1952), pp. 131–41.

[42] Olmsted to Bellows, July 13, 1862, Olmsted Papers, LC.

[43] Maxwell: *Lincoln's Fifth Wheel*, p. 194; War Department Special Orders No. 397, December 16, 1862, *Official Records*, Series 3, vol. II, p. 947.

[44] Bellows: "The U.S. Sanitary Commission," *Johnson's New Universal Cyclopaedia* (4 vols., New York, 1875–77), vol. IV, p. 74.

[45] Edward Jarvis: "Sanitary Condition of the Army," *The Atlantic Monthly*, vol. X (1862), p. 473.

[46] Bellows et al. to Lincoln, July 21 and August 5, 1862, *Official Records*, Series 3, vol. II, pp. 237, 298.

than criticize and admonish. First on the Western rivers and then on a more ambitious scale during the Peninsular campaign of 1862, it equipped and staffed ships to carry the sick and wounded from combat areas to general hospitals in the North. The transport service for the Army of the Potomac, costing about $20,000 a month, was the most expensive operation the commission had yet undertaken, and it proved to be the "most arduous and harassing duty" performed by the agency during the war.[47] Olmsted, who took personal charge of the work, was disappointed in the result. "It is not practicable," he wrote, "for government agents, in the tumult and occupation of war, to avail themselves of assistance and instruction offered by anyone to whom they are not officially responsible." The summer's work paid for itself in lives saved and pain alleviated, but in Olmsted's judgment the chief value of the experience was negative, "as indicating what our function is not." No voluntary organization could satisfactorily perform tasks which, because of their magnitude and importance, could be discharged only by government.[48]

One of Olmsted's comrades in the hospital transport service, nurse Katharine Prescott Wormeley, took a more positive view of the operation. She asserted:

> This expedition, if it has done no other good, has made a body of life-long friends. We have a period to look back upon when we worked together under the deepest feelings, and to the extent of our powers, shoulder to shoulder, helping each other to the best of our ability, no one failing or hindering another. From first to last there has been perfect accord among us; and I can never look back to these months without feeling that God has been very good to let me share in them and see human nature under such aspects. It is sad to feel that it is all over.[49]

In a book written while these memories were fresh in mind, Wormeley declared that the task of an agency like the Sanitary Commission was to "lead the way." What it asked, she said, was "not the gift of power but that the government should come

[47] Stillé: *History of the United States Sanitary Commission*, p. 159.
[48] Olmsted to Bellows, July 13, 1862, Olmsted Papers, LC.
[49] Katharine Prescott Wormeley: *The Other Side of War* (Boston, 1889), p. 205, quoting a letter Wormeley wrote in the summer of 1862.

forward and take the work away from it by doing it thoroughly."[50]

In hospital transports, as in earlier plans for pavilion hospitals and later in developing a railway ambulance car, the Sanitary Commission inaugurated and demonstrated useful services subsequently adopted by military authorities.[51] Through willingness or effrontery in presuming to "lead the way" it not only made important contributions to the welfare of soldiers but also clarified the function of philanthropy. Quartermaster General Montgomery C. Meigs, a friend of the Sanitary Commission and a vigorous champion of the army, defined the function (and accurately characterized the commission's work) as supplying a little leaven to the government's "large lump of dough."[52]

---

[50] Wormeley: *The United States Sanitary Commission*, p. 92.

[51] On the hospital transports see Frederick Law Olmsted: *Hospital Transports, A Memoir* . . . (Boston, 1863), and Newberry: *U.S. Sanitary Commission in the Valley of the Mississippi*, pp. 484–93; on the Sanitary Commission's work in developing a railway ambulance car see Newberry: pp. 474–83, and Bellows: "U.S. Sanitary Commission," *Johnson's New Cyclopaedia*, vol. IV, p. 74.

[52] Meigs to Henry I. Bowditch, October 30, 1862, *Official Records*, Series 3, vol. II, pp. 702–03.

Chapter 3

Philanthropic Warfare

The efforts for which the United States Sanitary Commission became best known lay neither in innovation nor in prevention, but in the auxiliary work of relief. The shift in emphasis from prevention to amelioration was almost imperceptible because, after the first year of war, mounting military activity blurred the distinction between the two functions. As in epidemics or disasters, succor of the afflicted and protection of the threatened seemed equally imperative. Whatever maintained or restored the vigor of the fighting forces and gave civilians a more vital sense of participating in the war was worth doing. The Sanitary Commission's far-flung activities ranged from battlefield relief to regular attendance in camp and hospital and special services in "homes," "lodges," and "refreshment saloons" for sick and needy soldiers, recruits, discharged veterans, and paroled prisoners of war. In addition, the commission maintained allotment, pension, and back-pay offices, a directory of the names and locations of men in general hospitals, and a bureau of vital statistics that collected and analyzed data on the background and condition of recruits and the effect of military service on their health and mortality. Operating this diversified program required the paid services of relief agents, hospital visitors, cooks, clerks, storekeepers, teamsters, carpenters, laborers, physicians, and statisticians. By 1864 the commission's employees numbered about 450 and the monthly payroll amounted to $28,000. Frederick Law Olmsted, who supervised the expansion of field operations, answered criticism of the use of paid workers by saying the scope of the work required that it be handled as a business and administered on a business basis.[1]

Behind the paid workers, making or collecting supplies that eventually reached soldiers in camp or hospital, were tens of thousands of volunteers, mainly women, for whom the war unleashed "emotions, energies, and talents even they did not realize they possessed."[2] Publicists described the Sanitary Commission as "the great artery which bears the people's love to the people's army" and wrote feelingly of the commission's "constant, never ceasing care for the health and comfort of the Army. . . ."[3] Cornelia Hancock, a young Quaker who volunteered her services as an army nurse, wrote her family shortly after Gettysburg: "Uncle Sam is very rich, but very slow, and if it was not for the Sanitary, much suffering would ensue."[4] For the most part, however, the commission discharged its tasks with acumen rather than sentiment. "The work of relieving the soldier," observed Charles J. Stillé in his history of the organization, "was found in practice to be a very hard, continuous and prosaic one." Goods collected, made, or purchased by members of 7,000 local auxiliaries flowed to twelve branch or regional offices to be sorted, acknowledged, reported to headquarters, and repacked; from branch depots supply shipments moved, as needed, to central distributing points in Washington or Louisville, thence to hospitals, hostels, and field relief agents, one of whom was assigned to each army corps.[5] The Sanitary Commission refused to accept contributions for designated units and recognized no distinction between soldiers of different states. On the other hand, the commission cautioned its agents against furnishing assistance in "gratuitous superfluity" and required them to observe certain rules in distributing supplies: "First the need must be plain; second, some satisfactory explanation must be given of the cause

---

[1] J. Foster Jenkins to Alfred J. Bloor, July 26, 1864, U.S. Sanitary Commission Papers, New-York Historical Society (hereafter cited as NYHS); Olmsted to Mrs. John Olmsted, January 26, 1863, Olmsted Papers, LC.

[2] Mary Elizabeth Massey: *Bonnet Brigades* (New York, 1966), p. 25.

[3] Katharine Prescott Wormeley: *The United States Sanitary Commission, A Sketch of Its Purposes and Its Work* (Boston, 1863), p. 1; Charles J. Stillé: *History of the United States Sanitary Commission* (Philadelphia, 1866), p. 253.

[4] Henrietta Stratton Jaquette, ed.: *South After Gettysburg, Letters of Cornelia Hancock, 1863–1868* (New York, 1956), p. 13.

[5] Stillé: *History of the United States Sanitary Commission*, pp. 251, 255–56, 258.

of the need; and third, a voucher must be secured from the surgeon showing that he had called for aid."[6]

Principle rather than parsimony dictated stringency in the administration of relief. Bellows was as critical of "imprudent benefactions" in war as in peace. The commission resolved not to take upon itself burdens properly belonging to government; it shunned interference with military procedures and was anxious to avoid duplicating supplies normally furnished by the army. Elisha Harris, one of its founders and mainstays, warned that public channels of assistance might shrink or dry up if the springs of private benevolence ran too copiously. "Will not officials neglect their duties," he asked, "if they find other people ready to do them in their stead?"[7] The question was rhetorical since government officials were as loath to shift their obligations to a voluntary agency as the Sanitary Commission was unprepared to assume them. "No nation," declared Quartermaster General Meigs, "has ever . . . made such large, such prodigious provision for its sick and wounded soldiers. It is the greatest charity on earth."[8]

Sanitary Commission leaders agreed that only government had the funds, stores, transportation, and authority necessary to meet the needs of soldiers. It was everywhere "the soldier's richest, ablest, and most constant friend," and supplies issued by its agencies always bore a gigantic ratio to the assistance furnished by outside benevolence. But next to the government, and foremost among voluntary efforts, stood the United States Sanitary Commission.[9] Or so the commission contended. In the winter of 1862–63 and during the first half of 1863, however, the Sanitary organization was racked by internal dissensions resulting in Olmsted's resignation as general secretary.[10] Meanwhile, the Sanitary Commission's dominance was being challenged by a

[6] Henry W. Bellows: "The U.S. Sanitary Commission," *Johnson's New Universal Cyclopaedia* (4 vols., New York, 1875–77), vol. IV, pp. 75–76.
[7] "The Sanitary Commission," *The North American Review*, vol. XCVIII (1864), pp. 178–79.
[8] M. C. Meigs to Henry I. Bowditch, October 30, 1862, in U.S. War Department: *The War of the Rebellion: A Compilation of the Official Records of the Union and Confederate Armies* (70 vols., Washington, D.C., 1880–1901), Series 3, vol. II (1899), p. 702 (hereafter cited as *Official Records*).
[9] Bellows to Mrs. Clara J. Moore, March 1863, U.S. Sanitary Commission Papers, NYPL.
[10] Bellows to Olmsted, August 10, 13, 18, 1863, Olmsted Papers, LC.

new organization, also designated a "commission" but with a religious rather than a medical or scientific orientation.

The United States Christian Commission was organized in November 1861 at an informal convention of delegates from fifteen Young Men's Christian Associations. The twelve commissioners appointed by the convention were clergymen and laymen from evangelical Protestant churches in New York, Philadelphia, Boston, Chicago, Cincinnati, Buffalo, and Washington. Most of the commissioners were active in YMCA work, and the permanent chairman, George Hay Stuart, a Philadelphia dry goods merchant, was chairman of the Central Committee of the YMCA. The objects of the Christian Commission, as stated in its first circular, were to promote "the spiritual good of the soldiers in the army, and incidentally their intellectual improvement and social and physical comfort." Despite expressions of approval for these objectives from President Lincoln, Secretary Cameron, and General George B. McClellan, the Christian Commission attracted little attention and neither attempted nor accomplished much during the first year of its existence.[11] Late in 1862, following removal of headquarters from New York to Philadelphia and appointment of W. E. Boardman as general secretary, the organization took on new vigor. Boardman, a Methodist minister, declared that John Wesley's preachers had carried the Gospel to British troops a century before Florence Nightingale went to heal their bodies; the Christian Commission, he rejoiced, was the first agency to minister to the soldiers' spiritual as well as physical needs.[12]

The new commission won powerful support among religious, business, and political leaders. Its management resembled an interlocking directorate of the national benevolent societies since former officers and agents of the Bible, Tract, Temperance, and Sunday school societies occupied key posts in the organization.[13] The Union's most prominent financier, Jay Cooke, served on the executive committee; William E. Dodge, the celebrated "Chris-

[11] Robert Ellis Thompson, ed.: *The Life of George H. Stuart, Written by Himself* (Philadelphia, 1890), pp. 129–32; Lemuel Moss: *Annals of the Christian Commission* (Philadelphia, 1868), pp. 107–09, 116–21.

[12] Timothy L. Smith: *Revivalism and Social Reform in Mid Nineteenth Century America* (New York and Nashville, 1957), p. 175.

[13] Clifford S. Griffin: *Their Brothers' Keepers, Moral Stewardship in the United States, 1800–1865* (New Brunswick, N.J., 1960), pp. 248–49; James H. Moorehead: *American Apocalypse, Yankee Protestants and the Civil War, 1860–1869* (New Haven and London, 1978), pp. 65–66.

tian merchant," was chairman of the New York branch. The commissioners included four Protestant bishops: two low-church Episcopalians and two Methodists. One of the latter, Bishop Matthew Simpson, reputed to be President Lincoln's favorite preacher, was a friend of Stanton and Salmon P. Chase. Another commissioner, the Reverend Heman Dyer, had known Stanton since his college days at Kenyon. Schuyler Colfax, Speaker of the House of Representatives, was another member. Anniversary meetings of the organization met in the hall of the House of Representatives and were attended by the President, Chief Justice, secretaries of executive departments, Senators and Congressmen, and representatives of the army and navy.[14]

The Christian Commission, although more loosely organized than the Sanitary Commission, also divided the home front into branches, located in major cities, that served as collection and distribution points for contributions raised by hundreds of local aid societies. As a general rule the local societies were affiliated with Protestant evangelical churches. The "Christians" conducted field operations by assigning paid general agents to each army, and station agents to each army corps and by commissioning volunteer delegates, who agreed to work under supervision of the permanent agents for periods of six weeks. Responsibility for camp and hospital programs rested with the paid agents, but the strength of the Christian apparatus lay in the delegate system. Delegates, who were clergymen or members in good standing in orthodox churches, received their commissions either from the central headquarters or from individual branches. Among the approximately 5,000 delegates sent to the field were the evangelist Dwight L. Moody, Washington Gladden (later famous as a leader of the social gospel movement), and Charles Loring Brace of the New York Children's Aid Society. As "ambassadors for Jesus" the delegates, in their field service, preached, held prayer meetings, distributed Bibles, tracts, hymn books, hospital stores, and comfort articles; on the home front the reports and sermons of returning delegates publicized the Christian Commission's work and stimulated fresh exertions for its support.[15]

The Christian Commission, like the Sanitary, regarded col-

[14] Moss: *Annals of the Christian Commission*, pp. 216–17.

[15] *Ibid.*, pp. 145, 541–638, especially p. 545. Field activities of the delegates can be followed through the daybooks of Christian Commission stations in the U.S. Christian Commission Papers, National Archives, Record Group 94.

lection and distribution of relief supplies as incidental to its major objective. But just as Sanitary inspectors believed that relief, properly administered, helped prevent sickness, suffering, and death, Christian agents and delegates maintained that alleviating bodily needs facilitated the great work of religious exhortation, instruction, and consolation. Sanitarians provided antiscorbutics to keep the army in fighting condition; Christian "ambassadors for Jesus" bestowed gifts as a means of spreading spiritual grace. "It was easy to converse with those men concerning their eternal well-being," a delegate said of soldiers aided by the Christian Commission. "They could not oppose a Christianity that manifested such concern for their bodily comfort":

> Farina, oranges, lemons, onions, pickles, comfort-bags, shirts, towels, given and distributed in the name of Jesus, though designed for the body, gave strength to the soul. To the quickened senses of a wounded soldier parched with fever, far from home and friends, an onion was a stronger argument for the religion which bestowed it than the subtle reasoning of Renan, and a pickle sharper than the keenest logic of Colenso![16]

Christian delegates became as well and favorably known for supplying coffee (served from a patented, mobile coffee wagon), comfort bags or "housewives" (made by Sunday school children), writing paper, and books as for furnishing "messages of mercy" and "words of comfort."[17]

The charitable public, as leaders of both commissions early discovered, was more interested in getting material assistance to volunteers than in preventing disease or promoting religion. Relief, therefore, became an essential activity for each commission, not only to serve troops but to attract and hold home-front supporters. In camps, in hospitals, and on battlefields representatives of the two agencies often cooperated with each other; behind the lines, however, Christian and Sanitary organizations competed for supplies and funds. Their rivalry was sharpened by religious animosities, personal and social antagonisms, and jealousy for

[16] Charles C. Coffin: *The Boys of '61 or, Four Years of Fighting* (Boston, 1880), p. 373.

[17] Mrs. W. E. Boardman: *Life and Labours of the Rev. W. E. Boardman* (New York, 1887), pp. 119–26; Jaquette, ed.: *South After Gettysburg*, pp. 138–39, contrasts the style of Christian and Sanitary agents in the field.

public recognition. Early in 1863, Bellows advised William E. Dodge of the Christian Commission that the country could not support two major relief organizations. "I think," Bellows warned, "the Christian Commission, without accomplishing its own object, will weaken and defeat ours."[18]

Priority of establishment, a strong system of branches and auxiliaries, and, in particular, bountiful financial contributions from California and other Far Western states and territories gave the Sanitary Commission an advantage over its rivals. In the autumn of 1862, through the efforts of Thomas Starr King, a popular Unitarian minister in San Francisco, magnificent gifts from the West Coast began to enrich the Sanitary treasury. "We *like* the California style . . ." Bellows wrote to King after receiving one of several drafts of $100,000 from the San Francisco Sanitary Fund Committee. "Can anything be more terse, succinct, intelligible, dignified, elegant, & sublime?"[19]

King's death early in 1864 sent Bellows hastening to California to keep the state loyal to the Sanitary Commission. On his arrival in San Francisco he discovered "a desperate effort, thoroughly organized & supported by the illiberal clergy of the Pacific Coast, . . . to divert the interest and weaken the confidence of the people in our cause." A society of 300 women from evangelical sects met thrice weekly "to gossip over the infidelity & wicked character of the U.S. Sanitary Commission, & to roll up their eyes over the holiness of the Christian Commission." The San Francisco Sanitary Fund Committee, an organization of forty businessmen with the mayor as chairman, was neither organized nor recognized as an agency of the Sanitary Commission; it could, if it chose, send the money it raised into other channels, and at least half its members were sympathetic to the Christian Commission. "You would be very much surprised," Bellows wrote his fellow commissioners, "if you knew how accidental and impulsive the enthusiasm has been under which the vast sums raised in California have been collected." Once or twice a year representatives of the San Francisco committee went through the city soliciting donations from wealthy merchants. "They have

[18] Bellows to Dodge, February 12, 1863, U.S. Sanitary Commission Papers, NYPL.

[19] Bellows to King, November 14, 1862, Bellows Papers, MHS; on King's skill in fund raising see the memoir by Edwin P. Whipple in Thomas Starr King: *Christianity and Humanity* (Boston, 1877) p. li.

a way of banding together 4 or 5 gentlemen, & settling down before a refractory non-payer until he surrenders in the term they consider he ought to subscribe to the Sanitary Fund!!" Because liberality to the fund influenced credit ratings, some merchants pledged more than they could afford. "To keep this so," Bellows cheerfully acknowledged, "is my great labor."[20]

In September 1864, after three months of strenuous organizing and exhorting, Bellows reported the California situation in hand. Having succeeded in converting the San Francisco committee into a branch of the Sanitary Commission, he proposed extending the assessment system to the entire state by having soldiers' aid societies in each town collect 10 cents a month from every man, woman, and child in the population. California was the philanthropic prize of the war. By holding the West in the Sanitary column, Bellows assured the continued flow to its treasury of funds needed to meet the cost of distributing supplies contributed by other sections of the country.[21]

Meanwhile, the pressure of mounting military demand and increasing competition from the Christian Commission forced Sanitary agents in the East and Midwest to adopt stringent methods of raising money and securing supplies. The Soldiers' Aid Society of Palatine, Illinois, assessed a graduated tax ranging from 5 cents to $1 per month on each inhabitant of the town.[22] Children's "Alert Clubs" in Norwalk, Ohio, and Irvington, New York, divided their communities into districts and canvassed each household for a minimum subscription of 20 cents a month.[23] To promote such neighborly excursions and to stimulate additional giving, the Sanitary Commission employed a staff of professional canvassers (eleven in the spring of 1864, twenty at the start of 1865), whose salaries, averaging $100 per month, were approximately twice as large as the pay of relief agents in

[20] Bellows to Strong, June 30, 1864, Bellows to Standing Committee, U.S. Sanitary Commission, June 22, August 11, September 2, 1864, Bellows Papers, MHS.

[21] Bellows to Standing Committee, U.S. Sanitary Commission, September 2, 1864, Bellows Papers, MHS; Bellows: "The U.S. Sanitary Commission," *Johnson's New Universal Cyclopaedia*, vol. IV, pp. 79–80. California contributed $1,200,000 or about 25 percent of the total cash receipts ($4,900,000) of the Sanitary Commission.

[22] *The Sanitary Commission Bulletin*, vol. III (1864), p. 826.

[23] *Ibid.*, vol. I (1863–64), pp. 208, 370–71.

the field.[24] In the circumstances, an English visitor commented
—more in admiration than in condemnation—it was "a dangerous matter for a man, in seeming good circumstances, to refuse
giving a donation when called upon." Only Englishmen and
Americans, declared James Dawson Burn, would have been able
and willing to subject themselves to such a drastic process of
"financial pumping."[25]

In both Union and Confederacy charitable fairs, familiar fund-
raising diversions in peacetime, yielded spectacular returns when
war fused patriotism and philanthropy. In the spring of 1862, in
the wake of the *Monitor-Merrimack* encounter, a wave of "gunboat fairs" swept the South. Mary Boykin Chesnut, who donated
a string of pearls to be raffled, jubilantly noted that the Columbia, S.C., fair made "bushels of money" for the purchase of a
gunboat. In Charleston slaves assisted the local gunboat fund by
contributing the proceeds of a concert by the "Confederate
Ethiopian Serenaders." At approximately the same time the
Columbus, Ohio, Soldiers' Aid Society arranged a "Grand Union
Bazaar and Tableaux."[26] All previous efforts of this kind were
overshadowed, however, by a succession of fairs held in Northern
cities and towns in 1863 and 1864 for the benefit of the U.S.
Sanitary Commission, its branches and auxiliaries. If Boston's
prewar fairs for the education of the blind and the antislavery
cause were the antecedents of these charitable extravaganzas,
Chicago's Great Northwestern Fair of October–November 1863
was their immediate inspiration. George Templeton Strong described the organizers of the Chicago fair, Mrs. A. H. Hoge and
Mary Livermore (both of whom were carried on the Sanitary
Commission payroll as canvassers), as "fearful and wonderful
women whose horse power is to be expressed in terms of droves
of horses." With little encouragement from national headquarters
and in the face of local disparagement, the two women turned
the Chicago fair into a regional "harvest home," eliciting support

[24] *Ibid.*, vol. I, p. 292; vol. III, p. 945.

[25] *Three Years Among the Working Classes in the United States During
the War* (London, 1865), pp. 238, 242.

[26] Mary Boykin Chesnut: *Diary from Dixie*, ed. by Ben Ames Williams
(Boston, 1949), pp. 210–11; E. Merton Coulter: *The Confederate States of
America, 1861–1865* (Baton Rouge, La., 1950), p. 256; Francis P. Weisen-
burger: *Columbus During the Civil War* (Columbus, Ohio, 1963), pp.17–
18.

of farmers and townspeople of northern Illinois, Wisconsin, and Iowa and making gifts to the commission synonymous with loyalty to the Union.[27]

During the winter of 1863–64 and in the spring of 1864, in emulation of Mrs. Hoge and Mrs. Livermore, committees in nearly every major city in the North staged fairs, each of which, according to local reports, surpassed all others in magnificence of arrangements and in monetary or patriotic returns. Since the financial returns of the fairs were treated as indices of wealth and civic spirit, each city sought to match or outdo the munificence of rivals. Brooklyn, whose fair was long remembered as the city's "first great act of self-assertion," was determined to "beat Boston"; promoters of the Metropolitan Fair of New York City were even more ambitious: their aim was to secure a larger amount of money than the aggregate raised by all previous fairs.[28]

The ingenuity of local managers gave each fair a special character, but the general pattern was the same: committees scoured cities and tributary areas for commodities useful to the commission and ransacked the community for articles that could be sold, auctioned—or where sentiment permitted—raffled, for the benefit of the commission or the sponsoring branch. Cincinnati's fair, with 16 major committees and 70 subcommittees, secured the cooperation of 200 separate organizations.[29] Fairs in New York City and Philadelphia, largest and most glamorous of the species, attracted contributions from friends of the Union in England, France, Italy, and Russia. All of the fairs welcomed farmers' and housewives' homely gifts of potatoes, onions, pickles, and jellies, but each sought to obtain salable items of patriotic or historical significance. President Lincoln, a lukewarm friend of the Sanitary Commission in its field operations, contributed drafts of the Emancipation Proclamation and the

[27] George Templeton Strong: *The Diary of George Templeton Strong,* ed. by Allan Nevins and Milton Halsey Thomas (4 vols., New York, 1952), vol. III, p. 562; *The Sanitary Commission Bulletin,* vol. I, pp. 66–71; Albert J. Bloor to Miss Ellen Collins, November 10, 1863, U.S. Sanitary Commission Papers, NYPL.

[28] George E. Waring, comp.: *Report on the Social Statistics of Cities* (2 vols., Washington, D.C., 1886), vol. I, p. 471; William Quentin Maxwell: *Lincoln's Fifth Wheel: The Sanitary Commission* (New York, 1956), pp. 224–25; Linus P. Brockett: *The Philanthropic Results of the War in America* (New York, 1864), p. 69.

[29] William J. Jacobs: "Quiet Crusaders, A History of the Cincinnati Branch of the United States Sanitary Commission" (unpublished M.A. thesis, University of Cincinnati, 1956), pp. 72–80.

Gettysburg Address to be sold for the benefit of various fairs. Along with members of his Cabinet, he supplied hairs from head or beard to "feather" a cardboard eagle donated to the New York fair. This enterprise also received and disposed of Fanny Kemble's album of presidential autographs, curios like James Bowie's knife, a manuscript by James Fenimore Cooper, and a trotter from the stables of the publisher Robert Bonner.[30] At Philadelphia in 1864 and in Chicago in 1865, managers of the fairs launched drives to collect one day's wages, earnings, or profits from every workman, farmer, industrialist, business or professional man within reach of their appeals. Everywhere, according to the Sanitary Commission organ, the *Bulletin*, the magic, money-producing word was "ORGANIZE."[31]

While procedures for collecting contributions for the Sanitary Commission were highly effective, methods of allotting funds were less than satisfactory, at least to the central organization. The net product of the fairs approached $2,750,000, but the branches retained the lion's share of this sum to finance their individual activities. The national office of the commission, although relieved of the expense of buying material to be made into clothing or bedding by the branches, received only a modest part of the fairs' cash proceeds to help meet the mounting expense of distributing supplies, conducting camp and hospital inspections, operating soldiers' homes and relief stations, and maintaining technical services such as information offices, hospital directories, and the statistical bureau. In May 1864 the *Sanitary Commission Bulletin* complained that the success of the fairs had put the commission as a whole in peril; the popular assumption seemed to be that the immense sums they raised rendered regular and less spectacular efforts superfluous.[32] "Gigantic spasms" of giving, exhausting canvassers and contributors alike, were followed by periods of torpor, in which only trickles of supplies reached the commission's depots. The Sanitary Commission wanted "quiet, persistent, methodical work," but the spirit of the times, as Mary Powers of Abington, Massachusetts,

[30] Strong: *Diary*, vol. III, pp. 417–28. The Thomas Haines Dudley Papers in the Henry E. Huntington Library contain useful information on English contributions to the New York, Philadelphia, and second (1865) Chicago fairs.

[31] *The Sanitary Commission Bulletin*, vol. III (1864), p. 826.

[32] *Ibid.*, vol. II (1864), pp. 417–19.

noted, favored "steam and impulse" rather than system.[33] Fortunately the Sanitary organization included women like Louisa Lee Schuyler and Ellen Collins of the Women's Central in New York City, whose patient, businesslike attention to logistical problems, day in and out, month after month, helped carry it through the last hard year of the war.[34]

None of the major military relief commissions succeeded in enlisting the unqualified support of all soldiers' aid societies in the North or entirely overcame forces of state and local particularism. Numerous societies gave more or less impartially to Sanitary and Christian commissions, meanwhile supplying state relief commissions and making contributions to individual agents whose appeals roused their sympathies. Citizens of almost every state, whether Massachusetts or Connecticut, Indiana or Ohio, felt that *their* soldiers had first claim on their benevolence. Nearly every society had pet regiments, hospitals, or almoners; practically all wanted to know where their boxes went, who received them, and how gratefully they were accepted. Women in Lynn, Massachusetts, for example, preferred to send contributions to a woman of their acquaintance at Finley Hospital in Washington rather than direct them into the impersonal supply channels of the Sanitary Commission.[35] The Soldiers' Aid Society of Bridgeport, Connecticut, determined to know "just where the contents of our boxes are received and the disposition made of articles," addressed boxes to known friends at designated hospitals. In return donors, including P. T. Barnum, received "many delightful reports of the hearts we have cheered" and repeated assurances of the everlasting gratitude of recipients.[36]

Foremost among the mavericks operating outside the Sanitary and Christian commissions was Clara Barton. She was a person to reckon with because, although a volunteer without official standing, she enjoyed and did not hesitate to make use of the friendship and support of Henry Wilson, chairman of the

---

[33] Mary L. Powers to Ida M. Gray, February 4, 1864, U.S. Sanitary Commission Papers, NYPL.

[34] Maxwell: *Lincoln's Fifth Wheel*, pp. 224–25.

[35] M. L. Newhall to Ida Gray, February 8, 1863, U.S. Sanitary Commission Papers, NYPL.

[36] Soldiers' Aid Society, Bridgeport, Connecticut: *First Annual Report*, pp. 8, 17.

Senate Committee on Military Affairs. Her service as nurse, cook, comforter, and provider for Union troops began, like Dorothea Dix's, in the very first days of the war, when she met and cared for men of the Sixth Massachusetts Regiment—"my early school-mates," as she described them—on their arrival in Washington after the affray in Baltimore. A spinster of forty, Barton was a tiny, ardent woman who had learned habits of command as a schoolmistress and ways of self-advancement as a Patent Office clerk. She was the youngest of five children of a veteran of Anthony Wayne's post-Revolutionary Indian campaigns. In childhood Clara had liked her father's stories "about the war and how the soldiers lived" better than fairy tales or nursery rhymes.[37] Beginning life as the little sister of a high-spirited, enterprising family, Clara grew up to become everybody's loving and demanding old-maid aunt. During the war, always insisting on having her own way, pouting or storming when denied it, she tended soldiers as though they were nephews, established sisterly relations with quartermaster and medical officers, and found and nursed an ailing brother. The war was to her, as to the nation as a whole, a family affair.[38]

Clara Barton's courage, zeal, and compassion were matched only by her ability to describe her efforts in prose that made her contributors feel they shared her heroism. Until the last year of the war she directed her appeals not to the public but to groups with which she had some personal connection. In reporting the disposition of two boxes of supplies sent by friends in Hightstown, New Jersey, she wrote:

> I carried them myself, and with my own hands wrapped them about the mangled, bleeding forms, or fed them to the thirsting, famished soldiers just brought from the field of blood and strife. Your wine brought strength to the fainting; your cloths staunched the blood of the dying. . . . I felt that every shred was consecrated, and my own heart assures me that they have drawn Heaven's choicest blessings on you.

[37] Ishbel Ross: *Angel of the Battlefield: The Life of Clara Barton* (New York, 1956), p. 4.

[38] The Barton Papers, Huntington Library, reveal the texture of Clara Barton's relations with her brothers, sisters-in-law, and nephews and the familial nature of her war mission. See, for example, Barton's letters to Amelia Barton, September 17, 1863, to Samuel Rich Barton, December 3, 1863, October 30, 1864, and to Stephen Barton, December 1864.

Today I am empty handed, and hourly expecting tidings of another battle. From all I gather, it must come soon, and to meet its terrible necessities I have only my empty hands.

Can you help fill them again for me? I shall go at the first sound of the battle, and do with my might what my hands find to do. Of all that you can send me I will see that not one shred is lost, and I will give it with my own hands where the need is greatest and the pain keenest.[39]

Eventually, private sources of supply proved inadequate to the need. Barton's first public appeal for support, issued in May 1864, was like an announcement that extreme adversity had forced a proud woman, previously assisted by friends and relations, to go on relief. Characteristically, Barton presented her need as a personal matter demanding general and immediate attention:

For the first time in the history of the war, the magnitude and intensity of the suffering and want are so appalling as to wring from me a public call for aid.

I have just returned from Fredericksburg where I have used and sent my last pound of supplies. . . . I ask you to aid in filling my hands that I may help meet the distress crowded within the dingy streets of that city of suffering and death. . . . There is time for all to labor and grow weary in well doing.

Send food, suitable for the wounded or money to buy it, the appeal concluded, to the Treasurer's Office, U.S. Treasury, Washington, D.C., FOR CLARA BARTON.[40]

Armed with the favor of Senator Wilson, Barton had little need, and no inclination, to subject her efforts to the control of either the Sanitary or the Christian Commission. "It would *seem,*" she wrote Secretary of War Stanton in April 1864, "that the two enormous Commissions that are driving the charitable world mad of late, must be equal to every contingency."[41] Barton, perhaps correctly, thought otherwise. In June 1864 she explained

[39] Clara Barton to "Ladies of the Soldiers' Relief Society of Hightstown, New Jersey," August 19, 1862, Clara Barton Papers, LC.

[40] Printed Circular, *To the Clergy and Soldiers' Friends: A Call to You from Our Suffering Wounded,* May 16, 1864, Clara Barton Papers, LC.

[41] Clara Barton to Stanton, April 29, 1864, Barton Papers, LC.

to a correspondent that because of her long experience in the field, she felt compelled to maintain an independent organization: "If, by practice, I have acquired any skill, it belongs to me to use discretionary, and I might not work as efficiently, or labor as happily, under the direction of those of less experience than myself."[42]

Among the numerous relief workers who shared Barton's familial view of the war and her disdain for impersonal, organized benevolence was Walt Whitman. He was about Barton's age and in his family played the roles of mother's boy, big brother, and bachelor uncle. Whitman's ministry to soldiers commenced relatively late, toward the end of 1862, when he went to Fredericksburg in search of an injured brother ten years his junior.[43] Unlike Barton, whose missions, as she remembered them, involved toiling in front of armies and endurance of Spartan hardships, Whitman, although no stranger to battlefields, usually rendered his service behind the lines, in Washington. He prepared for his hospital visits by bathing, donning clean clothes, eating a good meal, and putting on a cheerful appearance. "I found it was in the simple matter of personal presence and emanating ordinary cheer and magnetism," he wrote in *Specimen Days*, "that I succeeded and helped more than by medical nursing, delicacies, or gifts of money. . . ."[44] The delicacies and money Whitman sometimes distributed came from friends in Brooklyn, New York City, Providence, Salem, and Concord.

In later years Whitman recalled his three years of hospital visiting as "the greatest privilege and satisfaction . . . and, of course, the most profound lesson of my life." By serving as almoner for others, Whitman said, "I learned one thing conclusively—that beneath all the ostensible greed and heartlessness of our times, there is no end to the generous benevolence of men and women in the United States, when once sure of their object." Even to a poet as frank as Whitman, that genial lesson seemed more appropriate to poetic expression than the darker knowledge

[42] Clara Barton to Mrs. D. C. Alling, June 2, 1864, Barton Papers, LC.

[43] Whitman may have been associated with the Christian Commission for a few weeks early in 1863, but by March 1863 he was, in his own words, "A self-appointed missionary," Charles I. Glicksberg, ed.: *Walt Whitman and the Civil War* (Philadelphia, 1933), pp. 3–4; Daniel Aaron: *The Unwritten War, American Writers in the Civil War* (New York, 1973), pp. 63–65.

[44] *The Poetry and Prose of Walt Whitman*, ed. by Louis Untermeyer (New York, 1949), p. 621.

he possessed of the war as a monstrous slaughterhouse in which devils and butchers butchered each other. The latter was Whitman's vision of "the real war," which he predicted would never get in the books.[45]

To Clara Barton, "the real war" meant the engagements at which she had been present, all the others she would have attended had she been able, the anguish she had soothed, the unremembered and anonymous deaths denied her care and witness. She could never say, as Whitman did, "And so goodbye to the war," because the war was her life and livelihood. Before the fighting ended, while mourning the deaths of a brother and a nephew, she offered to find and mark the graves of Union prisoners of war, a service for which Congress (at the instance of Senator Wilson) paid her $15,000. As was the case in most of Barton's earlier and later humanitarian efforts, this mournful but congenial task involved her in acrimonious contests for precedence.[46] In conjunction with it she undertook an arduous series of lectures describing her own war experiences. In addresses entitled "Work and Incidents of Army Life" and "How the Republic Was Saved, or War Without the Tinsel," like the shade of her father, she told stories of how the soldiers lived and how some of them died in her arms.[47]

The Christian Commission was the first of the major relief organizations to leave the field. In February 1866 "The Christians" held a farewell meeting of prayer and self-praise in the House of Representatives with Speaker Colfax presiding and Chief Justice Chase and members of the Cabinet in attendance. Bishop Simpson, who had taken a prominent part in Lincoln's obsequies, read the eulogy: "The Christian Commission has led a noble life. It was baptized in prayer, worked amid suffering and affliction, leaned on the affections of the wise and pure, received aid from all classes and ministered to multiplied thousands."[48] After the

[45] *Ibid.*, pp. 643, 649; George M. Fredrickson: *The Inner Civil War, Northern Intellectuals and the Crisis of the Union* (New York, 1965), p. 94.

[46] William E. Barton: *The Life of Clara Barton, Founder of the American Red Cross* (2 vols., New York, 1922), vol. I, pp. 304–34; Ross: *Angel of the Battlefield*, pp. 84–95.

[47] Barton, *Life of Clara Barton*, vol. I, pp. 342–46. Barton netted $12,000 from her postwar lectures.

[48] George R. Crooks: *The Life of Bishop Matthew Simpson of the Methodist Episcopal Church* (New York, 1891), p. 404.

war, leaders and members of the Christian Commission enlisted their militant piety in the cause of religious revivals, home and foreign missions, campaigns against alcohol, and crusades for the suppression of vice.

The Sanitary Commission received no thanks from the government it had instructed, advised, and nagged. More or less against the wishes of Bellows, who favored a slow and gradual suspension of operations, and in accordance with the desire of Treasurer Strong, the U.S. Sanitary Commission resolved to close down swiftly. For such a large concern, however, going out of business was a time-consuming process. Some of its important statistical and medical reports were not published until 1869, and as late as 1873 the commissioners were still meeting occasionally to try to wind up affairs. William Quentin Maxwell, historian of the organization, gives May 8, 1878, as the date of its demise. A dozen years later, surviving commissioners scorned the suggestion that they receive pensions for their services. "Imagine being *paid* for what we did!" Wolcott Gibbs wrote to Olmsted.[49]

The longest-lived of the commissions was the Western Sanitary Commission, which was still in operation and well fixed financially twenty years after the war. In the postwar period the St. Louis organization endowed soldiers' homes and orphanages, relieved soldiers' widows and families of disabled veterans, and contributed funds to Washington University for a scholarship fund—still in existence—for children or descendants of Union soldiers.[50]

Across the country, women enrolled in local soldiers' aid societies either disbanded their organizations or turned their hands to other work. To end associations which had linked members to a larger service, and given leaders unexampled opportunities to manage large affairs, was a hard decision. Some of the societies expressed willingness to go on making shirts, drawers, socks, and wrappers indefinitely. On the other hand, Louisa Lee Schuyler, the principal supply officer of New York City's Women's Central Association of Relief, saw no point in having the work drag on and at last dwindle into insignificance. "I go for winding up quickly and thoroughly," she wrote in the summer of

[49] Strong: *Diary*, vol. IV, p. 503; William G. Eliot: *The Story of Archer Alexander* (Boston, 1885), p. 120; Maxwell: *Lincoln's Fifth Wheel*, pp. 290–91.

[50] Western Sanitary Commission: *Final Report* (St. Louis, 1886), pp. 143–44.

1865. "These 'last' days are tough."[51] Finally, on August 12, 1865, Schuyler and her assistant, Ellen Collins, put the office in Cooper Union in order. They were too busy to indulge in sentiment.

> By a sort of tacit consent [Schuyler told a friend] we never mentioned the words "last day," never alluded to it that whole day. . . .
>
> I waited to see the last cover put on the last box, the little flags taken down, and lastly the window curtains removed. Then I walked home. Not sadness, or regret— those were not the feelings, only the deepest gratitude to God for having been permitted to see that work through, and do what I could for it from beginning to end.[52]

Within a few weeks a china and glass store occupied the former office of the WCAR and there was nothing to indicate that the space had sheltered and nourished the seed from which the Sanitary Commission had grown.

[51] Schuyler to Angelina Post, June 7, July 11, 1865, Louisa Lee Schuyler Papers, NYHS.
[52] Schuyler to Post, October 1, 1865, Schuyler Papers, NYHS.

Chapter 4

The Army at Home

The least anticipated result of the Civil War was sensational prosperity for the North. The now-familiar experience of war-induced affluence was then an astounding phenomenon, all the more surprising because the secession crisis of 1860–61 had interrupted recovery from the prewar depression, and the outbreak of hostilities plunged the Northern economy into another and, at first, catastrophic decline. Charles Loring Brace of the New York Children's Aid Society predicted that the year 1861 would be remembered as "probably the most disturbed and disastrous which will ever occur in the history of the Republic." A Boston correspondent advised Dorothea Dix in March 1861 that uneasiness and apprehension had paralyzed commerce and suspension of business activity was causing intense suffering among the city's poor. Later that year, William E. Dodge told a Washington audience that in New York City despairing merchants were checking off the names of insolvent customers, while clerks idled over newspapers and brooded about what would happen to their wives and children if they were discharged.[1]

Economic gloom and confusion persisted into the early months of 1862 and even longer in the lower Midwest, previously dependent on Southern markets, and in militarily exposed areas like Missouri. But by 1863, in most parts of the North, the eco-

[1] New York Children's Aid Society: *Ninth Annual Report* (New York, 1862), p. 21; G. S. Hillard to Dorothea Dix, March 11, 1861, Dix Papers, HLHU; Arthur Train, Jr.: *Incidents in the Lives of Anson Greene Phelps and William Earl Dodge* (n.p., n.d.), p. 46.

nomic clouds had lifted. Government orders and transfer payments, the siphoning of excess manpower into the armed forces, currency inflation, and larger-than-usual European purchases of agricultural products brought increased demands and rising prices for commodities and labor. The want and waste of an immense army and the needs of distressed Europe stimulated Northern agriculture. Meanwhile, Northern industry proved capable of producing both swords and plowshares; from Maine to Missouri, workshops clanged and hummed in response to calls for military requirements and civilian necessities and furbelows.

In the Confederacy, the course of economic events was the reverse of that in the Union. Confederate state governments, anticipating hostilities, began to place orders to supply and equip troops while Northern businessmen and statesmen were still unwilling to acknowledge the likelihood of conflict. Consequently, secession and the threat of war animated rather than paralyzed Southern commerce. After the war began, however, everything went wrong for the Confederate economy. The South, predominantly agricultural, looked to the sun and the rain for prosperity. When sunshine and showers failed, as they intermittently did, the results were frosts and failing harvests; when they came, they came excessively, either parching or drenching the soil.[2] Meanwhile, the Northern blockade tightened and military operations plunged deeper into the South, impoverishing affected areas and disrupting lines of communication and transportation.

Lack of confidence in the central government—a problem in both Union and Confederacy—depreciated the value of Northern currency but rendered that of the South almost worthless. Thus, while the North enjoyed and thanked a Warrior God for the boon of blood-bought prosperity, the South experienced the hardships and tribulations traditionally associated with war: shortages of food, clothing, and medicine; ruinous inflation and burdensome taxation; military devastation and foraging by invaders and defenders alike. Toward the end of the war only Biblical allusions seemed adequate to describe the plight of the Confederacy. In January 1865 Mary Chesnut privately acknowledged that the charitable fair in Columbia, South Carolina, the arrangements of which had occupied her for months, would be superfluous. "The Bazaar will be a Belshazzar affair," she wrote in her diary. "The

[2] Paul W. Gates: *Agriculture and the Civil War* (New York, 1966), pp. 86–87, 116, 119–21.

handwriting is on the wall." James Shaw, a Methodist minister from Northern Ireland who spent the war years in America, likened the Confederacy to Egypt and the Union to the land of Goshen. "The difference between the Jews and the Egyptians in the times of Exodus," said Shaw, "could scarcely be greater than that of the South and North. . . ."[3]

The war could not have been fought if fighting men had been required to support dependents out of their own meager, uncertain wages. The pay of privates, originally $11 a month in both armies, was respectable by European standards, but it was usually in arrears and, even if it had been paid on time, would not have constituted a living wage for a family man in the United States. In the rush of patriotic ardor after Fort Sumter Northerners and Southerners, each expecting a short war, vowed to maintain the welfare of volunteers' families as zealously as the well-being and comfort of the volunteers themselves. Throughout the war, individuals and associations, North and South, invoked a variety of charitable expedients, including soup kitchens, free markets, and cooperative purchasing arrangements to help soldiers' dependents. Although assistance to servicemen's families never proved as glamorous as military relief, soldiers' aid societies held balls, concerts, bazaars, and fairs for the benefit of needy families. "We have recently undertaken . . . to strengthen the arms of our men in the field, by caring for their families at home" reported the Hartford, Connecticut, Soldiers' Aid Association in 1863. The Hartford group, like most of those in larger cities, contributed not directly to the poor, but to established charitable agencies; in smaller communities, however, soldiers' aid societies themselves distributed coal, wood, provisions and money to needy families. Early in the war, enterprising women like Katharine Prescott Wormeley of Newport and Caroline Kirkland of New York City established sewing rooms and obtained government contracts for clothing and hospital supplies to provide jobs for wives of volunteers.[4]

[3] Mary Boykin Chesnut: *A Diary from Dixie*, ed. by Ben Ames Williams (Boston, 1949), p. 472; James Shaw: *Twelve Years in America* (London, 1867), p. 187.

[4] Hartford Soldiers' Aid Association: *Second Annual Report* (Hartford, 1863), p. 10; Katharine Prescott Wormeley: *The Other Side of War* (Boston, 1889), pp. 185–86; Caroline Kirkland to Alexander Dallas Bache, June 9, 29, 1862, Bache Papers, Huntington Library.

Public officials on both sides commended such voluntary efforts, but the needs and demands of wives, children, and parents of men who volunteered for or were hustled into military service far exceeded the resources of private charity. Aid for servicemen's families, an issue in all the states, was everywhere recognized as a major factor in military and civilian morale. In 1862 a Mississippian, addressing the governor of his state, expressed the common concern of both belligerents: "Another army besides that in the field must be supported—*the army at home. . . .* Their preservation and their comfort are as essential to our success as that of soldiers in the field."[5] Patriotic, humanitarian, and political considerations induced governors and state legislatures to depart from the long-established principle that poor relief was strictly a local function. In both North and South efforts to relieve indigent families of servicemen brought an outpouring of tax-supported benevolence and an expansion of state welfare activities.

In the North bounties offered recruits by federal, state, and local governments and public assistance financed by state, county, and municipal tax levies or specially authorized bond issues eased, but did not entirely alleviate, the hardships of families whose breadwinners entered military service.[6] After 1862 desire to avoid imposition of the draft replaced humanitarian considerations in bestowal of bounties; payments became larger, but the principal beneficiaries were more likely to be unscrupulous adventurers than needy families of patriotic men.[7]

Aid for soldiers' dependents supposedly constituted a dis-

[5] W. H. Hardy to Governor John J. Pettus, December 2, 1862, in Charles W. Ramsdell: *Behind the Lines in the Southern Confederacy* (Baton Rouge, La., 1944), p. 30.

[6] Carl Russell Fish: "Social Relief in the Northwest During the Civil War," *American Historical Review*, vol. XXII (1916–1917), pp. 309–24; David M. Schneider: *The History of Public Welfare in New York State, 1609–1866* (Chicago, 1938), pp. 281–86; Joseph E. Holliday: "Relief for Soldiers' Families in Ohio During the Civil War," *Ohio History*, vol. LXXI (1962), pp. 97–112; John Niven: *Connecticut for the Union, The Role of the State in the Civil War* (New Haven, 1965), pp. 59–60, 319; Merle Curti: *The Making of an American Community: A Case Study of Democracy in a Frontier County* (Stanford, Calif., 1959), pp. 289–90.

[7] Fred Albert Shannon: *The Organization and Administration of the Union Army, 1861–1865* (2 vols., Cleveland, 1928), vol. II, pp. 50–52; Eugene C. Murdock: *Ohio's Bounty System in the Civil War* (Columbus, Ohio, 1963), p. 10, and "New York's Civil War Bounty Brokers," *Journal of American History*, vol. LIII (1966), pp. 259–60.

tinct category of public assistance without the stigma of pauper
ism; in practice it was administered in much the same fashion
and spirit as poor relief. Applicants had to pass stringent eligibil-
ity and means tests and might be exposed to reinvestigation to
ascertain whether aid was still required; the maximum allow-
ances—ranging from about $5 per week for a wife with four
children in New York City to about $4 per month in the rural
West—were geared to a minimum standard of living, and these
modest payments stopped when soldiers were discharged or
killed. In some areas, and according to some observers, too much
was done for families of servicemen; a Sanitary Commission document decried the "profuse and injurious relief" offered such
families in New York. But in New York, as elsewhere, expenditures for relief were small compared to bounty payments.[8]

In the Confederacy, obstacles to civilian relief proved
insurmountable. To assist indigent families of servicemen, several
states adopted public assistance programs without precedent in
Southern history and that, in comparison to available resources,
dwarfed similar efforts in the North. Beginning with laws permitting counties to pass tax levies for needy soldiers' families,
Southern legislatures proceeded to appropriate state funds for
relief; as the value of Confederate currency declined and goods
became scarcer, legislatures imposed taxes in kind and, near the
end of the war, authorized requisition and impressment of supplies to feed and clothe servicemen's families. Southern newspapers, like those in the North, sometimes asserted that as a
result of enlarged public and private philanthropy, the poor had
never been as generously treated as in the midst of war. Richard
McIlwaine, a clergyman in Farmville, Virginia, declared that he
could not recall a single instance of beggary in his community in
all the years of the war. Few sections of the Confederacy were as
fortunate. The South had pockets of plenty, but in the region as a
whole, crop failures and disruption of transportation, resulting in
shortages of supplies and inflated prices, made relief impossible.
Since the millions of Confederate dollars appropriated for relief
were nearly valueless and the goods they were intended to pro-

8 U.S. Sanitary Commission: *Documents* (2 vols., New York, 1866), vol.
II, Document No. 95, December 15, 1865; Schneider: *Public Welfare in
New York State*, pp. 285–86; John L. Gillin: *History of Poor Relief Legis-
lation in Iowa* (Iowa City, 1914), pp. 93–97.

"Crossing Sweeper." *Packard's Monthly*, Vol. I (1869), p. 22.

Panic of 1857: Wall Street half past 2 o'clock, October 13, 1857.
Museum of the City of New York. Reproduced by permission.

"State Emigrant Landing Depot, Castle Garden, N.Y." Friedrich Kapp, *Immigration and the Commissioners of Emigration of the State of New York* (New York, 1870), facing p. 108.

"Lynn Shoemakers' Strike." *Frank Leslie's Illustrated Newspaper*, Vol. IX (1860), pp. 242–43.

"The Cotton Famine: Group of Mill Operatives at Manchester."
Illustrated London News, Vol. XLI (1862), p. 564.

"Great Meeting of the Ladies of New York at the Cooper Institute on Monday, April 29, 1861, to Organize a Society to Be Called 'Woman's Central Association of Relief,' to Make Clothes, Lint, Bandages, and to Furnish Nurses for the Soldiers of the Northern Army." *Frank Leslie's Illustrated Newspaper*, Vol. XI (1860–61), p. 412.

Executive Committee of the U.S. Sanitary Commission. Photograph by Mathew B. Brady, 1864. Courtesy of the New York Academy of Medicine.

"I keep the Brady picture of the 'Standing Committee' on my table, & look up every little while to exchange glances with each & every one of my well-beloved yoke-fellows—with Gibbs and Van Buren (the heavy men) sitting in their chairs, & Agnew & Strong, the lightweights, standing in their shoes. I wouldn't sell for a thousand dollars, the comfort, cheer & fellowship, I have had out of that picture these last three months. . . . I have enjoyed oh how many cheerful laughs with my own heart, in recalling the hours we have spent together & looking forward to their happy renewal."

Henry W. Bellows to Executive Committee of the U.S. Sanitary Commission, August 11, 1864. Bellows Papers, Massachusetts Historical Society. Quoted by permission of the Massachusetts Historical Society.

"Aid Society's Store-room." Charles C. Coffin, *The Boys of '61, or Four Years of Fighting* (Boston, 1881), p. 16.

"The Christian Commission in the Field." Coffin, *The Boys of '61*, p. 176.

Women working in the Cooper Union headquarters of the Women's Central Association of Relief. *Left to right:* Unidentified woman, Mrs. William B. Rice, Louisa Lee Schuyler, Mrs. William Preston Griffin, Mrs. Theophile Marie d'Oremieulx, Ellen Collins. Museum of the City of New York. Reproduced by permission.

"Union Refugees from Western Missouri Entering
St. Louis." *Harper's Weekly*, Vol. V (1861), p. 817.

"The Effects of the Proclamation." *Harper's Weekly*, Vol. VII (1863), p. 116.

"The Riots at New York—The Rioters Burning and Sacking the Colored Orphan Asylum." *Harper's Weekly*, Vol. VII (1863), p. 493.

Pension Building, Washington, D.C., U.S. Public Buildings Service, *Historical Study No. 1, Pension Building* (Washington, D.C., 1964). Montgomery C. Meigs (1816–1892), quartermaster-general of the Union army, was the architect of the building, which was completed in 1887.

"The Story of a Waif, Second Thought."
Harper's Weekly, Vol. XVI (1872), p. 233.

"Major General Howard. (From a photograph taken after the battle of Gettysburg.)." *Autobiography of Oliver Otis Howard* (2 vols., New York, 1908), Vol. I, p. 448.

"St. Philip's Church, Richmond, Virginia—School for Colored Children." *Harper's Weekly*, Vol. XI (1867), p. 321.

Susie King Taylor. *Reminiscences of My Life in Camp* (Boston, 1902), frontispiece. In 1862, Susie King, a fourteen-year-old fugitive who had learned to read and write in a clandestine school, volunteered to teach the freedmen of the Sea Islands. Later she was laundress, teacher, and nurse for the first Negro regiment in the Union army.

"My Schoolhouse in Savannah." Taylor, *Reminiscences of My Life in Camp*, facing p. 54. When her husband died after the war, Susie King Taylor supported herself for several years by teaching in this school.

Samuel Gridley Howe
(1801–1876), "the
Friend of Humanity."
Laura E. Richards, ed.,
*Letters and Journal of
Samuel Gridley Howe*
(2 vols., Boston,
1906–09), Vol. II,
frontispiece.

"McAlisterville School, Juniata County, Pa." James L. Paul,
Pennsylvania's Orphan Schools (Harrisburg, Pa., 1877), p. 196.

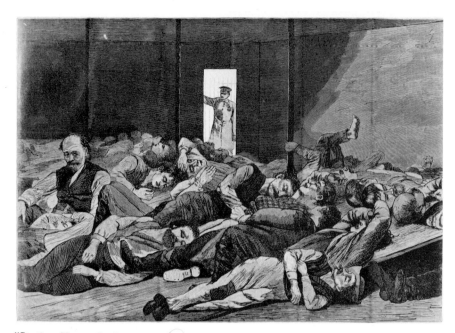

"Station House Lodgers.—
From a Drawing by Winslow Homer."
Harper's Weekly, Vol. XVIII
(1874), p. 132.

"The Newsboys' Lodging-House,
Sketched by Charles G. Bush,"
Harper's Weekly, Vol. XI
(1867), pp. 312–13.

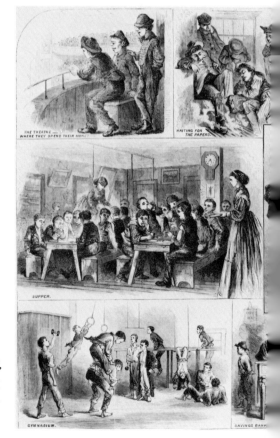

"Tramps and Their Ways."
Harper's Weekly, Vol. XXII
(1878), p. 348.

George Peabody. *The American
Annual Cyclopaedia*, Vol. VII
(1867), frontispiece.

Catharine Lorillard Wolfe.
Oil on canvas by
Alexandre Cabanel.
The Metropolitan Museum
of Art, Purchase, 1887.
Reproduced by permission.

"Clara Barton, From a Portrait
Taken about 1875."
Clara Barton, *The Red Cross*
(Washington, D.C., 1898),
frontispiece.

"Josephine Shaw Lowell.
From a Bas-Relief by
Augustus Saint-Gaudens,
1899." William Rhinelander
Stewart, *The Philanthropic
Work of Josephine Shaw
Lowell* (New York, 1911),
frontispiece.

vide were usually unavailable, the benefits—impressive on paper
—were negligible in practice.[9]

Even in North Carolina, where Governor Zebulon B. Vance
promoted vigorous programs of state assistance, soldiers' wives
clamored: "We have not Drawn nothin but want in three months
an without help we must starv." During the final years of the
war, bread riots led by war-weary women erupted from Richmond to Mobile. Refugees from areas threatened, overrun, or
occupied by Union forces further complicated an impossible
situation by creating a displaced-person problem with which neither the Confederate Congress nor state governments could cope
and to which private philanthropy afforded only spasmodic
relief.[10]

The pitiful condition of the army at home, communicated in
family letters, was a factor in desertions from Southern units in
the field. In December 1864 a destitute Virginia mother of four
children wrote her husband, who was on duty with General
George Pickett:

> Christmas is most hear again, and things is worse and
> worse. . . . I don't want you to stop fighten them Yankees
> till you kill the last one of them, but try to get off and
> come home and fix us all up and then you can go back
> and fight them a heep harder than you ever fought them

[9] Paul D. Escott: " 'The Cry of the Sufferers': The Problem of Welfare in
the Confederacy," *Civil War History*, vol. XXIII (1977), pp. 231–32;
Ramsdell, *Behind the Lines in the Southern Confederacy*, pp. 62–68, 82;
Clement Eaton: *A History of the Southern Confederacy* (New York, 1954),
pp. 240–43; Clyde O. Fisher: "The Relief of Soldiers' Families in North
Carolina During the Civil War," *South Atlantic Quarterly*, vol. XVI (1917),
pp. 60–72; E. B. Coddington: "Soldiers' Relief in the Seaboard States of
the Southern Confederacy," *Mississippi Valley Historical Review*, vol.
XXXVII (1950), pp. 17–38; William F. Zornow: "State Aid for Indigent
Soldiers and Their Families in Louisiana, 1861–1865," *Louisiana Historical
Quarterly*, vol. XXXIX (1956), pp. 375–80, and "Aid for Indigent Families
of Soldiers in Virginia, 1861–1865," *Virginia Magazine of History and
Biography*, vol. LXVI (1958), pp. 454–58; Richard McIlwaine: *Memories
of Three Score Years and Ten* (New York and Washington, 1908), pp.
209–10.

[10] Francis B. Simkins and James W. Patton: *The Women of the Confederacy* (Richmond, Va., 1936), p. 126; E. Merton Coulter: *The Confederate States of America, 1861–65* (Baton Rouge, La., 1950), pp. 422–24;
Mary Elizabeth Massey: *Refugee Life in the Confederacy* (Baton Rouge,
La., 1964), pp. 242–62.

before. We can't none of us hold out much longer down here.

After taking off to see his family without obtaining leave, the soldier was arrested, tried as a deserter, and condemned to death. He escaped execution through the intervention of General Pickett's wife and, because the offense was so common, a general reprieve of deserters.[11]

"The farms teem, the workshops and the factories whir, and bustle of trade fills the streets," declared a *New York Times* editorial on July 2, 1863, just as the Battle of Gettysburg began and only eleven days before the start of the New York City draft riots. "Labor was never in greater demand, or more largely paid. . . . Taking all classes of society into account, it may, with very little risk, be averred that in no year in the history of the country has there been so little destitution and so much physical comfort throughout the North, as has prevailed thus far in this third year of the war." As in all the periods of booming prosperity, however, portions of the population lagged behind the general advance. By the end of the war the doubling of living costs, which was the price Northern civilians paid for war prosperity, had canceled gains workers obtained from full employment and higher wages.[12] Mounting prices for food, fuel, and shelter bore especially hard on women in the needle and handicraft trades, on men and women too old or infirm to work, on families with small fixed incomes, and on all the categories of the poor who regularly depended in whole or part on charity or relief. Charity agents in Eastern cities, while agreeing that cases of "suffering from indigence" were fewer in war than in peace, reminded the affluent that people who were poor were worse off than ever. "Poverty—stark poverty—lurks or creeps amongst us unreached by the copious, refreshing rills from the monstrous outflow of public and private treasure," asserted a Boston missionary to the poor. In

[11] Katharine M. Jones, comp.: *Heroines of Dixie: Confederate Women Tell Their Story of the War* (Indianapolis, 1955), p. 348; Escott, " 'The Cry of the Sufferers,' " pp. 239–40.

[12] Wesley Clair Mitchell: *A History of the Greenbacks* (Chicago, 1903), pp. 347–51, 391; Clarence D. Long: *Wages and Earnings in the United States 1860–1890* (Princeton, N.J., 1960), p. 61; Niven: *Connecticut for the Union*, p. 344.

1864 the minister at large in Lowell, Massachusetts, advised his supporters that as a result of the high cost of living, he had never known so many people to "live so low." "Some," he said, "come down to two meals a day, and others to only one."[13] As the war dragged on, widows and orphans, distressed families of servicemen who could not meet settlement or other requirements for local or state aid, freedmen and loyal refugees from the South, sufferers or survivors of wartime epidemics, and disabled, unemployed veterans with unsatisfied claims for pay or pensions swelled the ranks of the needy. "We have found dwellings where there are sick, shivering, hungry soldiers; more destitute, perhaps, than on the field of Gettysburg," reported a Boston society. These men and their families, according to the report, were reluctant to ask for help and had to be sought out and quietly relieved.[14]

Resources of non-war-related charities, both public and private, reflected the fortunes and misfortunes of war. At the start of the secession crisis the superintendent of the Eastern Kentucky Lunatic Asylum wrote Dorothea Dix: "States as well as individuals are feeling the pressure of the times, and if the 'irrepressible conflict' is to go on I fear that our means will be demanded for other than charitable purposes." Throughout most of 1861 the superintendent's prediction seemed likely to be realized. Excitement of war and mobilization pushed civilian needs into the background. Construction of buildings and additions to state institutions authorized before 1861 continued, but after the outbreak of the war, projects for new state schools, prisons, and asylums were set aside. Ohio, for example, defeated an appropriation for a new school for the deaf, drastically reduced support for the state's three hospitals for the insane, and cut salaries of teachers and staff at the school for the blind by nearly 20 percent. Under the pressure of short funds mental hospitals in state after state began returning "incurable" patients to their home counties in order to make room for more hopeful cases. "Here-

[13] Boston Benevolent Fraternity of Churches: *Twenty-ninth Annual Report* (Boston, 1863), pp. 7–8; Lowell Missionary Society: *Twentieth Annual Report of the Minister at Large* (Lowell, Mass., 1865), p. 5.

[14] Young Men's Benevolent Society: *Thirty-fifth Annual Report* (Boston, 1863), pp. 4–5; see also New York Association for Improving the Condition of the Poor: *Twenty-second Annual Report* (New York, 1865), p. 31; Society for the Relief of Poor Widows with Small Children: *Sixty-eighth Annual Report* (New York, 1865); Niven: *Connecticut for the Union*, pp. 307–08.

after," acknowledged one superintendent, "public hospitals of palatial size and costly administration for the demented and chronic insane are out of the question."[15]

Established private charities also suffered in the uncertain months just before and immediately after the start of the war. Receipts of the American Bible Society, ordinarily the best supported of the national benevolent societies, declined in 1860–61 and fell lower in 1861–62. In September 1861 the American Board of Commissioners for Foreign Missions, anticipating a period of hard times, ordered expenditures in Near Eastern missions reduced by one-third.[16] "In view of the present and prospective state of the treasury, arising from the disturbed and distressing state of political affairs," the executive committee of the Boston Children's Mission to the Children of the Destitute decided to dispense with the services of two of its five missionaries and to discontinue boarding children at its expense. The New York Children's Aid Society, also experiencing a drop in receipts, had to discharge four of its six visitors and close several of its industrial schools.[17]

The situation changed rapidly after 1862. In the later years of the war civilian charitable societies in the North recorded large increases in contributions for their various activities. "Indeed," observed Charles Loring Brace, an experienced and aggressive fund raiser, "it seems easier for people to support charitable institutions now . . . than before the war. They have learned to levy on their own pockets, to pay voluntary as well as involuntary taxes."[18] In the midst of domestic tribulations, Northern workmen, merchants, and financiers found the means to send supplies valued at $350,000 to distressed textile workers in Lancashire. Diplomatic considerations no doubt influenced and spurred the Yankee effort to relieve distress arising from

[15] W. L. Chipley to Dorothea Dix, December 19, 1860, Dix Papers, HLHU; Blake McKelvey: *American Prisons* (Chicago, 1936), p. 32; "Reports of American Asylums," *American Journal of Insanity*, vol. XVII (1860–61), p. 84; vol. XIX (1862–63), p. 105.

[16] *Fifty-fifth Annual Report of the American Bible Society* (New York, 1871), p. 148; Henry Harris Jessup: *Fifty-three Years in Syria* (2 vols., Chicago, 1910), vol. I, pp. 304–05.

[17] Minutes of the Executive Committee, Boston Children's Mission to the Destitute, May 29, July 31, 1861, Children's Mission to Children, Boston, Massachusetts; New York Children's Aid Society: *Ninth Annual Report* (New York, 1862), pp. 19–24.

[18] New York Children's Aid Society: *Tenth Annual Report* (New York, 1863), p. 35.

Lancashire's cotton famine, but as the *Times* (London) magisterially observed, "It was a generous deed, and it was generously received."[19] Orphan homes, asylums for the aged and indigent, hospitals, and dispensaries were among the beneficiaries of war prosperity. Churches burdened with debt at the start of the war burned their mortgages in the course of it. Receipts of the major benevolent societies—usually an accurate barometer of philanthropic pressure—rose to new highs in 1864 and 1865. Contributions to home and foreign missions quadrupled during the war, and colleges and theological schools added $1,500,000 to their endowments, Yale alone garnering more than $400,000. "I say it is a most remarkable fact," declared William E. Dodge, one of the most active and generous philanthropists of the period, "that we have not only sustained this war, but the institutions of this country as they never were sustained before." Linus P. Brockett, the first historian of Civil War charities, observed that the war had aroused eagerness in all classes to "taste the luxury of doing good" and concluded that philanthropy seemed to find its widest sphere of activity in time of war.[20]

Northern public institutions, although benefiting less than private charities, shared in the largesse of war prosperity. In 1864 the Ohio legislature, reversing its action of 1861, appropriated funds for a costly new school for the deaf. State officials interpreted the action as proof that Ohio was not only first among her sisters in military efforts but queen of the states in "designs and deeds of philanthropy."[21]

Between 1861 and 1864, admissions to Northern state hospitals for the insane either declined slightly or remained at pre-war levels. The Board of Visitors of the Government Hospital for the Insane in Washington, D.C., interpreted statistics on admissions as evidence that war, dispelling "the apathies and self-

[19] The *Times* (London), December 12, 1864; Merle Curti: *American Philanthropy Abroad: A History* (New Brunswick, N.J., 1963), pp. 67–72; John A. Carpenter; "The New York International Relief Committee, A Chapter in the Diplomatic History of the Civil War," *The New York-Historical Society Quarterly*, vol. LVI (1872), pp. 239–52.

[20] William E. Dodge: *Influence of the War on Our National Prosperity* (New York, 1865), p. 24 et seq.; Linus P. Brockett: *The Philanthropic Results of the War in America* (New York, 1863), pp. 14, 26–27, and "Philanthropy in War Time," *Methodist Quarterly Review*, vol. XLVII (1865), p. 65.

[21] *Laying of the Cornerstone of the New Building for Ohio Institution for the Education of the Deaf and Dumb, October 31, 1864* (Columbus, Ohio, 1864), p. 7.

indulgences" of peace, had raised the mind of the country to "a healthier tension and more earnest devotion to healthier objects." Other observers attributed stabilization of admissions not to the nation's mental health, but to the hospitals' exclusion of the so-called incurables and to refusal of local officials and taxpayers to foot the cost of sending indigent insane to state institutions when they could be kept more cheaply in county jails or almshouses.[22]

After 1863, expenditures of state hospitals began to increase mainly as a result of higher operating costs but partly because of introduction of amenities such as gaslights, bowling alleys, work-shops, and chapels. As in prewar years, some of these improve-ments were paid for out of gifts and legacies from private donors. The high cost of institutional care tempted legislators to seek ways of making asylums self-supporting by getting patients to work at agricultural or industrial employments. A proposal to establish a workshop at the Worcester, Massachusetts, Hospital led Dr. Isaac Ray, superintendent of the Butler Hospital in Prov-idence, Rhode Island, to scoff: "After they have had a few stab-bings & cuttings & sunk a few thousand dollars, they will probably allow [the superintendent] to set his patients to work in his own way."[23]

While the war was in progress, New York set an example for other states by opening the first special institution for confine-ment of the criminal insane, and both New York and Massachu-setts took steps toward founding asylums specifically for the chronic insane. To balance such advances in institution founding, New York offered a horrible example of institution management. Toward the end of the war, inmates of New York City's Lunatic Asylum on Blackwell's Island, in addition to mental illness, suf-fered from endemic typhus and scorbutus. Because cotton was scarce and expensive, they had to do without sheets and under-wear. The woolen garments they wore were "so deficient in quantity that they often could not be spared for the necessary washings." Moreover, as the superintendent acknowledged, "the

---

[22] Isaac Ray to Dorothea Dix, May 1863, Dix Papers, HLHU; "Reports of American Asylums," *American Journal of Insanity*, vol. XIX (1862–63), p. 194, vol. XX (1863–64), pp. 432, 504, vol. XXII (1865–66), pp. 73, 529–30; Gerald N. Grob: *Mental Institutions in America, Social Policy to 1875* (New York, 1973), p. 162.

[23] W. S. Chipley to Dorothea Dix, April 29, 1863; Isaac Ray to Dorothea Dix, May 1863, Dix Papers, HLHU; "Reports of American Asylums," *American Journal of Insanity*, vol. XVIII (1861–62), pp. 103–04, vol. XX (1863–64), pp. 476, 498, vol. XXI (1864–65), p. 236.

amount of clothing has never been sufficient to compensate for deficiencies in artificial heat. Nor is the diet sufficiently varied."[24]

"A state of war is a school of violence and crime," reported the commissioners of New York's Metropolitan Police in 1864. Nevertheless, commitments of male offenders to state prisons fell off sharply during the war. The reason, according to one warden, was that in wartime the penalty of crime was "to enlist in the army and get a large bounty." Some offenders secured freedom on condition that they enlisted; others joined the army to escape arrest. From the point of view of wardens, the decline in prison populations was unwelcome because prisons did not "pay" unless they furnished contractors with abundant and cheap convict labor. Prisoners arriving at the Ohio Penitentiary in Columbus in 1864 were so few and "useless" that the warden wondered whether "prosecuting attorneys for the state have remitted the practice of bringing able-bodied men to trial." In the absence of "usable" manpower, most Northern prisons operated in the red during the war years. Shortages of able-bodied male labor also impeded efforts to make county almshouses and workhouses or reformatories self-supporting, except where older boys could be pressed into service.[25]

In the South and border regions, public charitable institutions sometimes found themselves in the path of military operations. At the start of the war rebel bands broke into the Missouri State Lunatic Asylum, stole equipment, and dispersed the patients. Union forces destroyed the Tennessee Blind School near Nashville and converted the Deaf and Dumb School at Knoxville into a military hospital. Federal troops burned the Georgia state prison; Confederates fired on the Mississippi State Insane Asylum near Jackson, mistakenly believing it had been occupied by Union forces. Even when buildings and occupants were not harmed, institutions suffered from devastation of the surrounding country and were not spared seizure or impressment of livestock

[24] "Reports of American Asylums," *American Journal of Insanity*, vol. XIX (1862–63), p. 102, vol. XXII (1865–66), pp. 127–30, 192–216, vol. XXIII (1866–67), pp. 485–87.

[25] New York (State) Board of Commissioners of the Metropolitan Police: *Annual Report* (Albany, N.Y., 1865), p. 7; E. C. Wines and Theodore W. Dwight: *Report on the Prisons and Reformatories of the United States and Canada* (Albany, N.Y., 1867), pp. 267, 312–13; *Annual Report of Directors and Wardens of the Ohio Penitentiary, 1864* (Columbus, Ohio, 1865), p. 550.

and supplies. The superintendent of the Western Lunatic Asylum in Taunton, Virginia, after reciting the trials of trying to operate the asylum in a theater of war, reported the following incident:

> On the 4th of March last [1862] a detachment from General Sheridan's command made an assault upon the meat house, flour house, store room and other buildings, bearing off and destroying about 180 barrels of flour, 10,600 pounds bacon, 300 bushels corn—a considerable quantity of hay—135 bushels rye and oats—wagon and carriage harness—50 pairs coarse shoes—many articles of wearing apparel from the laundry, and 3 valuable mules. I promptly and earnestly announced to the officer in command the character and object of the institution, cited the number of the unfortunate insane under our care, apprised him of the difficulties we had encountered in obtaining these supplies, and the danger that, if removed, they could not be replaced—but without avail! It is gratifying to add, that none of this party ever intruded within the buildings occupied by patients of either sex— a happy circumstance: for which I felt well assured, from careful observation, we were more indebted to the forbearance of the privates than to any restraints imposed by their officers.[26]

At the other side of Virginia the venerable asylum at Williamsburg passed under the control of Union forces early in the war and was thereafter administered and supplied by the army, with the Sanitary Commission contributing supplementary comfort articles.[27]

When the Confederates captured the region around the Kentucky Eastern Lunatic Asylum in September 1862, the superintendent, Dr. W. L. Chipley, expressed fear that the hospital would experience "the blasted fortunes of similar institutions within the limits of the Confederacy whose inmates have been driven from their comfortable abodes to suffer and to perish. . . ."

[26] "Reports of American Asylums," *American Journal of Insanity*, vol. XXII (1865–66), pp. 130, 519–21; Henry Mills Hurd, ed.: *Institutional Care of the Insane in the United States and Canada* (3 vols., Baltimore, 1916), vol. III, pp. 598–99, 639, 727, 872; McKelvey: *American Prisons*, p. 33; *American Annual Cyclopaedia, 1865*, vol. V (1865), p. 780.
[27] "Reports of American Asylums," *American Journal of Insanity*, vol. XX (1863–64), pp. 350–52; *The Sanitary Commission Bulletin*, vol. II (July 15, 1864), p. 566.

In fact, however, behind Confederate lines in the Southeast the insane continued to be admitted to asylums. When legislative appropriations were inadequate, superintendents and trustees begged or borrowed funds to keep their institutions operating. Thus, at the State Hospital for the Insane in Columbia, South Carolina, the number of patients declined by only about one-fourth between 1862 and 1865, but the expense of operating the institution increased fivefold. In February 1865, when Sherman's army burned Columbia, the asylum escaped destruction and became a refuge for homeless people of the city. After the war the doughty superintendent boasted to Dorothea Dix that the State Hospital for the Insane was the only public institution in South Carolina that had survived the war.[28]

The Civil War erupted in the midst of a period of growing interest and activity in child welfare. The exigencies of war, far from curtailing this interest, sharpened and augmented it. From the very outset experts had predicted the war would greatly increase the number of orphaned, destitute, neglected, and delinquent children. To meet the demand for services, children's charities, growing for a generation before 1861, expanded rapidly during the war decade. Accepting the premise that orphans of war were the children of the state, Pennsylvania, Illinois, Kansas, Minnesota, Ohio, Indiana, Iowa, Wisconsin, and New Jersey organized or subsidized institutional "homes" for soldiers' and sailors' orphans. Senator Samuel Clarke Pomeroy of Kansas proposed but failed to secure passage by Congress of a bill that would have granted as much public land to each state for the support of education of soldiers' orphans as had been appropriated for agricultural education under the Morrill Act. Promoters of the state orphan homes recommended that in physical arrangements and discipline "Spartan frugality and severity be tempered by Christian philanthropy."[29] Indiana maintained its soldiers' orphan home in the same building and under the same management as

---

[28] "Reports of American Asylums," *American Journal of Insanity*, vol. XX (1863–64), p. 500; Dr. F. W. Parker to Dorothea Dix, May 5, 1868, *Dix Papers*, HLHU.

[29] *Congressional Globe*, 38 Cong., 1 Sess., p. 694 (February 17, 1864), p. 2777 (June 11, 1864); Theodore Sedgwick Gold: *A Plan for the Mental, Moral and Physical Development of Children* . . . (Hartford, Conn., 1864), p. 1.

the school for feebleminded. Protestant denominations, Roman Catholic orders, and fraternal societies were no less active than official bodies in establishing asylums for children of their respective faith or affiliations. As many orphanages were founded in the 1860s as the combined total for the two preceding decades.[30] The increase, however, failed to keep pace with the number of children orphaned or reduced to destitution by the war. In 1864 and 1865 poorhouses and juvenile reformatories reported significant increases in the admission of dependent and delinquent children. An investigatory commmission in New Jersey found an eleven-year-old orphan boy who had been put in a county jail because there was no other institution to shelter him.[31]

The rise in institutional population, occurring in a time of inflated prices, embarrassed superintendents who liked to cite low per capita costs to prove the efficiency of their operations. On the other hand, advocates of home placement as opposed to institutional care used the war experience as proof of the superior economy of their method of caring for dependent children. "The *cheapness* of this charity [home placements] is one of its most remarkable features," Charles Loring Brace of the New York Children's Aid Society told a London audience in 1865. Brace's society, like a number of other New York benevolent institutions, was assisted during the war years by large gifts from an Indiana philanthropist, Chauncey Rose, whose generosity was often held up as an example for Manhattan's allegedly tightfisted millionaires.[32] After 1862 the demand for farm labor made it easier for the New York Children's Aid Society and similar organizations to find "places" for city children in the West. In the opinion of agents of such societies the double service performed in removing children from the city and in supplying farmers' needs for labor entitled the organizations to generous subsidies from both state legislatures and city councils.

Early in 1865 a Michigan correspondent advised one of sev-

[30] Homer Folks: *The Care of Destitute, Neglected, and Delinquent Children* (New York, 1902), pp. 101–02.

[31] New York Society for the Reformation of Juvenile Delinquents: *Fortieth Annual Report, 1864* (New York, 1865), p. 6, and *Forty-first Annual Report, 1865* (New York, 1866), pp. 6–7; for the case of the New Jersey orphan see "Report of Commissioners on Reform of Juvenile Offenders" (1864), in New Jersey Prison Inquiry Commission: *Report* (2 vols., Trenton, N.J., 1917), vol. II, p. 583.

[32] New York Children's Aid Society: *Thirteenth Annual Report* (New York, 1866), p. 52, and *Fifteenth Annual Report* (New York, 1868), p. 59.

eral Boston societies engaged in Western placements: "My friends want children between the ages of ten and fourteen, smart, active, and intelligent. I think that I could dispose of a whole carload of boys and girls if you could send them to me soon." A common complaint of child placement agencies in the war period was that children between six and ten years of age, less suited to farm labor, found few takers.[33]

The children of greatest concern to reformers and city officials were homeless, vagrant boys and girls who, in every city, managed to elude the police and truant officers and escape the nets of child welfare agencies. In 1863, estimates of their number ranged as high as 6,000 in Boston and 30,000 in New York.[34] Not all were orphaned, abandoned, or from destitute homes; some were runaways who, in a time of social dislocation, found the excitement of the streets more congenial than the routine and discipline of home and school. War prosperity made it comparatively easy for these voluntary exiles to make a little money by selling apples or matches or running errands.[35] In 1863 the New York legislature chartered the Roman Catholic Protectory to receive truant, vagrant, and delinquent children whose parents or guardians requested the courts to commit them to a Catholic establishment rather than to the House of Refuge or other predominantly Protestant institutions. A contemporary observer, presumably Protestant, described protectory children as "ignorant and spoiled" and making large demands on the patience of their teachers. "Most of them are returned to their parents, and many return the second time to the Institution. Parents who have neglected children to their ruin, rarely exhibit much improvement on a second trial."[36]

Although alarm over the growth of rootless, alienated youth antedated 1863 by many years, reformers used the New York

[33] *The Little Wanderers' Advocate* (Boston), vol. I (1865), p. 3; Boston Children's Mission to the Children of the Destitute: *Thirteenth Annual Report* (Boston, 1862), p. 4, *Fourteenth Annual Report* (Boston, 1863), p. 10; Boston Children's Friend Society: *Twenty-ninth Annual Report* (Boston, 1862), p. 11.

[34] *Monthly Record of Five Points House of Industry* (New York), vol. VI (1862–63), p. 217; *The Little Wanderers' Advocate*, vol. I (1865), p. 118.

[35] Boston Children's Mission to the Children of the Destitute: *Fourteenth Annual Report*, pp. 10–11.

[36] John Francis Richmond: *New York and Its Institutions, 1609–1872* (New York, 1872), pp. 349–53.

City draft riots of that year to focus wider attention on the problem. "Those terrible days in July," exclaimed Charles Loring Brace, "provided the first dreadful revelations to many of our people of the existence among us of a great, ignorant, irresponsible class, who were growing up here without any permanent interest in the welfare of the community or the success of the government. . . ." *Harper's Weekly* reported that boys from fifteen to eighteen years of age took a leading part in the riots and that children from eight to eighteen were responsible for at least half the arson and theft. Among the buildings plundered and burned by the mob was the Colored Orphan Asylum, the 233 occupants of which, ranging in age from two to twelve, found shelter first in a police station and later (when they had to be evacuated to make room for arrested rioters) in the city almshouse. Brace was not surprised at such outrages, maintaining that the perpetrators were "merely *street-children* grown up." A decade earlier he had predicted that in eight or ten years New York would pay a fearful price for neglecting street boys and girls. "Then let society beware," he had warned in 1854, "when the outcast, vicious, reckless multitude of New York boys, swarming now in every foul alley and low street, come to know their power and use it!"[37]

A merchants' committee collected approximately $40,000 for the relief of sufferers from the riots. Working with pastors of Negro churches and visitors of the Association for Improving the Condition of the Poor, it distributed food, clothing, and furniture, provided for widows, orphans, and other dependents of those killed in the riots, and helped those who had lost property prosecute claims against the city. Vincent Colyer, secretary of the committee, compared New York's Negro population with the "contrabands" he had recently worked with in New Bern, North Carolina:

> The free colored people, are very much the superiors of their southern brethren, in education, cultivated intelligence, refinement, and in a quick and independent way of maintaining and asserting their rights. While in kindness toward each other—patience under trial and affliction—

[37] New York Children's Aid Society: *Eleventh Annual Report, 1863–64* (New York, 1864), pp. 3–4; *Harper's Weekly*, vol. VII (July 25, 1863), p. 466; Adrian Cook: *The Armies of the Street: The New York City Draft Riots of 1863* (Lexington, Ky., 1973), pp. 78–79.

cheerfulness, willingness to labor, and an entire absence
of everything like revenge, or a cherishing of ill will
towards those who have injured them, both those of the
North and the South are alike remarkable.[38]

In the wake of the draft riots, reformers in other Northern
cities, alarmed by "thronging evidence of youthful depravity" in
their own communities, called for the establishment, enlarge-
ment, or improvement of reform schools for juvenile delinquents.
Civic leaders in New York City, however, acting on the assumption that sanitary neglect produced social degradation, turned
their attention to the overcrowded tenements and filthy streets
from which the rioters had emerged to terrorize the city. During
1864 the Council of Hygiene and Public Health, a group of
physicians working under the auspices of the prestigious Citizens' Association of New York, conducted a comprehensive
investigation of sanitary conditions in the metropolis. The council included men like Elisha Harris, Stephen Smith, and Valen-
tine Mott, who had been active in the medical activities of the
United States Sanitary Commission; the inquiry, conducted by a
staff of thirty-one physicians who inspected and reported on
conditions in assigned sanitary districts, followed procedures similar to those developed by the Sanitary Commission for the
inspection of military camps and hospitals.[39]

The council's report, edited by Elisha Harris and published
in 1865, emphasized the extent of preventable death and sickness
in New York and called attention to "the physical sufferings, the
want, the neglect, the sickness, the orphanage and pauperism"
resulting from New York's disregard for public health. In a style
reminiscent of Sanitary Commission pronouncements the report
dwelt on the possibility of saving a "vast number of precious
lives," on "the preventable causes of disease," and on "public
peril from removable evils." "We must reap that which we sow,"
warned the physician in charge of the inspection of Gotham
Court and other notorious rookeries. Occupants of "such confined
and filthy premises," he reported, exhibited a "state of physical,
mental, and moral decline . . . so well recognized and its causes so

[38] *Report of the Committee of Merchants for the Relief of Colored People,
Suffering from the Late Riots in the City of New York* (New York, 1863),
p. 28; Cook: *Armies of the Streets*, pp. 174–75.

[39] On the sanitary investigation of New York see George Rosen: *A History of Public Health* (New York, 1958), pp. 243–48, and Stephen Smith:
The City That Was (New York, 1911), pp. 40–49.

well understood, that it has received a name, less elegant than expressive: it is called the Tenant-House Rot. . . . Pestilence and crime are fungi of hideous growth, which spring side by side from such pollution as we allow to rankle in our midst."[40]

A bill incorporating the council's recommendations for hygienic improvements and creating the Metropolitan Board of Health passed the state legislature in 1866. In March 1865, when the measure was presented to the legislature, Dr. Stephen Smith issued a statement asserting: "The poor population of New York is to-day but an immense army in camp, upon small territory, crowded into old filthy dwellings, and without the slightest police regulation for cleanliness."[41]

In the postwar years the sanitary and social condition of the army at home would require as serious and thoughtful attention as that given wartime troops in the field. But even while the war went on, succor had to be provided for new armies of want composed of freedmen, refugees, and the destitute people of the South.

[40] Citizens' Association of New York: *Report of the Council of Hygiene and Public Health . . . upon the Sanitary Condition of the City* (New York, 1865), pp. xi–xvii, 64–65.
[41] Smith: *The City That Was*, pp. 127–28.

Chapter 5

Refugees, Contrabands, and Freedmen

The relief problems facing the victorious North in April 1865, although of unprecedented magnitude, were as old as the war. From the beginning of hostilities, the needs of destitute people in occupied portions of the Confederacy, refugees, and escaped or abandoned slaves demanded the attention of Northern military commanders, civilian officials, and agents of the major relief commissions. As Confederate territory came under Union control, army authorities attempted to provide the distressed with rations, fuel, housing of a sort, and medical assistance. General Henry W. Halleck in St. Louis, Military Governor Andrew Johnson in Nashville, and General Ben Butler in New Orleans levied special taxes on wealthy secessionists to obtain funds for poor relief. During the summer and autumn of 1862 Butler's war on poverty and dirt in occupied New Orleans involved the unwilling city in the largest public works and sanitation programs in its history. In October 1862 Butler notified Secretary of War Stanton that he had put 1,000 of the unemployed poor to work cleaning the streets and wharves, was distributing food to 32,450 persons daily, was sustaining five orphan asylums, and was aiding the Charity Hospital at the rate of $5,000 a month. Butler established a relief agency which, frankly seeking to encourage or win loyalty to the Union, investigated the political sympathies as well as the economic condition of applicants; the agency discriminated in favor of "Federals" but did not exclude needy families of soldiers serving in the Confederate army from assistance until March 1863, when General Nathaniel Banks, Butler's successor, ordered that such families be denied relief.[1] After the fall of Natchez the Union provost marshal donated funds to the local supervisors of the poor for relief of the destitute and provided a building, wood, and rations for children from the Protestant Orphan Asylum whose institution had been seized for military purposes.[2]

Throughout the war the St. Louis-based Western Sanitary Commission supplemented army relief for thousands of refugees who streamed into Missouri from the lower Mississippi Valley. Many of the refugees went on to other parts of the West, but the old, infirm, infant, and indigent—ineligible for local or state assistance—became charges of army chaplains and the Western Commission. The general pattern was for the army to furnish rations and barrack housing to the refugees while the commission, supported in part by friends in Boston and New England, added "incidentals" which could not be obtained through official channels. "No one can imagine what war is, who has not seen it with his own eyes," wrote a young army chaplain, Frederick Wines, who was superintendent of refugees at Springfield, Missouri. "There are families of women and children who are afraid to stay at home while their husbands and brothers are absent in the army, living in tents, all around the town, sleeping on the bare ground." The army kept them and other destitute women and children in the town from starving, and the Western Sanitary Commission provided bedding, clothing, and other necessities.[3] Toward the end of the war the Union commandant at Rolla, Missouri, reported:

> There are at this post about 150 destitute families, nearly all women and children. They can only be subsisted here by the Government. If they could be sent to the northern

[1] Butler's letter to Stanton is in U.S. War Department: *War of the Rebellion: A Compilation of the Official Records of the Union and Confederate Armies* (70 vols., Washington, D.C., 1880–1901), Series 3, vol. II (1899), pp. 720–25 (hereafter cited as *Official Records*); Butler's relief program is discussed in Elizabeth Joan Doyle: "Civilian Life in Occupied New Orleans" (unpublished Ph.D. dissertation, Louisiana State University, 1955), pp. 150–55; Hans L. Trefousse: *Ben Butler: The South Called Him Beast!* (New York, 1957), pp. 119–20; and Peyton McCrary: *Lincoln and Reconstruction, The Louisiana Experiment* (Princeton, N.J., 1978), pp. 77–82.

[2] A. L. Mitchell to John Eaton, March 6, 1865, Eaton Collection, U.S. Army Chaplains Archives, Fort Hamilton, N.Y. (hereafter cited as Eaton Collection).

[3] *The International Record of Charities and Correction*, vol. II (1887), p. 55; Western Sanitary Commission: *Report on the White Union Refugees of the South* (St. Louis, 1864), pp. 19–22.

districts, where farms are being worked and such labor of value, I think the greater number of these could obtain homes and support. To discontinue the issue of subsistence, if [they are] retained here, would entail much suffering. I have tried to get the county court to establish a county farm for the care of a per centum that would be counted their own poor, but they claim to be bankrupt. I would suggest the sending of these people under charge of the chaplain of the post to different points in North Missouri, that homes and employment may be found for them. The crippled and blind can be provided for in Saint Louis. A large number of them are the families of soldiers now in our army, or who have died in the service. The removal of them from a military post will be a charity to them and a great saving to the Government.[4]

Refugee relief was a frustrating experience for both recipients and donors. Resources were seldom adequate to need; those who received help thought they deserved more, and their attitude antagonized would-be benefactors. After a tour of refugee camps along the Mississippi in the summer of 1864, Frances D. Gage, an agent of the Western Sanitary Commission, complained that the objects of the commission's benevolence despised rule, authority, order, and work.

> Of the Union Refugees, as I found them in June [wrote Mrs. Gage], nothing can be said but that their condition is deplorable. They were sick, suffering and dying, in hovels, sheds, barns, caves, tents and fields, helpless and I might almost say, hopeless, with far less power to help themselves than the negro, and far less will to do so, yet everywhere, proud, arrogant, and *exacting*.[5]

Many refugees, unloaded on the wharves of Cairo, Louisville, Cincinnati, and other border cities "meanly clad, well nigh starved, and almost heart-broken," found that because of settlement laws, the only public institutions that would receive them were police stations. During the spring and summer of 1864 the Refugee Relief Commission of Ohio (a private society despite its

[4] Colonel E. C. Catherwood to Major General G. M. Dodge, Department of the Missouri, March 14, 1865, *Official Records*, Series 1, vol. XLVIII (1896), p. 1172.

[5] Western Sanitary Commission: *Report on White Union Refugees of the South*, p. 41.

official-sounding name) raised $13,000 for the relief of distress, converted an abandoned schoolhouse in Cincinnati into a "refugee rest," and sent boxes of clothes and bedding to refugee camps in the South. The commission, the headquarters of which were in Cincinnati, favored and, where possible, followed the policy of passing refugees along to friends, relatives, and employers in other communities and states. "Border towns," it asserted, "should not be exclusively taxed with the care and expense of relieving a common burden brought about by a common cause."[6]

The American Union Commission, founded in New York in 1864, undertook the task of nationalizing refugee relief. The Union Commission, modeling itself after the Sanitary and Christian commissions, sought to systematize within one organization local and spasmodic efforts for the estimated 80,000 refugees within Union lines. By February 1865 it boasted branches in Boston, Cincinnati, and Chicago and maintained local agencies at Cairo, Louisville, Nashville, and Memphis. At a meeting held in the hall of the House of Representatives on February 12, 1865, the Reverend Joseph Parrish Thompson, president of the commission, issued an appeal for $150,000 to meet the needs of refugees during the winter and spring of 1865 and called on Congress to supply seed corn to suffering loyalists of Tennessee and Virginia. "We must feed the hungry; we must clothe the naked," declared Thompson, who was minister of the Broadway Tabernacle, a leading Congregational church in New York City. "But, in administering your charities . . . , we will guard most carefully against creating a long state of dependence and holding these people as paupers." He described the commission's policy of "deporting" refugees to places where labor was in demand as a "work of humanity, which at once helps the industry of this country, and relieves the government of the care of these needy people."[7]

Displaced Southerners who elected to remain within the contracting boundaries of the Confederacy constituted a major and eventually insuperable relief burden for local communities.

[6] First Semi-Annual Report of the Refugee Relief Commission of Ohio, 1864 (Cincinnati, 1864), pp. 4–7.

[7] The American Union Commission: Speeches of Hon. W. Dennison, Rev. J. P. Thompson . . . and Gen. J. A. Garfield . . . (New York, 1865), pp. 19, 21. On the origin of the American Union Commission see Ira V. Brown: Lyman Abbott: Christian Evolutionist (Cambridge, Mass., 1953), p. 38; Henry Lee Swint: The Northern Teacher in the South, 1862–1870 (Nashville, Tenn., 1941), pp. 10–11; The American Union Commission: Its Origin, Operations and Purposes (New York, 1865), p. 1.

Each year of the war brought an exodus of people driven from their homes by disaster, such as the Charleston fire of 1861, by military operations, or by enemy occupation. Texas and Florida probably benefited by the influx of newcomers, black as well as white, but hard-pressed cities like Charleston, Richmond, Columbia, and Savannah, with limited housing facilities and meager food supplies, were ill equipped to receive additions to their populations. Southern newspapers conducted energetic fund drives for the relief of refugees from Charleston, Fredericksburg, New Orleans, and Atlanta. In 1863 George Trenholm, reputedly the richest man in the Confederacy, arranged for the removal of children from the Charleston orphanage to an institution he had purchased for their use in Orangeburg, South Carolina; when that building burned in 1864, the 260 occupants again became subjects for relocation. The Confederate Congress, debating political, military, and diplomatic issues, gave scant heed to refugees; but after 1863 state legislatures became increasingly concerned with the problem. Georgia established a log cabin colony, Fosterville, for families driven from Atlanta. In most Southern states, however, public aid was available only to displaced indigent families of soldiers or their widows and orphans. Mary Elizabeth Massey, whose *Refugee Life in the Confederacy* provides a full and authoritative account of the subject, concludes that despite the efforts of individuals, local organizations, organized groups, and the Confederate army, most Southern refugees received no regular assistance from any source. "What was usually given was in the form of charity, which they resented, and token gifts which were insufficient to their needs."[8]

One of the most widely supported and highly organized civilian relief operations of the war years came in 1864 in response to the miserable condition of the population of East Tennessee, a Union enclave in the Confederacy. The region had been devastated by the traversing of opposing armies, both living off the land, and further impoverished by successive occupations by the rival forces. Crops, seed, and livestock had been destroyed, consumed, or carried off. Residents demanded assistance from the federal government, and sympathizers as far away as Maine dunned neighbors for contributions and petitioned state legislatures for appropriations for Tennessee relief. Agents of the East

[8] Mary Elizabeth Massey: *Refugee Life in the Confederacy* (Baton Rouge, La., 1964), p. 261; see also Paul W. Gates, *Agriculture and the Civil War* (New York, 1965), pp. 25–27.

Tennessee Relief Association solicited money, food, and clothing in Ohio, Pennsylvania, Massachusetts, Maine, and New York. The Western Sanitary Commission, the United States Sanitary Commission, and the Christian Commission enlisted their branches and auxiliaries in the campaign. The Hartsville (Pennsylvania) Ladies Aid Society raised $50 for the cause, and the New York Children's Aid Society sent C. C. Tracy, its "emigration agent," to Cincinnati to shepherd forty Tennessee orphans to foster homes in Ohio.[9]

In the last winter of the war political and commercial considerations as well as philanthropic motives contributed to Northern efforts to relieve destitution in Savannah. The city's trade had suffered severely from the war and blockade. Its capture in December 1864 by General William T. Sherman rendered Confederate currency worthless, cut the city off from normal sources of supply, and left the 20,000 inhabitants (as Mayor R. D. Arnold said) "with no means to purchase provisions and no provisions to purchase." Sherman's occupation policy, influenced by the hope of fostering peace sentiments in the rest of the Confederacy and abetted by the tractable behavior of the mayor and leading citizens, was mild and generous. He authorized distribution of quartermaster supplies to the needy and approved the mayor's proposal to send an agent to New York to negotiate the exchange of a quantity of confiscated rice for bacon, pork, lard, sugar, and other commodities. At a meeting of the New York Chamber of Commerce held on January 5, 1865, the agent, Julian Allen, declared: "Knowing the generosity of the citizens of New York and the Chamber of Commerce, I have no doubt that you will give the citizens of Savannah the requisite provisions, and tell them to keep their rice." The chamber accepted Allen's suggestion and appointed a committee to receive money and goods to be sent to Savannah for distribution by the mayor. Merchants in Boston and Philadelphia took similar action. Before the end of January provisions valued at more than $115,000 began to reach Savannah. Although the immediate objective was to tide the city over a difficult period, both donors and recipients expressed the hope that the gift was a harbinger of peace and of resumption of

9 Thomas William Humes: *The Loyal Mountaineers of Tennessee* (Knoxville, Tenn., 1888), pp. 316–33; James B. Campbell: "East Tennessee During the Federal Occupation, 1863–1865," *The East Tennessee Historical Society's Publications*, vol. XIX (1947), pp. 71–75; New York Children's Aid Society: *Twelfth Annual Report* (New York, 1865), pp. 11–12.

prewar commercial ties. The Savannah relief fund was the last of many causes to which Edward Everett contributed his eloquence for fund-raising purposes. Everett's valedictory, delivered at Faneuil Hall in Boston less than a week before his death, asked Bostonians to give to Savannah "not in the spirit of almsgiving, but as a pledge of fraternal feeling."[10]

While in Savannah, Sherman issued Special Field Order No. 15, reserving the Sea Islands and the abandoned rice plantations of Georgia and South Carolina for settlement by Negroes. Sherman's purpose was to rid his forces of the encumbrance of thousands of blacks who had attached themselves to the army during the March to the Sea.[11]

As Sherman's forces, after leaving Savannah, advanced through the Carolinas, displaced whites became a problem. In March 1865 the commanding officer at Wilmington, North Carolina, disposed of part of the burden by sending 400 white Southerners to New York City on the steamer *General Sedgwick*. General Joseph R. Hawley advised the chief quartermaster in New York that these refugees were

> a small portion of those accumulated by Major General Sherman during his late march. When the general reached Fayetteville, finding the multitude impeding his march and eating all the food within reach, he turned the caravan toward Wilmington under guard. In his written instructions he said that he desired to have the white refugees sent to New York to the commissioners of immigration. Even if they are all to be fed by the government, it can be done much cheaper there. Here they get but imperfect rations, which, with the exposure and crowding, threatens to bring pestilence. They impede and endanger military operations. Supplies cannot be gathered from the surrounding country. We have large numbers of the residents of this vicinity on our hands already.[12]

[10] John P. Dyer: "Northern Relief for Savannah During Sherman's Occupation," *Journal of Southern History*, vol. XIX (1953), pp. 457–72; Edward Everett: *Orations and Speeches on Various Occasions* (4 vols., Boston, 1850–68), vol. IV, p. 753.

[11] For Special Field Order No. 15, January 16, 1865, see *Official Records*, Series 1, vol. XLVII (1895), part 2, pp. 60–62; Martin Abbott: *The Freedmen's Bureau in South Carolina, 1865–1872* (Chapel Hill, N.C., 1967), pp. 7–8.

[12] General Joseph R. Hawley to General S. Van Vliet, March 28, 1865, *Official Records*, Series 1, vol. XLVII (1895), part 3, p. 51.

*   *   *

"For blacks," declares Louis Gerteis, "Reconstruction began in 1861 when Union forces occupied positions in Tidewater Virginia and in the Sea Islands of South Carolina." Before the war was over nearly a quarter of a million former slaves came under direct control of military authorities and more than one million were within Union lines.[13] Providing shelter and rations for thousands of fugitive or abandoned slaves was an unwelcome and onerous burden for army commanders, who often lacked supplies for their troops and were more interested in getting on with the war than in devising relief and rehabilitation projects. "We cannot now give tents to our soldiers," wrote General William T. Sherman from Memphis in September 1862, "and our wagon trains are a horrible impediment, and if we are to take along and feed the negroes who flee to us . . . it will be an impossible task." Shortly before issuing the Preliminary Emancipation Proclamation of September 22, 1862, President Lincoln expressed concern lest the proclamation induce a new influx of black refugees to Union camps. "What should we do with them?" he asked. "How can we feed and care for such a multitude?" There was agreement, however, that some sort of relief was essential, as a matter of military necessity, to save the Army, if not the refugees, from disease and demoralization.[14]

Proposals to move the black refugees, like white ones, to new homes and jobs in the North ran afoul of Northern opposition to Negro migration.[15] The solution adopted was to herd former slaves into a series of "contraband" camps scattered from the outskirts of Washington, D.C., down the Atlantic seaboard to South Carolina and along the Mississippi and its tributaries from Cairo, Illinois, to New Orleans. Conditions in the camps varied. The African village constructed by the army in 1864 for 2,800

[13] Louis Gerteis: *From Contraband to Freedman, Federal Policy Toward Southern Blacks, 1861–1865* (Westport, Conn., 1973), pp. 6, 193. The fullest account of the impact of the war on Southern blacks is Leon F. Litwack: *Been in the Storm So Long, The Aftermath of Slavery* (New York, 1979).

[14] Rachel Sherman Thorndike, ed.: *The Sherman Letters, Correspondence Between General and Senator Sherman from 1837 to 1891* (New York, 1894), p. 161; Roy P. Basler, ed.: *The Collected Works of Abraham Lincoln* (9 vols., New Brunswick, N.J., 1953–55), vol. V (1953), p. 420; Martha Mitchell Bigelow: "Freedmen of the Mississippi Valley, 1862–1865," *Civil War History*, vol. VIII (1962), p. 39.

[15] Gerteis: *From Contraband to Freedom*, pp. 17, 24.

blacks in New Bern, North Carolina, was deemed a model institution, carefully laid out and healthfully situated. At Corinth, Mississippi, working under an able superintendent, freedmen built log cabins, numbered them, laid out streets, divided the camp into wards, and constructed a school, church, commissary, and hospital.[16] Most of the camps, however, provided crowded, makeshift accommodations in which the refugees suffered and succumbed to exposure, unsanitary surroundings, lack of medical attention, and want of food and clothing. Many years after the war an aged former slave recalled: "We was freed and went to a place that was full of people. We had to stay in a church with about, twenty other people and two of the babies died on account of the exposure. Two of my aunts died, too, on account of exposure. . ."[17] In 1863 James Yeatman of the Western Sanitary Commission reported that at Helena, Arkansas, upwards of 3,000 blacks were either quartered in tents, caves, and bush shelters in Camp Ethiopia or packed 16 to 20 to a room in the poorer houses of the town. Throughout the Mississippi Valley Yeatman found living and working conditions so appalling that he concluded: "It would seem, now, that one-half are doomed to die in the process of freeing the rest."[18]

Self-help was the cornerstone of Union policy toward former slaves. "It is folly merely to receive and feed the slaves," advocates of emancipation advised Lincoln. "They should be welcomed and fed, and then, according to Paul's doctrine, that they who eat must work, be made to labor and to fight for their liberty and ours."[19] From the summer of 1861, contraband camps were recruiting grounds for labor, and after 1862 for enlistment in the armed services. Able-bodied men were in particular demand, but women as well as men, and children as well as adults, worked as

---

[16] Horace James: *Annual Report of the Superintendent of Negro Affairs of North Carolina, 1864* (Boston, 1865), pp. 7–8; Cam Taylor: "Corinth, The Story of a Contraband Camp," *Civil War History*, vol. XX (1974), pp. 7–8.

[17] Matilda Hatchett, North Little Rock, Arkansas, quoted in George P. Rawick, ed.: *The American Slave: A Composite Autobiography* (19 vols., Westport, Conn., 1972), vol. IX, p. 199.

[18] James E. Yeatman: *A Report on the Condition of the Freedman of the Mississippi* (St. Louis, 1864), pp. 1–16; W. R. Hodges: *The Western Sanitary Commission* (St. Louis, 1906), p. 10; George R. Bentley: *A History of the Freedman's Bureau* (Philadelphia, 1955), p. 26.

[19] William W. Patton and John Dempster, in "Reply to Emancipation Memorial," in Basler, ed.: *Collected Works of Abraham Lincoln*, vol. V, p. 423.

servants, cooks, nurses, and laborers at military camps and hospitals or made crops on government-operated or leased plantations. Unfortunately, as authorities often complained, illness, disability, old age, and infancy rendered a considerable number of blacks unfit for labor. The approved practice was to deduct a portion of the wages paid (or owed) able-bodied black workers as a charge for the support of the sick and disabled. Thus, under an order issued by General John E. Wool in the autumn of 1861, able-bodied Negro men working at Fortress Monroe, Virginia, were to be allowed $10 a month and boys $5. "But," explained a member of General Wool's staff,

> this money was not to be paid to the negroes earning it, but was to be turned over to the Quartermaster to be added to the fund . . . for the support of the women and children and those other negroes unable to work. As an incentive to good behavior, however, each able-bodied negro was allowed two dollars a month, and each negro boy one dollar a month for their own personal use.[20]

The first voluntary agency to extend aid to the contrabands was the American Missionary Association, which, since 1848, had maintained a mission for fugitive slaves in Canada. The AMA entered the field in September 1861 by sending a missionary to serve the contrabands around Fortress Monroe. The immediate stimulus was a letter from a chaplain of the New York State Volunteers deploring the "destitute and desolate" condition of the religious life of the blacks in the vicinity of the fort. General Benjamin Butler had earlier advised Lewis Tappan of the AMA of the Fortress Monroe contrabands' need for shoes and "substantial cheap clothing fit for winter service" but had discouraged missionary activity.[21]

[20] Le Grand B. Cannon: *Personal Reminiscences of the Rebellion, 1861–1866* (New York, 1895), pp. 57–58; see also Gerteis: *From Contraband to Freedom*, pp. 19–20.

[21] Richard B. Drake: "The American Missionary Association and the Southern Negro, 1861–1888" (unpublished Ph.D. dissertation, Emory University, 1957), pp. 7–9; Robert Stanley Bahney: "Generals and Negroes: Education of Negroes by the Union Army, 1861–1865" (unpublished Ph.D. dissertation, University of Michigan, 1965), pp. 94–98; Butler's letter to Tappan, dated August 10, 1861, is in American Missionary Association Manuscripts (Amistad Research Center, Dillard University, New Orleans, Louisiana), Virginia, Roll 1. This microfilm collection will hereafter be cited as AMA Mss.

In the winter of 1862, both the AMA and specially organized groups in Boston, New York, and Philadelphia responded to General W. T. Sherman's official appeal for philanthropic assistance for abandoned and fugitive slaves in the Port Royal, South Carolina, area:

> The helpless condition of the blacks inhabiting the vast area in the occupation of the forces of this command calls for immediate action on the part of a highly-favored and philanthropic people. . . .
> As the blacks are now in great need of suitable clothing, if not other necessities of life, which necessity will probably continue and even increase . . . the benevolent and philanthropic of the land are most earnestly appealed to for assistance in relieving their immediate wants.[22]

The Boston, New York, and Philadelphia societies, like the AMA, were more interested in developing religious and educational programs for freedmen than in administering physical relief. In practice all groups engaged in freedmen's aid found the gathering and distribution of relief supplies, mainly shoes and clothing but also medicine, garden seeds, tools, and farm implements, a necessary and long-continuing part of their work. In March 1863 Colonel John Eaton, superintendent of freedmen in the Mississippi Valley, acknowledged arrival in Memphis of "marvelous supplies of clothing" from the AMA. "There is a great need of clothes of every kind," reported an AMA agent in Grand Junction, Tennessee, in April 1863. "These the gov't does not furnish, and the destitution has been very great. The people of the North have done much—the approaching summer will do more, and when winter comes again God will provide."[23]

Care of orphans and other children without adult guardians presented problems of unusual difficulty for military authorities. After the War Department ordered removal of contraband families from Washington, D.C., to Arlington Heights, about fifty

[22] General Orders No. 9, Headquarters Expeditionary Corps, Hilton Head, South Carolina, February 6, 1862, in *Official Records*, Series I, vol. VI (1882), pp. 222–23; for the origins and development of freedmen's aid in the Sea Islands see Willie Lee Rose: *Rehearsal for Reconstruction, The Port Royal Experiment* (Indianapolis, 1964).

[23] John Eaton to George Whipple, March 14, 1863, Joel Grant to Professor Henry Cowles, Oberlin, Ohio, April 10, 1863, Tennessee Roll 1, AMA Mss.

children, belonging to no families, remained in the deserted camps in utter desolation. Mrs. S. C. Pomeroy, wife of the senator from Kansas and a veteran of the drought and famine of 1860–61, headed a group of Republican women who organized an asylum to shelter them as well as aged colored refugees. In John Eaton's territory, the first to assume responsibility for orphans were "Aunt Maria," a colored woman, and Eliza Mitchell, "one of the earliest to hasten to the aid of the destitute people flying from slavery," who managed an asylum on President's Island near Memphis. By 1864, similar institutions were in operation at Memphis, Helena, Arkansas, and Natchez, Mississippi. Eaton, who did not regard their combined efforts as "commensurate with the necessities of the Department," would have preferred a "large and central institution" to bring together all needy Negro orphans under his jurisdiction; no single society was willing to undertake the task, and no joint venture of the competing aid societies could be arranged.[24]

Wherever located, the asylums sent out urgent calls for bedding and clothing. The matron of an AMA institution for children in Norfolk, Virginia, told her headquarters in September 1863 that lack of supplies made it impossible to take in more orphans. "It has been very cold here for one week," she wrote. "Miss D——— loaned me six warm blankets which has been a great help. My boys has [sic] nothing but ragged pants to wear . . . we put patch upon patch but they are generally thin."[25]

Except among abolitionists and in strong antislavery circles, aid to freedmen did not initially enlist broad support in the North. "The war engrossed all minds," declared officials of the New York National Freedmen's Relief Association, recalling the early days of the organization.

> The masses of people had never been anti-slavery in
> sentiment. The number was small of those who had faith
> in the black man's capacity, or hope in his future, or
> interest in his fate. The Sanitary Commission was pressing

[24] U.S. Commissioner of Education: "History of Schools for the Colored Population," in *Special Report of the Commissioner of Education on Improvement of Public Schools in the District of Columbia, 1871* (reprinted, New York, 1969), p. 233; John Eaton: *Report of the General Superintendent of Freedmen, Department of the Tennessee, 1864* (Memphis, Tenn., 1865), pp. 87–88.

[25] R. G. Patten to William E. Whiting, September 2, 1863, Virginia, Roll 2, AMA Mss.

its plea for money to aid and comfort the sick and wounded soldiers. Few heard the freedmen's sigh; few that heard it heeded it. He was regarded as a hopeless vagabond, who had no health in him, and whom it would be foolishness to attempt to aid. Some said the money would be thrown away; some said that it would be worse than thrown away, for it would go to perpetuate pauperism.[26]

Possibly to forestall such criticism, and certainly in sharp contrast with it, the freedmen's aid societies adopted an unsentimental, businesslike stance. Not charity, but leading the freedmen "to form habits of cheerful voluntary labor in place of the constrained toil of slavery, teaching them to read and write, and interesting them in lessons of honesty and frugality" were the tasks assumed by the Educational Commission of Boston (later named the New England Freedmen's Aid Association). Founders of the New York Association, including William Cullen Bryant and the philanthropist Francis George Shaw, agreed at an organizational meeting that fugitive and abandoned slaves at Port Royal should be treated as freedmen, required to "earn their livelihood, as we do, and not be dependent upon charity. . . . No idlers will be allowed among them, but all must work who can." In an appeal for funds and donations of clothing, medicine, and books, the American Freedmen's Friend Society, organized by blacks in New York City and Brooklyn, listed as its objectives not only furnishing physical help to the freedmen but also promoting their loyalty, patriotism, and service to government.[27]

Application of these principles was left to missionaries, teachers, and plantation supervisors, who disposed of goods by gift or sale according to the need and condition of individual applicants. The process, as the superintendent of Negro affairs in North Carolina observed, required "at once judgment, penetration, firmness, and great kindness."[28] Susan Walker, a Bostonian,

[26] *Fourth Annual Report of the New York National Freedmen's Relief Association with a Sketch of Its Early History* (New York, 1866), p. 9.

[27] Pamphlet and Constitution of the Educational Commission of Boston, quoted in Henry Noble Sherwood: "Journal of Miss Susan Walker, March 3rd to June 6th, 1862," *Quarterly Publications* of the Historical and Philosophical Society of Ohio, vol. VII (1912), p. 9; *First Annual Report of the National Freedmen's Relief Association* (New York, 1863), p. 1; American Freedmen's Friend Society: Appeal [1863], James Morison Mackaye Papers, LC.

[28] James: *Annual Report of the Superintendent of Negro Affairs of North Carolina,* 1864, p. 13.

and one of the first women volunteers to reach Port Royal, complained of clothing too poor to sell or give away:

> Yesterday I was all day assorting old clothes sent from New York for the Negroes. Such old shoes and men's clothing filled with dust and dirt! Women's soiled gowns, etc. and *rags* I would not give to a street beggar, have been sent at government expense, to be *handled* and assorted by ladies! Some new but more old. Could not the large charity of New York furnish new materials?[29]

Laura M. Towne, another early volunteer, who was to remain on the Sea Islands for almost forty years, reported on a typical problem:

> The question of today is how to dispose of clothing to the poor people. They are willing to buy generally, but the supply is too small to admit of all they want. . . .
>
> They say, "Guv'ment is fighting for us and we will work for Guv'ment. We don't ask money; we only ask clothes and salt and sweetins."[30]

Miss Walker dealt with a difficult case:

> Katy has 7 ragged, dirty children, what shall be done? No husband and *nothing*. Some clothes are given for her children—one naked, and must have it at once. Is Katy lazy? Very likely. Does she tell the truth? Perhaps not. I must have faith and she must, at least, cover her children. She promises to make her cabin and herself clean and to wash her children before putting on new clothes. Will she do it? I will see her again.

If some of the freedmen, in Miss Walker's opinion, were lazy, others struck her as grasping. "They like to hoard," she commented and then asked herself: "Does this desire of acquisition indicate providence or selfishness? If the former we should hail it and encourage such good omen as will lead to self care and provision for the future."[31]

---

[29] Sherwood, ed.: *Journal of Miss Susan Walker*, p. 15.

[30] Rupert Sargent Holland, ed.: *Letters and Diary of Laura M. Towne Written from the Sea Islands of South Carolina, 1862–1884* (New York, 1969; first published 1912), p. 16.

[31] Sherwood, ed.: *Journal of Miss Susan Walker*, pp. 21, 31.

In the early stages of the work both missionaries and teachers performed a variety of functions. An AMA agent in South Carolina advised his headquarters: "I am teacher, doctor, & minister, besides assisting . . . in giving out rations, writing passes, etc."[32] Another missionary, S. G. Wright, who was commended by John Eaton as "a man who knows his business, the lifting of a race," described his daily routine in Memphis: "I visit hours every day among the 1500 here in camp and give out tickets with which they can draw clothing. Take my testament and read and speak as I find opportunity. Sometimes stop and teach awhile."[33] Teaching was not confined to classrooms or the young. Eaton noted: "Soldiers and laborers carry their speller or reader, and are frequently overheard reciting to each other." Soldiers in black regiments attended classes conducted by chaplains or by teachers whose salaries they paid themselves. While awaiting construction of a schoolhouse, Lucinda Humphrey, formerly a visitor for the Home for the Friendless in Chicago, acted as a friendly visitor imparting "essential ideas" to Memphis blacks. Lucy and Sarah Chase of Worcester, Massachusetts, who were sent to the Sea Islands by the New England Freedmen's Aid Association, were strong believers in training for self-reliance. They attached alphabet cards to walls so that black women could learn their letters while making beds or doing other household chores. The sisters also reported a successful experiment in uniting study with sewing, so that heads and fingers could be kept busy at the same time.[34]

Freedmen's aid publications justified expenditures for education as "the quickest and shortest way to relieve ourselves of the burden of contributing to the relief" of former slaves. The freedmen's faith in the efficacy of education matched that of their benefactors. Nearly all the teachers and missionaries commented on the Negroes' eagerness to learn to read. "They oftener ask for books than for clothes," declared Susan Walker. Moreover, from the beginning, blacks contributed to the cost of building and

[32] Reverend Fitch, Pinckney Island, South Carolina, to AMA, May 8, 1862, South Carolina, Roll 1, AMA Mss.

[33] Eaton to G. Whipple, March 14, 1863, Wright to S. S. Jocelyn, March 27, 1863, Tennessee, Roll 1, *ibid.*

[34] Eaton: *Report of the General Superintendent of Freedmen*, p. 68; John W. Blassingame; "The Union Army as an Educational Institution for Negroes, 1861–1865," *Journal of Negro Education*, vol. XXXIV (1965), p. 155; Henry L. Swint, ed.: *Dear Ones at Home: Letters from Contraband Camps* (Nashville, Tenn., 1966), p. 21.

operating schools. In December 1861 L. C. Lockwood, the first AMA missionary to the contrabands, noted that black laborers at Fortress Monroe, working for the government for lodging, rations, clothing, and the promise of $2 per month in cash, had subscribed $125 toward the cost of a church and schoolhouse. "If this is not giving of poverty what is?" observed Lockwood. "And if Northern charity would give in equal proportion of abundance, not only the means for building this house would be forthcoming, but every other call of benevolence would be met."[35]

Some of the teachers, like Mary Peake, a free Negress who in September 1861 established the AMA's first school for contrabands at Fortress Monroe, were recruited in the South. Most, however, were Northerners selected and paid by the freedmen's aid societies. Their salaries (about $15 a month and often in arrears) were supplemented by transportation, subsistence, and, sometimes, quarters furnished by the government. Relations with officers in charge of contraband affairs were of crucial importance in determining the quality and extent of facilities and services provided for educational and religious programs. Relations with white Southerners were ordinarily hostile, and relations among teachers themselves and between teachers and missionaries were not always harmonious. In the Sea Islands, missionaries engaged in sectarian and doctrinal squabbles, while representatives of the Boston and New York societies—the former predominantly Unitarian, the latter staunchly evangelical —regarded each other with suspicion. In Natchez, black teachers complained of discrimination in housing, school buildings, and allocation of school supplies; their white colleagues were affronted by the freedmen's preference for teachers and preachers of their own race.[36]

As would be expected, the missionaries, teachers, and other freedmen's aid workers were of uneven ability and dedication. The historian Willie Lee Rose, noting the peccadilloes committed by some of the missionaries at Port Royal, South Carolina,

---

[35] *The Freedman's Record*, January 1866, quoted in Thomas H. Smith: "Ohio Quakers and the Mississippi Freedmen—'A Field to Labor,'" *Ohio History*, vol. LXXVIII (1969), p. 161; Sherwood, ed.: *Journal of Susan Walker*, p. 20; L. C. Lockwood, Fortress Monroe, to AMA, December 23, 1861, Virginia, Roll 1, AMA Mss.

[36] Rose: *Rehearsal for Reconstruction*, pp. 218–21. Bertram Wyatt-Brown: "Education, Religion, and Racial Friction: The Yankee Mission to Mississippi Freedmen, 1865–1866" (paper presented at Ohio Academy of History, Columbus, Ohio, April 26, 1975).

concludes that a number of the missionaries sent to that area were "incompetent, dishonest, or at best extremely foolish." Edward Philbrick, "an aggressive entrepreneur" who came to the Sea Islands with the first boatload of representatives of the New England Freedmen's Aid Association, said some of his fellow passengers "look like broken-down schoolmasters or ministers who have excellent dispositions but not much talent." Several months after arriving at Port Royal, Philbrick expressed regret that little had been accomplished in the teaching department. "It is difficult to get people to stick to it," he said, "especially in the summer and during the unhealthy season."[37] The following spring, referring to the Memphis area, John Eaton wrote: "I tremble as I see some of the persons who offer themselves as teachers." Joel Grant, superintendent of freedmen at Grand Junction, Tennessee, described a teacher who may be taken as fairly typical:

> He is a young man of little knowledge of the world, but of large benevolence—willing to be directed, and is doing good. The Negroes try his patience by their dullness in some cases, but more by their inconstancy. But few men will expect all Negroes to thirst for a knowledge of letters with the same eagerness through the months and years necessary to attain it.[38]

Quite a different picture emerges of the matron of an AMA asylum for black orphans in Norfolk. Her associates charged her with "angry and repeated stamping of the foot at the table—shaking the fist in the face of Miss Doxey, and striking a big colored girl in the face till the blood flowed, etc., etc., etc."[39]

Even the most worldly-wise, experienced, and even-tempered teachers might have been discouraged by the problems encountered in teaching in overcrowded, unsanitary contraband camps. Schoolhouses were poorly heated if at all, without lights, and badly ventilated. Books, blackboards, and other educational materials were in desperately short supply. Lucinda Humphrey opened her first school in a windowless slab building without

[37] Rose: *Rehearsal for Reconstruction*, p. 221; Elizabeth Ware Pearson: *Letters from Port Royal* (New York, 1969), pp. 2, 110; the characterization of Philbrick is from James M. McPherson's introduction to the volume, p. iii.

[38] Eaton to Whittle, March 14, 1863, Grant to Professor Henry Cowles, April 10, 1863, Tennessee, Roll 1, AMA Mss.

[39] W. H. Woodbury to AMA, September 1, 1863, Virginia, Roll 2, *ibid.*

benches, desks, or blackboards and with only three books.[40] Elizabeth Hyde Botume, who began teaching in Beaufort, South Carolina, in November 1864, was fortunate in having a new school building, built with funds sent by an English freedmen's aid society and boasting the luxury of six glazed windows. On approaching it for the first time, she saw a crowd of children

> . . . all screaming and chattering like a flock of jays and blackbirds in a quarrel. But as soon as they saw me they all gave a whoop and a bound and disappeared. When I reached the door there was no living thing to be seen: all was literally "as still as a mouse"; so I inspected my new quarters while waiting for my forces. . . .
>
> The furniture consisted of a few wooden benches, a tall pine desk with a high office stool, one narrow blackboard leaning against a post, and a huge box stove large enough to warm a Puritan meetinghouse in the olden times. The pipe of the stove was put through one window. . . .
>
> Inspection over, I vigorously rang a little cracked hand-bell which I found on the desk. Then I saw several pairs of bright eyes peering in at the open door. But going towards them, there was a general scampering, and I could only see a head or a foot disappearing under the house. Again I rang the bell, with the same result, until I began to despair of getting my scholars together. When I turned my back they all came out. When I faced about they darted off. In time, however, I succeeded in capturing one small urchin, who howled vociferously, "O Lord! O Lord!" This brought out the others, who seemed a little scared and much amused. I soon reassured my captive, so the rest came in. Then I tried to "seat" them, which was about as easy as keeping so many marbles in place on a smooth floor. [As I went] towards half a dozen little fellows huddled together on one bench, they simultaneously darted down under the seat, and scampered off on their hands and feet to a corner of the room, looking very much like a family of frightened kittens. Hearing a noise and suppressed titters back of me, I looked around, and saw four or five larger boys rolling over and over under the benches towards the door. Whether for fun or freedom I could not tell; but as the first boy sprang to his feet and out of the

---

[40] L. Humphrey to Chaplain Fiske, post superintendent of contrabands, Memphis, Tennessee (1863), Tennessee, Roll 1, *ibid.*

door, I concluded they all planned escape. But I "halted" the rest, and got them on to their feet and into their seats. Then I looked them over. They saw I was not angry, but in earnest, so they quieted down. The runaway peeped in at the door, then crept along and sat down by his companions. There was not a crowd of them—not half as many as I supposed from all the clatter they had made.

All the children, Botume recalled, were "black as ink and shy as wild animals." They "had been born and bred in troublous times. They had always been surrounded by conflict and confusion. Irrepressible? That's tame! They were in a constant state of effervescences."[41]

Not only among Botume's students but everywhere, pupils' attendance was irregular because of the demands of work or sickness at home; their attention was adversely affected by hunger, cold, and bad health. Schools sometimes had to close because of widespread sickness in the community. An Arkansas teacher was grateful that only two of his students succumbed in an epidemic that killed one-eighth of the black population of the area.[42] "The poor negroes die as fast as ever," Laura Towne wrote from the Sea Islands in the last winter of the war. "The children are all emaciated to the last degree and have such violent coughs and dysenteries that few survive. It is frightful to see such suffering among children." The only part of Towne's work that was easier than at the start was distribution of relief. Formerly, she said, "it was hard to tell who were needy and who were not, but now we know all are alike in poverty. . . ."[43]

If self-help and education were the pillars of wartime policy for freedmen, thrift was intended to be the capstone. During 1863 and 1864, as thousands of freedmen entered the armed forces and tens of thousands more found work with the Union government and armies, military commanders like Thomas W. Higginson, colonel of the first Negro regiment in the Union army, and Generals Saxton, Banks, and Butler established banks to encourage saving by soldiers and civilian employees and to provide safe

[41] Elizabeth Hyde Botume: *First Days Amongst the Contrabands* (Boston, 1893), pp. 41–45.
[42] David Todd, Monthly Report, School for Colored Children in the Vicinity of Pine Bluff, Arkansas, June 1864, Arkansas, Roll 1, AMA Mss.
[43] Holland, ed.: *Letters of Laura M. Towne*, pp. 153–54.

places of deposit. In January 1865 in New York City, a group of businessmen and philanthropists held the first of a series of meetings leading, on March 3, 1865, to approval by Congress of an act incorporating the Freedmen's Savings and Trust Company. The Freedmen's Savings Bank, as it was usually called, was founded in much the same spirit and with similar expectations—although on a much larger scale—as the savings bank at the Newsboys' Lodging House of the New York Children's Aid Society. It was a nonprofit concern designed to receive deposits of freedmen, invest them in government securities, and return the profits to depositors in the form of interest. The idea for the Freedmen's Savings Bank originated with John Alvord, a Congregational minister and secretary of the American Tract Society, who knew how useful savings banks had been to workingmen in the North. Supporters of Alvord's plan included officers of the American Missionary Association, Chief Justice Chase, Senators Henry Wilson and Charles Sumner of Massachusetts, Peter Cooper, William Cullen Bryant, Samuel Gridley Howe, and a long list of men eminent in business, finance, and reform. Lincoln died before giving the bank his endorsement, but President Johnson praised its objectives and directed government officials to facilitate its operation. The bank went into business just as the war was coming to an end with William A. Booth, who was president of the American Trust Society and the New York Children's Aid Society, as president and John Alvord as corresponding secretary. For the next five years, while also working for the Freedmen's Bureau, Alvord vigorously promoted the interests of the Freedmen's Savings Bank not as a benevolent undertaking, but as an agency for helping former slaves win economic independence and prosperity.[44]

[44] Carl R. Osthaus: *Freedmen, Philanthropy and Fraud: A History of the Freedmen's Saving Bank* (Urbana, Ill., 1976), pp. 1–14; James M. McPherson: *The Abolitionist Legacy, from Reconstruction to the NAACP* (Princeton, N.J., 1975), pp. 74–75.

Part Two

RECONSTRUCTION
AND AFTER

Chapter 6

The Freedmen's Bureau:

Relief and Education

While freedmen's aid workers in Union-occupied parts of the South were distributing relief and improvising schools, leaders of the societies in the North joined other emancipationists in mounting a campaign for establishment of a governmental bureau specifically charged with protecting and promoting the welfare of freedmen. A public meeting held in New York City in mid-November 1863 unanimously adopted a resolution urging President Lincoln to call on Congress to create a Bureau of Emancipation "whose duty it should be, at the expense of the nation, to superintend the transition of the freedmen . . . from a state of compulsory labor to a condition of self-supporting industry."[1] The resolution was proposed by Henry W. Bellows on behalf of the National Freedmen's Relief Association of New York. Shortly thereafter Bellows drafted a letter to Lincoln, signed by representatives of the New York, Boston, Philadelphia, and Cincinnati freedmen's aid societies, spelling out the case for more concerted governmental action for the freedmen and indicating the relationship the voluntary societies expected to bear to the proposed Bureau of Emancipation. "It is the magnitude, not the nature of the work, that appals us, and drives us to government for aid and support," explained Bellows and the cosigners of the letter.

> It is plain to us, with our experience, that the question is too large for anything short of government authority, government resources, and government ubiquity to deal

[1] *Cleveland Morning Leader*, November 14, 1863.

with. The plans, the means, the agencies, within any volunteer control, are insignificant in their adequacy to the vastness of the demand. Our relief associations have discharged their highest duty in testing many of the most doubtful questions touching the negroes' ability, and willingness to come under direction when direction has lost its authorative character. They have proved the freedman's diligence, docility, and loyalty, his intelligence, and value as a laborer. They have alleviated much want and misery also. But were their resources ten times what they are, and ten times what they can be made, they would be no substitute for the governmental watchfulness, and provision which so numerous a race under such extraordinary circumstances requires.

Just as the Sanitary Commission channeled its aid to servicemen through the Medical Bureau of the War Department, so the freedmen's aid societies would "carry their complaints, their suggestions, . . . their supplementary assistance" to the Bureau of Emancipation.[2]

Bellows's letter, which Lincoln transmitted to Congress with a noncommittal message, was neither the first nor the last petition that advocates of a government agency for the freedmen sent to Washington. The American Freedmen's Inquiry Commission, an investigatory group appointed by Secretary of War Stanton in 1863, took a strong stand in support of such an agency. "We need a freedmen's bureau," declared the commissioners in their final report submitted in May 1864, "but not because these people are negroes, only because they are men who have been, for generations, despoiled of their rights."[3] In 1863 and 1864, Congress intermittently debated the need for and constitutionality of the proposed bureau and whether it should be placed in the War or

[2] The letter is printed in *Senate Executive Documents*, 38 Cong. 1 Sess., No. 1 (1863), pp. 1–7 (serial 1176). Bellows stated that he was the author of the document in a letter to Jonathan Sturges, December 12, 1863, Bellows Papers, MHS.

[3] "Final Report of the American Freedmen's Inquiry Commission," in U.S. War Department: *The War of the Rebellion: A Compilation of the Official Records of the Union and Confederate Armies* (70 vols., Washington, D.C., 1880–1901), Series 3, vol. IV (1900), p. 381 (hereafter cited as *Official Records*). Members of the commission were Robert Dale Owen, James McKaye, and Samuel Gridley Howe. On abolitionist influence in the movement for the Freedman's Bureau see James W. McPherson: *The Struggle for Equality, Abolitionists and the Negro in the Civil War and Reconstruction* (Princeton, N.J., 1964), pp. 178–91.

Treasury Department. In March 1865, both houses approved and President Lincoln signed a hastily drafted compromise bill which lumped supervision of refugees, freedmen, and abandoned lands in one agency located in the War Department. The act made officials of the Bureau of Refugees, Freedmen, and Abandoned Lands responsible for "supervision and management of all abandoned lands" and "control of all subjects relating to refugees and freedmen from rebel states" but made no appropriation for discharge of these tasks and limited the life of the bureau to one year after the conclusion of the war. On the other hand, the act permitted the Secretary of War to issue provisions, clothing, and fuel for the temporary relief of refugees, freedmen, and their families, allowed the assignment of military officers to duty with the bureau, and authorized the commissioner of the bureau to lease and sell forty-acre plots of abandoned or confiscated land to loyal refugees and freedmen.[4]

The officer chosen to head the bureau was Major General Oliver Otis Howard, former commander of the Army of the Tennessee, whose reputation for piety had won him the sobriquet "the Christian soldier." Howard, a native of Maine and a graduate of Bowdoin College as well as of West Point, was thirty-four years old at the time of his appointment. He was well regarded by the freedmen's aid societies and, as a New England Congregationalist, had close ties to the American Missionary Association.[5] In his autobiography, published more than forty years after the founding of the Freedmen's Bureau, Howard asserted that establishment of the agency constituted an important step toward making the federal government "something to love and cherish and to give forth sympathy and aid to the destitute." He was aware, however, that the bureau's benevolent functions were of the sort "hitherto always contended against by our leading statesmen" and that its relief operations, "being abnormal to our system of government," were of a temporary nature.[6] In staffing

[4] "An Act to Establish a Bureau for the Relief of Freedmen and Refugees," *U.S. Statutes at Large*, vol. XIII (1863–65), pp. 507–09; for valuable comment on the act and the agency see Harold M. Hyman: *A More Perfect Union, The Impact of the Civil War and Reconstruction on the Constitution* (New York, 1973), pp. 286–87.

[5] On Howard see John A. Carpenter: *Sword and Olive Branch, Oliver Otis Howard* (Pittsburgh, 1964), and William S. McFeely: *Yankee Stepfather, General O. O. Howard and the Freedmen* (New York, 1970).

[6] *Autobiography of Oliver Otis Howard* (2 vols., New York, 1908), vol. II, pp. 203, 226.

the bureau, Howard selected as his chief assistants comrades-in-arms from the Army of the Tennessee and men like Colonel John Eaton and General Rufus Saxton, who had been in charge of or responsible for large concentrations of freedmen during the war. The bureau, which has been described as "only slightly less military than the army itself,"[7] was committed from its inception to speedy restoration of social order and economic productivity. Establishment of a legally free but economically compulsory labor system was the cornerstone of its program. During Howard's first month in office he issued a series of directives to bureau officers outlining a cautious and restrictive relief policy: assistance was to be furnished the aged, sick, and orphaned, but able-bodied freedmen were to be encouraged "and if necessary compelled" to support themselves by their own labor. The most comprehensive of these orders, dated May 30, 1865, stated that relief establishments were to be discontinued as soon as possible and that only the "absolutely necessitous and destitute" were to be aided.[8]

Given the chaotic conditions prevailing in the summer of 1865 and for some years thereafter, it was impossible for his subordinates to observe Howard's decrees to the letter. In any event, the number of persons "absolutely necessitous and destitute" vastly exceeded the bureau's capacity for assistance. The immediate effect of peace was to increase rather than lessen the sufferings of freedmen. Blacks of both sexes and all ages who, as contrabands, had had jobs of some sort during the war were stranded, often far from home, when the army demobilized, contraband camps shut down, and military hospitals closed.[9] Few able-bodied freedmen possessed the experience and training requisite for making a living in a competitive society, and destitute planters were unable to hire even the most willing workers except under onerous conditions. The old, infirm, and mentally defective no longer had any claim to support by former masters, who, even if charitably disposed, had no means to help. In nearly every Southern community, children without or separated from

[7] John Hope Franklin: *Reconstruction: After the Civil War* (Chicago, 1961), p. 36.

[8] McFeely: *Yankee Stepfather*, p. 60; Carpenter: *Sword and Olive Branch*, p. 94. For the relief provisions of Howard's order of May 30, 1865, see Walter Fleming, comp.: *Documentary History of Reconstruction* (2 vols., Cleveland, 1906), vol. I, p. 309.

[9] Constance McLaughlin Green: *The Secret City, A History of Race Relations in the Nation's Capital* (Princeton, N.J., 1967), p. 81.

parents, not "owned" by anybody, and too young to work required special assistance.

Bureau officials relieved some of the needy and averted worse calamity by distributing rations of food obtained from the commissary general and surplus clothes from quartermaster stores, by providing free shipment for relief supplies sent by freedmen's aid societies, and by granting free transportation to refugees and freedmen returning home or seeking friends, relatives, or places of employment. In August 1865 the bureau issued 148,000 rations per day, and at the end of the year it was still supplying 50,000 people with daily food.[10] Three months after the bureau went into operation, Howard and Surgeon General Joseph K. Barnes reached an agreement to regularize issuance of medical and hospital supplies to its officials tending the sick in hospitals and asylums.[11] In cities like Washington, D.C., New Orleans, and Charleston, where destitute freedmen were especially numerous, the bureau established institutions for the aged, unemployed adults, and dependent children. Conditions in some of these overcrowded, ill-equipped facilities were as bad as those in the wartime contraband camps. In the autumn of 1865 Josephine S. Griffing, militant friend of the freedmen and a bureau agent in Washington, antagonized her superiors by publiciz-

---

[10] George R. Bentley: *A History of the Freedmen's Bureau* (Philadelphia, 1955), p. 76. Freedmen's Bureau Circular No. 8, June 20, 1865, defined a ration as follows:

> Ration—Pork or bacon, 10 ounces, in lieu of fresh beef; fresh beef, 16 ounces; flour and soft bread, 16 ounces, twice a week; hard bread, 12 ounces, in lieu of flour or soft bread; corn meal, 16 ounces, five times a week; beans, peas, or hominy, 10 pounds to 100 rations; sugar, 8 pounds to 100 rations; vinegar, 2 quarts to 100 rations; candles, adamantine or star, 8 ounces to 100 rations; soap, 2 pounds to 100 rations; salt, 2 pounds to 100 rations; pepper, 2 ounces to 100 rations.

> Women and children, in addition to the foregoing ration, are allowed roasted *rye* coffee at the rate of ten (10) pounds, or tea at the rate of fifteen (15) ounces to each one hundred (100) rations. Children under fourteen (14) years of age are allowed half rations.

House Executive Documents, 39 Cong., 1 Sess., No. 11 (1865–66), p. 47 (serial 1255).

[11] Howard: *Autobiography*, vol. II, p. 258. In the first year the value of medical and hospital supplies issued to the bureau amounted to nearly $268,000, Gaines M. Foster: "U.S. Army Medical Department Participation in Disaster Relief" (unpublished monograph, Medical History Division, Chief of Military History and Center of Military History, Department of the Army, Fort Detrick, Maryland, [1977]), Chapter II, p. 56.

ing the inadequacy of Freedmen's Bureau care for the 20,000 blacks packed in unsanitary barracks in the capital city.[12] Even such meager assistance as the bureau and freedmen's aid societies were able to offer alarmed advocates of "workfare," who believed that charity deterred former slaves from going back to work for their old masters. In contrast with such criticism, Henry W. Bellows expressed the hope in August 1865 that the government would be "truly paternal" in its dealings with both blacks and whites in the coming winter. "Of course it will be cheated and bamboozled, and idleness and dependence will be encouraged," he wrote. "But in a flood it won't do to think that sending boats to the relief of millions will prevent some thousands from learning to swim."[13]

While wrestling with relief problems, Howard and his assistant commissioners attempted to carry out provisions of the Freedmen's Bureau act authorizing the agency to rent or sell parcels of confiscated and abandoned land to freedmen. Howard gave the program high priority because it was a way of encouraging and demonstrating freedmen's capacity for self-reliance and also, in the absence of appropriated funds, a prospective source of revenue for the bureau's other operations. In land distribution, as in relief, demand exceeded supply; neither the freedmen's desire for land nor the bureau's expectations of income from providing it were realized. Under the most favorable circumstances the quantity of confiscated and abandoned land (800,000 acres and 5,000 town properties) would have provided homesteads for only a tiny fraction of the black population of the South. And President Johnson's insistence that all confiscated land, except that condemned and sold by court order, be restored to prewar owners and that all abandoned land be returned to owners holding general or special pardons substantially reduced the amount available for distribution. In Mississippi, where there were 400,000 landless blacks, land at the disposal of the bureau shrank from 80,000 acres at the end of the war to 35,000 acres in December 1865. By 1868, in the South as a whole, the agency controlled only 140,000 acres, enough for 3,500 forty-acre homesteads. On the Sea Islands and coastal parts of Georgia and South Carolina, restoration of abandoned land to prewar owners pre-

---

[12] Bentley: *History of the Freedmen's Bureau,* pp. 77–78.
[13] Bellows to James Miller McKim, August 18, 1865, Bellows Papers, MHS.

sented knotty legal and poignant human problems. In the end, only 1,600 of 40,000 freedmen settled on forty-acre plots under General Sherman's wartime Special Order No. 15 received valid certificates for their holdings; in 1867 they were required, under pain of expulsion, to exchange these for tracts in the Hilton Head region, where the federal government could convey a clearer title.[14]

In July 1866, overriding President Johnson's veto, Congress extended the life of the Freedmen's Bureau for two years; at the expiration of that term, Congress gave the bureau until January 1, 1869, to complete all its activities except those connected with education and disbursement of moneys owed freedmen for military service. The 1866 law, while authorizing continuance of relief operations, contained a stern proviso: "no person shall be deemed 'destitute,' 'suffering,' or 'dependent upon the government for support,' . . . who is able to find employment, and could by proper industry or exertion, avoid such destitution, suffering, or dependence." The Army Appropriation Act of July 14, 1866, tacitly recognizing the failure of land distribution as a source of income, granted the bureau approximately $300,000 for administrative expenses, $1,170,000 for clothing, $3,106,250 for commissary stores, $500,000 for medical supplies and services, $500,000 for rent and repairs of schools and asylums, and $1,320,000 for transportation.[15]

From first to last, Howard smarted under accusations that lax bureau operations fostered idleness and promoted pauperism. Nothing was further from his intention. Like most of his countrymen in his own day and since, Howard had ambivalent feelings toward relief. Sympathetic and eager to respond to the need of "our destitute wards," he was suspicious of fraud and feared imposition. He approved the decision of one of his inspectors, General J. S. Fullerton, to close an orphan home in New Orleans the inmates of which, "mostly boys, some of whom were 12 to 16 years of age, and able to take care of themselves," had no occupation except "to lie around in the warm sun and play marbles." Fullerton ordered the boys to be apprenticed "to good and responsible persons in order that they might be properly cared for,

[14] Martin Abbott: "Free Land, Free Labor, and the Freedmen's Bureau," *Agricultural History*, vol. XXX (1956), pp. 150–53; Vernon Lane Wharton: *The Negro in Mississippi, 1865–1890* (Chapel Hill, N.C., 1947), p. 58.

[15] *U.S. Statutes at Large*, vol. XIV (1865–67), pp. 92, 173–74; vol. XV (1867–69), pp. 193–94.

and acquire habits of industry and morality"; he resented the allegation of "supposed friends of the freedmen" that his action reduced the orphans to slavery.[16] Through an adjutant, Howard charged agents investigating need in Georgia and Alabama in 1866 to:

> Remember that people who are able to walk from ten to twenty miles, and carry great loads of rations, are in no danger of starving without those rations; and the same exertion that they put forth to draw supplies from the Government, applied to some useful occupation, would earn enough to support wives and children that may really be destitute.[17]

Repeatedly, and prematurely, as it turned out, Howard sought to have responsibility for paupers, including indigent refugees and freedmen, restored to local officials. In August 1866, with the approval of the Secretary of War, he ordered that, effective October 1, the issue of rations be suspended except to the sick in regularly established hospitals and to orphan asylums already in existence. Trouble was expected, but failed to materialize, in areas like Hampton, Virginia, where large numbers of blacks had been fed since early in the war. "Their resource was surprising," reported a bureau official; "the Negro in a tight place is a genius."[18]

Deemphasis of the bureau's relief, land distribution, and welfare functions was accompanied by increasing efforts to get the freedmen back to work. In the words of W. E. B. Du Bois the freedmen's organization became "a vast labor bureau," the agents of which directed their energies to negotiating and enforcing contracts between planters and former slaves. The contracts generally provided that Negroes, in exchange for their labor, would receive rations and a share, ranging from one-tenth to one-third,

---

[16] Howard A. White: *The Freedmen's Bureau in Louisiana* (Baton Rouge, La., 1970), p. 79; for report of General J. S. Fullerton to General Howard, see *New York Times*, December 31, 1865, p. 3.

[17] Carpenter: *Sword and Olive Branch*, pp. 104–05.

[18] Circular No. 10, August 22, 1866, in "Report of the Commissioner of the Bureau of Refugees, Freedmen and Abandoned Lands, November 1, 1866," *House Executive Documents*, 39 Cong., 2 Sess., No. 1 (1866), p. 712 (serial 1285); Samuel C. Armstrong: *The Founding of Hampton Institute*, Old South Leaflets, No. 149 (Boston, n.d.,), p. 3.

of the crop harvested.[19] In practice in the immediate postwar years planters were unable to feed their workers, and only scanty and, in some localities, no crops at all were raised. Late planting and a host of other problems resulted in a short harvest in 1865. The next year was worse; flood, drought, and tornadoes caused the failure of both cotton and corn crops. By the winter of 1866–67 planters as well as laborers in vast areas of the South were in even more desperate straits than at the end of the war. A South Carolina poor law official advised a Northern correspondent in February 1867 that until new crops could be raised, "clothing and bread are both needed but more particularly the latter." James Yeatman and representatives of the St. Louis Board of Trade warned that new crops might not be planted; farmers were without money, provisions, or credit, and the merchants who ordinarily advanced supplies to them were unable to do so.[20]

On the same day (March 2, 1867) that Congress adopted the basic Reconstruction Act, officially entitled "An Act to provide for the more efficient Government of the Rebel States," the Senate Judiciary Committee asked Howard to provide an estimate of the extent of destitution and danger of starvation in the South. His reply, received about a week later, precipitated a Senate debate on the propriety of federal disaster relief, particularly when the prospective beneficiaries were former rebels. Howard estimated that 56,897 persons (32,662 whites and 24,235 Negroes) were in grave need, and that the cost of feeding them for five months would be $2,133,750, necessitating a $1,500,000 increase in the appropriation granted the bureau in July 1866. The Judiciary Committee trimmed his request to $1,000,000.[21] On March 30, 1867, both houses approved a joint resolution granting the bureau no additional appropriation but authorizing it to em-

---

[19] "The Freedmen's Bureau," *The Atlantic Monthly*, vol. LXXXVII (1901), p. 361; on the deemphasis of relief and welfare functions see J. Thomas May: "Continuity and Change in the Labor Program of the Union Army and the Freedmen's Bureau," *Civil War History*, vol. XVII (1971), p. 253; for provisions of labor contracts see Martin Abbott: *The Freedman's Bureau in South Carolina, 1865–1872* (Chapel Hill, N.C., 1967), pp. 69, 141–43.

[20] J. A. Schenck, Camden, South Carolina, to James Dunlap, February 28, 1867, Southern Famine Relief Committee Papers, New-York Historical Society, Box 2 (hereafter cited as SFRC Papers, NYHS); James E. Yeatman, George Partridge, and A. G. Brown, Petition to Congress, February 19, 1968, SFRC Papers, NYHS, Box 3.

[21] *Congressional Globe*, 40 Cong., 1 Sess., pp. 39–48 (March 9, 1867).

ploy unexpended funds from its existing appropriation "to issue supplies of food sufficient to prevent starvation and extreme want to any and all classes of destitute or helpless persons in those southern and southwestern States where a failure of the crops and other causes have occasioned widespread destitution."[22] After passage of the resolution Howard designated $500,000 of his 1866 appropriation for famine relief. Qualified adults were to receive eight pounds of meat and a bushel of corn per month; children under fourteen, half those amounts. According to Howard's figures, the number assisted per day for four months was 58,343, "no distinction being made between whites and blacks, loyal and disloyal."[23]

Voluntary efforts for the relief of destitute white Southerners commenced a year before Congress authorized federal aid. In April 1866 the Ladies' Southern Relief Association of Baltimore held a fair attracting support not only from Maryland but as far afield as California, Cuba, France, and England. The $165,000 raised by the fair and other solicitations were distributed among former Confederate states according to population and need.[24] In autumn 1866 a St. Louis group sponsored a "Fair and Tournament" for the relief of the suffering poor of the South, particularly widows and orphans of Confederate soldiers.[25] The New York Ladies' Southern Relief Association, organized in December 1866 by society women of Southern birth or family ties, garnered $71,000 for the cause through donations, balls, benefits, lectures, fairs, teas, contribution of one day's pay by post office clerks, and proceeds of a day's business at the Russian Baths,

---

[22] U.S. Statutes at Large, vol. XV (1867–69), p. 28. On the same day, in another joint resolution, Congress transferred $50,000 from the Freedmen's Bureau to the Department of Agriculture "for the purchase of seeds of improved varieties of vegetable and cereals and their distribution in the Southern States."

[23] Abbott: Freedmen's Bureau in South Carolina, pp. 42–43; White: The Freedmen's Bureau in Louisiana, pp. 70–71; "Report of the Commissioner Bureau Refugees, Freedmen &c, October 20, 1869," in U.S. War Department, Annual Report 1868–69 (2 vols., Washington, D.C., 1869), vol. I, p. 501.

[24] The association had a committee for each state with subcommittees in the various states to act as distributing agents. Part of the relief to South Carolina, Georgia, Alabama, and Mississippi was sent directly to the governors, Ladies' Southern Relief Association: Report (Baltimore, 1866); Alice B. Keith: "White Relief in North Carolina, 1865–1867," Social Forces, vol. XVII (1939), pp. 341–43.

[25] Keith: "White Relief in North Carolina," p. 344.

Broadway at Thirteenth Street.[26] Boston also supported Southern relief, but not enthusiastically. Robert Winthrop complained in February 1867 that "our people are not sufficiently alive to the danger of starvation . . . impending over many parts of the South." The feeling in Hartford, Connecticut, according to Frederick Law Olmsted's mother, was "let them starve!"[27]

New York merchants and shippers who, before the war, had profited by meeting the supply and carrying needs of the Southern economy, conducted the most businesslike canvass of Northern philanthropic resources. The Southern Famine Relief Commission, established in January 1867, represented the city's benevolent, mercantile, financial, and professional elite. Archibald Russell, a lawyer, who had been active in the American Bible Society and the Christian Commission, was chairman of the executive committee. Members of the committee included J. P. Morgan; Howard Potter, formerly treasurer of Sanitary Commission; and Nathan Bishop, who had been chairman of the executive committee of the Christian Commission. Frederick Law Olmsted was recording secretary.[28] The Famine Relief Commission, employing tactics developed by the wartime commissions, waged an aggressive fund drive that, in the space of four months, collected $220,000 in contributions from individuals, business concerns, and churches. Recalling actions taken during the Irish and Kansas famines, the commission petitioned the New York legislature to appropriate funds for Southern relief; it also proposed that England send the unexpended balance of the Lancashire Relief Fund to the American South. The commission declined to follow General Howard's suggestion that it supplement Freedmen's Bureau activities by supplying "comforts and delicacies." Instead, it used the money it collected to buy, bag, and ship corn, "the cheapest method of sustaining life, the most

[26] Anne Middleton Holmes: *Southern Relief Association of New York, 1866–1867* (New York, 1926), *passim.* Mrs. Algernon Sydney Sullivan, a Virginian by birth, took a leading part in the organization of the association; officers included Mrs. James I. Roosevelt, president, and Mrs. S. L. M. Barlow, vice-president; Mrs. Cyrus Hall McCormack was a member of the executive committee. The association used clergymen in the South as its agents and almoners; Francis R. Flournoy: *Benjamin Mosby Smith* (Richmond, Va., 1947), pp. 99–102.

[27] Winthrop is quoted in Keith: "White Relief in North Carolina," p. 345; Mrs. John Olmsted to Frederick Law Olmsted, February 26, 1867, Olmsted Papers, LC.

[28] On Russell see *New York Times*, April 21, 1871, p. 8.

easy of carriage, and the least liable to perversion." When possible, the Famine Relief Commission shipped supplies to Southern ports by naval transports. For distribution it used agencies created by military commanders and Southern state governors rather than officers of the Freedmen's Bureau. The commission justified a separate system of distribution on the grounds that its contribution would reach points not served by the bureau, and would be more likely to promote conciliation than if sent through bureau channels.[29]

The Famine Relief Commission wound up its work in autumn 1867 in the assumption that a kind Providence had promised abundant harvests. In fact, crop failures caused by heavy rains and caterpillar infestations left parts of Louisiana, South Carolina, Mississippi, and other Southern states under continued threat of starvation. On January 2, 1868, General Howard transmitted reports of severe distress to Secretary of War Ulysses S. Grant with a plea that the President and Congress provide "some thorough and practical mode of relief that will not have a tendency to pauperize the people."[30] In the absence of a better plan, bureau officials supplied planters with corn and meat, taking crop liens on the next year's crop, and fed the destitute in cities and towns at soup houses where "desiccated and mixed vegetables" provided sustenance at one-third the cost of rations.[31]

Howard's instructions regarding operation of soup kitchens in Richmond, Virginia, a city frequently visited by foreign dignitaries and newspapermen, showed unusual tenderness for the needy. "Please not to spare any pains in caring for the poor during these terrible days," he wrote the assistant commissioner on February 7, 1868.

> Do not have people who come for soup waiting in the streets. It occasions remarks of every kind for and against the colored people. . . . A yard with a floor upon it to stand upon or where they can get under cover, and such arrangements as will let them come and go with great rapidity will prevent this exposure. Be sure not to have an Irishman in

[29] SFRC, NYHS, Box 2, Report of the committee appointed to confer with General Howard, April 27, 1867; SFRC, NYHS, Box 3, undated document in Executive Committee Minutes.

[30] Howard to Grant, January 2, 1868, Bureau of Refugees, Freedmen, and Abandoned Lands Records, National Archives (cited hereafter as Freedmen's Bureau Records), Record Group 105, Entry 69, p. 220.

[31] Circular Letter, December 4, 1867, *ibid.*, p. 185.

charge of colored people. The deep rooted aversion of the Irish to the negroes is sufficient reason of this. Please see that the officer in charge of groceries has not his own interest involved in the issue of supplies. . . . Please not to make any reports but to do the work. If necessary employ another physician to visit those who are unable to come out of their houses.[32]

Bureau officials in more remote, less visible areas of the South conducted their work without such explicit and compassionate guidance. The novelist John W. De Forest, who was bureau chief in Greenville, South Carolina, in 1868, followed a tightfisted policy. "It was necessary," he wrote, "to convince the Negroes of the fact that the object of government was not to do them favors, but justice; and of the still greater fact that there is very little to get in this world without work." De Forest was equally stringent in his attitude toward "the low-down people," poor whites who had subsisted by beggary both before and during the war and who now flocked to the Freedmen's Bureau office, asking, " 'Anythin' to git?' " " 'Got anythin' for the lone women?' " " 'When is the next draw day?' " In response to such appeals De Forest took the view that "Charity is either an absolute necessity or an absolute evil." Noting the many demands made on a Freedmen's Bureau agent, he concluded that an agent "might be said to do best when he did least."[33]

In summarizing and defending bureau relief, Howard denied that it had been a "pauperizing agency." "The wonder," he wrote in 1869, "is not that so many, but that so few, have needed help." He estimated that out of 4,000,000 former slaves, only 1 in 200 freedmen had received assistance. Most of those helped, he asserted, were people whose circumstances would have made them objects of public charity in any state at any time.[34]

In view of the meager aid available and the suspicious attitude displayed toward applicants, it is not surprising that former slaves, looking back on the hard times after the war, expressed dissatisfaction with relief efforts. "Dem Yankees was mean folks,"

[32] Howard to General Orlando Brown, February 7, 1868, *ibid.*, pp. 282–83.

[33] John W. De Forest: *A Union Officer in the Reconstruction* (New Haven, Conn., 1948), pp. 38, 42, 141.

[34] "Report of the Commissioner Bureau Refugees, Freedmen, &c, October 20, 1869," in U.S. War Department: *Annual Report, 1868–69*, vol. I, p. 502.

recalled Sarah Debro of Durham, North Carolina. After seventy years she had not forgotten or forgiven the unpalatable rations:

> I was never hungry till we was free and de Yankees fed us. We didn't have nothin' to eat 'cept hard tack and middlin' meat. I never saw such meat. It was thin and tough with a thick skin. You could boil it all day and all night and it wouldn't cook done. I wouldn't eat it. I thought 'twas mule meat; mules dat done been shot on de battlefield, den dried. I still believe 'twas mule meat.

Not poor quality, but denial of assistance was what galled Lorenzo Ivy, a student at the Hampton Institute, who later became a teacher and principal in Virginia schools. Ivy said of the bureau officer who had denied his family help in the winter of 1865–66: "He had on Uncle Sam's clothes, but he had Uncle Jeff's heart."[35]

Educational activities of the Freedmen's Bureau began at least as early as relief operations and lasted longer. On May 19, 1865, in the first important circular issued from his headquarters, Howard pledged that the bureau would be attentive to the moral and educational condition of the freed people. The circular, drafted with the aid of Lyman Abbott, a young clergyman who had recently been appointed executive secretary of the American Union Commission, declared: "The utmost facility will be afforded to benevolent and religious organizations in the maintenance of good schools for refugees and freedmen until a system of free schools can be supported by recognized local government." According to the circular, the bureau's aim was not to supersede benevolent agencies already engaged in educational work, but "to systematize and facilitate" their efforts.[36] For the next five years these tasks were to occupy a leading place in the agency's efforts and expenditures.

When the bureau was established, about 750 teachers and

[35] Norman R. Yetman, ed.: *Life Under the "Peculiar Institution," Selections from the Slave Narratives* (Huntington, N.Y., 1976), p. 100 (Debro); John W. Blassingame, ed.: *Slave Testimony, Two Centuries of Letters, Speeches, Interviews and Autobiographies* (Baton Rouge, La., 1977), pp. 737–38 (Ivy).

[36] Howard: *Autobiography*, vol. II, pp. 271–72; Lyman Abbott: *Reminiscences* (Boston and New York, 1915), pp. 257–58.

missionaries were instructing 75,000 Negro children and adults in parts of the South occupied by Union forces.[37] They worked without coordination and often in competition. In early spring 1865, Abbott found representatives of four different associations teaching and proselytizing in a camp for 2,000 freedmen. "None can do much," he observed. "Each is jealous of the other."[38] On July 12, 1865, Howard took a step toward systematization by ordering the appointment in each state of a superintendent of education, who was instructed to "take cognizance of all that is being done to educate refugees and freedmen, secure proper protection to schools and teachers, promote method and efficiency, and correspond with the benevolent agencies which are supplying his field." In September 1865, Howard appointed the Reverend John W. Alvord, corresponding secretary and later president of the Freedmen's Savings Bank, inspector of finance and schools. Alvord, a member of Oberlin's first graduating class, formerly secretary of the American Tract Society, and, like Howard, well disposed toward the American Missionary Association, remained in charge of Freedmen's Bureau educational activities until the agency wound up most of its work late in 1870.[39]

During the bureau's first year—which, as far as was then known, might well have been its last—Howard lacked funds even to pay superintendents of education. In some states, e.g., Virginia, an army chaplain was detailed to the job; in others, such as South Carolina, a civilian paid by the benevolent associations received the appointment. Despite lack of an appropriation, the bureau fostered education in 1865 and 1866 by granting freedmen's aid associations rent-free use of barracks and other government buildings for schoolhouses, by providing free transportation to the field for teachers, books, and school supplies, and by helping teachers obtain military rations at cost.[40]

When Congress extended the bureau's life in July 1886, it appropriated further funds for transportation, $21,000 for sal-

---

[37] Bentley: *History of the Freedmen's Bureau*, p. 170.

[38] Abbott: *Reminiscences*, p. 250.

[39] T. D. Eliot: "Condition of the Freedmen," *House Reports*, 40 Cong., 2 Sess., No. 30 (1868), p. 22 (serial 1357); Carl R. Osthaus: *Freedmen, Philanthropy and Fraud: A History of the Freedmen's Savings Bank* (Urbana, Ill., 1976), pp. 12–13, 60–61; and Robert C. Morris: "Reading, 'Riting and Reconstruction" (unpublished Ph.D. dissertation, University of Chicago, 1976), pp. 91–94, discuss Alvord's background and friendship with AMA officials.

[40] Bentley: *History of the Freedmen's Bureau*, p. 171.

aries of superintendents of education, and, as noted earlier, $500,000 for rent and repair of schools and asylums.[41] The act authorized the bureau to "seize, hold, lease, or sell for school purposes" property of the former Confederate States of America, and it directed Howard to:

> cooperate with private benevolent associations of citizens in aid of freedmen, and with agents and teachers, duly accredited and appointed by them, . . . hire or provide by lease buildings for purposes of education whenever such associations shall, without cost to the government, provide suitable teachers and means of instruction and . . . furnish such protection as may be required for safe conduct of such schools.[42]

The misgivings and constraints limiting bureau relief operations did not apply in educational matters. By adopting a broad interpretation of "repair," Howard and his state superintendents were able not only to renovate barracks and other structures used for teaching freedmen but to assist in construction of new school buildings. Whenever freedmen's aid associations or, as frequently happened, Negro groups obtained land and started putting up schoolhouses, the bureau supplied funds for "repair"—i.e., completion of the buildings. By March 1869, 630 schoolhouses had been built with its aid. Although the agency was not authorized to pay teachers' salaries—which benevolent associations were supposed to provide "without cost to the government"—it "facilitated" the aid associations by "renting" buildings which, in many cases it had helped construct. In 1868 Howard devised a formula under which the bureau paid $10 per month in rent for each teacher instructing an average of thirty or more pupils.[43] Thus, the bureau subsidized both school construction and the cost of instruction. Historian Richard B. Drake estimates that it allotted nearly half ($5,262,000) of the $12,000,000 appropriated to it to benevolent associations for support of freedmen's education.[44]

[41] U.S. Statutes at Large, vol. XIV (1865–67), p. 92.

[42] Ibid., p. 176.

[43] Bentley: History of the Freedmen's Bureau, pp. 172–73; see also Henry Lee Swint: The Northern Teacher in the South, 1862–1870 (Nashville, Tenn., 1941), p. 6.

[44] Richard B. Drake: "Freedmen's Aid Societies and Sectional Compromise," The Journal of Southern History, vol. XXIX (1963), pp. 177, 179 n.

In 1866 the principal voluntary agencies serving freedmen were the American Missionary Association, active in the field since 1861, and the American Freedmen's Union Commission, a federation of the American Union Commission and the New York, Boston, Philadelphia, and other freedmen's aid associations.[45] In addition to the AMA and AFUC, each of the major Protestant denominations maintained its own freedmen's aid organization. The bureau was more successful in facilitating than in systematizing the work of these agencies. All were eager for assistance but intent on autonomy. Duplication of effort by competing organizations continued throughout the life of the bureau, with the result that some areas were oversupplied with schools for freedmen, while others were undersupplied or neglected altogether. Howard soon learned that "competition was almost as much the rule among the aid societies as . . . cooperation."[46]

Rivalry between the AMA and AFUC, like the wartime contest between the Christian and Sanitary commissions, involved conflicting styles and programs as well as competition for public acclaim, "benevolent revenues," and government recognition and aid. Both the AMA and the AFUC had abolitionist roots, the former stemming from the Weed-Tappan wing of the movement, the latter from the Garrison branch.[47] While the AMA confined its educational efforts to blacks, the AFUC, as an offshoot of the American Union Commission, was interested in educating whites as well as freedmen, and its schools, in theory, were open to both races.[48] The AMA, nominally nondenominational but supported mainly by Congregationalists, was committed to an evangelical program. "Our organization is a religious one, tho' an educational one also," its secretary advised Alvord, "and it will be impossible,

[45] On the American Union Commission see Chapter 5; on consolidation of the freedmen's aid societies see Julius H. Parmelee, "Freedmen's Aid Societies, 1861–1871," in Thomas Jesse Jones: *Negro Education: A Study of Private and Higher Schools for Colored People in the United States* (2 vols., Washington, D.C., 1917), vol. I, pp. 269–71.

[46] Bentley: *History of the Freedmen's Bureau*, p. 64.

[47] Drake: "Freedmen's Aid Societies and Sectional Compromise," p. 177; Morris: "Reading, 'Riting and Reconstruction," pp. 80, 94.

[48] In practice, the students were nearly all black; Morris: "Reading, 'Riting and Reconstruction," pp. 339–40, notes that in 1867 only thirty-eight whites were enrolled in the New England branch of AFUC schools in Maryland, Virginia, North Carolina, and Georgia.

suicidal, to subject our missionaries and teachers (both in one) to any body of men not of a religious character; and we cannot separate the educational from the religious element."[49] The AFUC, on the other hand, with a membership drawn from many denominations, including Unitarians and Universalists, adopted a secular approach. It told its teachers they "were neither 'missionaries, nor preachers, nor exhorters'; they must have nothing to do with 'churches, creeds or sacraments,' and were 'not to inculcate doctrinal opinions or take part in secretarian propagandism of any kind.' "[50] Lyman Abbott, who was secretary of the AFUC, later recalled: "We did not regard the South as a proper field for missionary effort. We went into the South . . . not to convert a non-Christian or imperfectly Christian people, but to aid a people impoverished by war in establishing the cornerstone of democracy—a public school system."[51]

Denominational jealousies and rivalries were too strong to permit the AMA to realize its aim of bringing all evangelical groups into its fold. For the same reasons, support for the AFUC began to erode shortly after its founding in 1866 as the Cincinnati and Chicago branches defected to the AMA and the Methodist Church established a separate Freedmen's Aid Society. The AFUC scored a propaganda victory in 1867, when William Lloyd Garrison hailed its achievements before an admiring audience at the World Anti-Slavery Conference in Paris. The AMA, however, had the advantage of an aggressive fund-raising apparatus with access to important collection channels in the North; it also enjoyed better relations with the Freedmen's Bureau. At peak strength in 1866 the AFUC maintained almost 775 teachers in more than 300 schools. By 1869, however, the commission's executive committee concluded that although the work of aiding in the education of the freedmen was not finished, the presence of many other agencies in the field made a national organization such as the AFUC no longer "necessary or expedient." The decision to disband at a time when the Freedmen's Bureau still had funds to disburse for education may have been influenced by Abbott's difficulties and disappointments in dealing with General Howard and his associates, who seemed better disposed toward

---

[49] Reverend Geo. Whipple to Reverend J. W. Alvord, September 5, 1865, Freedmen's Bureau Records, Box 162.

[50] Swint: *The Northern Teacher in the South*, p. 37.

[51] Abbott: *Reminiscences*, pp. 267–68.

the AMA and the denominational societies than to the nonsectarian AFUC.[52]

Both the Freedmen's Bureau and the benevolent associations expected and required freedmen to make substantial contributions to the support of education. Despite poverty, crop failure, and troubled social conditions, former slaves found the means to buy school sites, assist in erecting school buildings, furnish teachers with room and board, and pay tuition. In some cases they also pledged themselves to pay part or all the teachers' salaries.[53] In 1868 R. M. Manly, the Freedmen's Bureau superintendent of schools in Virginia, defended the levying of tuition charges of 10 to 50 cents a month as a way to "eliminate the worthless material, to improve the average attendance and punctuality, to increase the interest both of pupil and parent, and to develop in them a legitimate feeling of self-respect, in place of the debasing sense of the entire dependence."[54] Some children paid tuition in kind rather than currency. A teacher recalled that at Fortress Monroe, Virginia, "one 'har' " (rabbit), old or young, fat or lean, paid for a whole month's schooling; another teacher in Virginia, a Northern black, jotted in his diary: "The people sent for tuition 5 eggs and a chicken . . . from Rebecca Zander 5 eggs and 2 small chickens; from Mr. Towns 1 doz. eggs."[55] While the bureau provided desks and benches, benevolent organizations such as the American Tract Society supplied primers, spelling books, Scriptures, and cards for beginning readers. On the theory that students would prize books more if they helped pay for them, a Sunday school teacher in Virginia asked each child to donate an egg; a Tract Society colporteur forwarded the proceeds of the sale of the eggs—$2—to headquarters for catechisms.[56]

[52] *Ibid.*, p. 272; Richard B. Drake: "The American Missionary Association and the Southern Negro, 1861–1888" (unpublished Ph.D. dissertation, Emory University, 1957), pp. 16–24; Morris: "Reading, 'Riting and Reconstruction," p. 94.

[53] Parmelee: "Freedmen's Aid Societies, 1861–1871," pp. 291–92; see also W. E. Burghardt Du Bois and Augustus Granville Dill, eds.: *The Common School and the Negro American* (Atlanta, 1911), pp. 18–19.

[54] Quoted in William T. Alderson: "The Freedmen's Bureau and Negro Education in Virginia," *The North Carolina Historical Review*, vol. XXIX (1952), p. 80.

[55] Richard L. Morton, ed.: "Life in Virginia, by a 'Yankee Teacher,' Margaret Newbold Thorpe," *Virginia Magazine of History and Biography*, vol. LXIV (1956), p. 201; Pauli Murray: *Proud Shoes, The Story of an American Family* (New York, 1956), p. 182.

[56] Thos. L. Johnson to T. L. D. Walford, November 20, 1867, American Tract Society Correspondence, Huntington Library.

Of the 1,831 schools reporting to the Freedmen's Bureau for the year ending July 1, 1868, 1,325 were sustained wholly or in part by freedmen, who owned 518 of the buildings in which schools were held. About 40 percent of the approximately 78,000 children in daily attendance paid tuition.[57] Black self-help in education was especially important in rural areas and sparsely settled states like Florida and Arkansas, which, as an official report noted in 1871, did not offer "so inviting a field to philan-thropic efforts" as more populous and accessible parts of the South.[58] Florida, one of the few states to provide a system of education for freedmen before Radical Reconstruction, not only levied a tuition charge of 50 cents per month but also imposed a school tax of $1 a year on black males between the ages of twenty-one and fifty-five.[59] In Arkansas, voluntary activities by blacks in Little Rock resulted in the founding of the first free school ever established in the state; at Camden, Arkansas, black families planned a fair, concert, and exhibition to be held at the close of the 1868 school year to raise funds to fence the school lot, buy a school bell, and make repairs to the church.[60]

In 1869, at the peak of the benevolent associations' activity in education, 9,500 men and women were teaching freedmen; an estimated 5,000 came from the North. In a sample of 1,000 whose homes have been located, almost 50 percent hailed from Mas-sachusetts, Connecticut, and other New England states; the other half came in about equal proportions from New York, Pennsyl-vania, and other middle Atlantic states and from Ohio, Michigan, Indiana, Illinois, and states farther west. A handful of missionary

[57] Howard: "Report to the Secretary of War, October 14, 1868," in U.S. War Department, *Annual Report, 1867–68* (2 vols., Washington, D.C., 1868), vol. I, p. 1029. On problems encountered in the use of figures from Freedmen's Bureau school reports see Swint: *Northern Teacher in the South,* pp. 6–7.

[58] U.S. Commissioner of Education: "History of Schools for the Colored Population," in *Special Report of the Commissioner of Education on Im-provement of Public Schools in the District of Columbia, 1871* (reprinted, New York, 1969), p. 337.

[59] *Ibid.,* pp. 337–38. The law also provided for fine and imprisonment of "any white person" who taught freedmen without a state license; James Watson Davis: *The Civil War and Reconstruction in Florida* (New York, 1913), p. 420.

[60] Davis: *Civil War and Reconstruction in Florida,* p. 327; Jas. A. Scovill, Camden, Arkansas, to James R. Shipherd, May 21, 1868, American Mis-sionary Association Manuscripts (Amistad Research Center, Dillard Uni-versity, New Orleans, La.), Arkansas-Arizona, Roll 1.

teachers found their way to the South from England, Canada, and Hawaii.[61] The majority of Yankee teachers—probably 75 percent—were female and mostly single, although some accompanied husbands. One of the young women, Chloe Merrick of Syracuse, New York, who began teaching in Fernandina, Florida, in 1863 and subsequently kept school in North Carolina, moved from schoolhouse to executive mansion in 1869, when she married Harrison Reed, carpetbag governor of Florida.[62] Some of the Northern teachers served for as little as $15 a month, but those employed by the New England branch of the AFUC, one of the oldest and most active of the teacher recruiting agencies, received minimum monthly salaries of $35, with no distinction in pay between males and females.[63] Both the AMA and the more secular AFUC scrutinized the religious credentials of candidates, the AMA demanding "fervent piety" of its teachers, the AFUC settling for "a genuine spirit of love for God and man."[64] Neither agency accepted Roman Catholics.

Immediately after the war, Southern whites who taught freedmen usually presented themselves as Union sympathizers, but as demand for teachers increased and hard times continued, "lawyers, physicians, editors, ministers and all classes of white people," including Confederate veterans and widows of Confederate soldiers, applied for and obtained teaching positions.[65] A school inspector's report indicates the variety of white teachers serving blacks in one Southern community during Reconstruction. Canton, a town in central Mississippi, had three freedmen's schools, the only ones available to the 17,000 blacks in the county. The teacher of the first, "a white woman of the South," was characterized by the inspector as "without native or acquired ability"; the second school's teacher was a white South-

[61] Swint: *Northern Teacher in the South*, p. 3, Appendix III, pp. 175–200.

[62] Richard N. Current: *Three Carpetbag Governors* (Baton Rouge, La., 1967), pp. 11, 23.

[63] Morton, ed.: "A 'Yankee Teacher' in North Carolina," p. 577; "History of New England Branch, A.F.U.C.," Freedmen's Bureau Records, Entry 158, p. 340.

[64] Swint: *Northern Teacher in the South*, pp. 36–38; Morris: "Reading, 'Riting, and Reconstruction," p. 89.

[65] Alderson: "Freedmen's Bureau and Negro Education in Virginia," p. 74; E. Merton Coulter: *The South During Reconstruction, 1865–1877* (Baton Rouge, La., 1947), p. 84; Abbott: *The Freedmen's Bureau in South Carolina*, p. 95; Morris: "Reading, 'Riting, and Reconstruction," pp. 190, 195–96.

crncr, who frankly admitted he taught to make a living; at the
third, another white man, a Baptist minister "of fine reputation
and broad influence," conducted classes with the assistance of a
woman from the North.[66] In 1866 in Charleston, South Carolina,
an ex-Confederate chaplain, A. Toomer Porter, selected fifteen
"ladies" to teach in what he proudly called "the first large school
for colored children opened solely by the white people in the
South." Unlike some "ladies of refinement" in Virginia who
offered former slaves "gratuitous" lessons, Porter's teachers received $500 per year from funds contributed by Episcopalians in
the North.[67]

Black teachers ranged from the highly educated to the
barely literate. The Reverend Francis L. Cardozo, an AMA educator in Charleston, had studied in Glasgow, Edinburgh, and
London, and preached in New Haven. No less dedicated were
young men and women whose energy and enthusiasm exceeded
their academic preparation. George E. Stephens, for example,
born a slave in 1853, started his teaching career in the late 1860s,
several years before entering the Hampton Normal School:

> Having been sent to school all this time [three or four
> years] by my father, and attained an age when I could be
> of some benefit to him, I thought it no more than right
> that I should do something. I began to teach school about
> fifteen miles from home. Here I found difficulties that
> almost made me give up. I was placed among an ignorant
> people who I were to teach, and make some attempt,
> though small, to elevate; while not many miles from where
> I was teaching a preceptor had been hung for instructing
> his own race. When I went home on Saturday, I had to
> walk fifteen miles, and get back Monday to open school at
> nine o'clock. I continued my school for four months. I think
> I gave satisfaction, because they wanted me to teach again,
> but I took a school nearer home—only five miles off. To
> this I walked every morning—teaching six hours. I taught
> two sessions here, and enjoyed it very much, though it
> required considerable patience. In this way I helped my

[66] Report of John M. Langston, Canton, Mississippi, July 24, 1867,
Freedmen's Bureau Records, Entry 18, p. 69.

[67] A. Toomer Porter: Led On! Step by Step: Scenes from Clerical, Military, Educational, and Plantation Life in the South, 1828–1898 (New York,
1899), pp. 222–23; Alderson: "Freedmen's Bureau and Negro Education in
Virginia," p. 74.

father to build a house, and sent my sister to the Hampton Normal School.[68]

Benjamin Holmes, five years older than Stephens, taught school while attending Fisk University, which he entered in 1868. He told an interviewer in 1872 that commuting on foot to meet his various responsibilities as college student, schoolmaster, self-employed tailor, church deacon, Sunday school teacher, and member of a literary society made him feel he "lacked neither work nor exercise."[69]

Freedmen's Bureau officials often questioned the fitness of Southern teachers, whether white or black. The Georgia superintendent of education complained in 1867 that too many white applicants "appeared to think that *'anybody can teach niggers.'*" At about the same time Superintendent Manly of Virginia reported that poorly trained teachers made many rural schools only better than none at all; some of those in the towns in 1868, "worse than none." The bureau superintendent in Mississippi warned in 1868 that schools taught by unqualified blacks were "springing up like mushrooms all over the state since the teachers have learned that the Bureau will pay them more than they can earn at any other business."[70]

In addition to buildings, "repaired" by the bureau, freedmen's schools met in a variety of accommodations, including a former slave market, the dining room of the house of former Governor Henry A. Wise of Virginia, and in former President John Tyler's summer home. Through the intercession of President Johnson and General Howard, the Reverend Porter of Charleston obtained the former Marine Hospital in that city for his school for colored children.[71] At a time when school buildings throughout the country were described as too often "unsightly, inconvenient, and dilapidated," it is not surprising that

[68] Blassingame: *Slave Narratives*, pp. 741–42, reprinted from M. F. Armstrong and Helen W. Ludlow: *Hampton and Its Students* (New York, 1874), pp. 115–17.

[69] *Ibid.*, p. 620. The Holmes interview originally appeared in Gustavus D. Pike: *The Jubilee Singers and Their Campaign for Twenty Thousand Dollars* (Boston, 1873), p. 60.

[70] The three superintendents are quoted in U.S. Commissioner of Education: "History of Schools for the Colored Population," p. 341; Alderson: "Freedmen's Bureau and Negro Education in Virginia," p. 73; and Swint: *Northern Teacher in the South*, p. 8.

[71] Porter: *Led On!*, pp. 222–23; Howard: *Autobiography*, vol. II, p. 340.

physical conditions in schools for freedmen usually left much to be desired. The journalist J. T. Trowbridge found the situation in Tennessee similar to that in other states: schools held in old buildings and sheds good for little else, without proper seats or desks. "The pews of colored churches, or plain benches in the vestries, or old chairs with boards laid across them in some loft over a shop, or out-of-doors on the grass in the summer—such was the usual scene of the freedmen's schools." Yet even in a school that was physically but a shell and lacking maps and charts, able teachers and willing pupils could make progress.[72]

What students at the time thought about the poor facilities is hard to ascertain. Many years later, when interviewed in the 1930s for the WPA Slave Narratives project, the survivors had little to say about the physical conditions of the schools. They remembered their teachers' names, the books they had studied— *Webster's Blue-Backed Speller* and *McGuffey's Readers*—and one could still recite the words of a song learned seventy years earlier:

> *I am a happy bluebird*
> *Sober as you see;*
> *Pure cold water*
> *Is the drink for me.*
>
> *I'll take a drink here*
> *And take a drink there;*
> *Make the wood ring*
> *With my temperance prayer.*

Fanny Johnson of Hudgins, Arkansas, confessed that she "didn't learn nothing" from the young white lady who came down from the North:

> They had our school near what was the grave yard. I didn't learn cause I was too busy looking around at the tombstones. They was beautiful. They looked just like folks to me. Looks like I ought have learned. They was mighty good to send somebody down to learn us that way. I ought have learned, it looks ungrateful, but I didn't.[73]

[72] *American Annual Cyclopaedia*, vol. VII (1867), p. 284; J. T. Trowbridge: *A Picture of the Desolated States and the Work of Restoration, 1865–1868* (Hartford, Conn., 1868), p. 337.

[73] George Rawick, ed.: *The American Slave: A Composite Narrative* (19 vols., Westport, Conn., 1972), vol. IX, *Arkansas Narratives*, part 4, pp. 10, 88, 98–99.

Curriculum and discipline varied as widely as facilities. At St. Helena on the Sea Islands, Laura M. Towne gently but firmly guided students through reading, arithmetic, American history, civics, and geography. Teachers at Fort McGruder, near Williamsburg, Virginia, emphasized the basics:

> Next to reading and spelling, we consider writing of most importance, and hence have made more effort to teach writing than arithmetic. We considered, that processes of calculation will soon be acquired from doing business, but penmanship will not be. Without knowing how to write, no independent communication can be indulged in between distant friends, and no account be kept, or note taken of anything but by memory.[74]

Public schools in Charleston, South Carolina, followed what Alvord called the Southern plan, "strict in discipline but with less that cultivates the mind and heart." Thus, at the Franklin Street School a teaching staff of 12 white South Carolinians put 800 black students through a rigorous routine:

> A student who was tardy to class was given a number of demerits; if absent a total of ten or more days, whatever the cause, his class grade was lowered one rank; if absent ten consecutive days without permission he was expelled; if in his work he fell below the general average of the class, he was demoted to the grade below; and if insubordinate or willfully disobedient, he was immediately dismissed.[75]

At the other extreme, two "Yankee teachers" at a public school in Warrenton, North Carolina, reported that their school was in a constant state of genial disorder:

> We teach in a room with a single aisle running from end to end, long benches go from the aisle to the wall, and are so close that the children have not room to walk on the floor between them when seats are occupied; so when the children are called out for recitation they walk over

[74] Morton, ed.: "Life in Virginia," p. 182.
[75] J. W. Alvord: *Letters from the South Relating to the Condition of the Freedmen* (Washington, D.C., 1870), p. 7; Abbott: *Freedmen's Bureau in South Carolina*, p. 92.

each other, the walkers kicking and the sitters pinching, so
that our school appears as if always having recess.[76]

Freedmen's schools could survive disorder in the classroom;
scorn and hostility on the part of native whites were more serious, and in some cases, an insurmountable obstacle. "It is difficult
to describe the odium with which the excellent self-denying
school teachers are met," Howard reported in December 1865,
attributing the opposition in part to survival of wartime animosities, but "mostly . . . to prejudice against educating the blacks
and the belief that teachers are fostering social equality."[77] On
the basis of observations made during a tour of the South in
autumn 1865, Alvord, the bureau's chief education officer,
warned that only military force could save established schools
from being broken up, enable others to be started, and provide
the order and security needed for teaching and learning.[78] Subsequent events bore out the accuracy of his predictions; despite
efforts to enforce provisions of the renewal act of 1866, which
charged the bureau with protecting schools, the disruption of
classes, harassment of teachers and pupils, and destruction of
school buildings continued throughout the life of the agency.
Howard's autobiography contains a state-by-state catalogue of
attacks on teachers, students, and schools by the Ku Klux Klan
and similar groups. "But for the presence of Bureau officers, sustained by a military force," he maintained, "there would have
been no one to whom these victims of cruelty and wrong could
have appealed for defense." Even more important than the cases
redressed by the bureau, in Howard's opinion, were the acts of
violence prevented by the mere fact of its existence as an agency
to preserve order and enforce justice.[79]

Generalizations about popular attitudes toward education of
blacks, whether in the South or the North, are subject to qualifi-
cation and contradiction. Bureau officials were eager to find and
quick to cite instances of toleration or approval by "the better
class" of whites, but such cases were usually balanced by other
examples of obstruction and opposition. The reporter J. T.

[76] Morton, ed.: "A 'Yankee Teacher' in North Carolina," p. 570.

[77] "Report of the Commissioner of the Bureau of Refugees, Freedmen,
and Abandoned Lands . . . December 1865," p. 13.

[78] Alvord to Howard, Jan. 1, 1866, in *Senate Executive Documents*,
39 Cong., 1 Sess., No. 27 (1866), p. 120 (serial 1238).

[79] Howard: *Autobiography*, vol. II, pp. 37, 374–89.

Trowbridge declared indifference to be the prevailing attitude among whites who did not actively oppose freedmen's schools. "Visiting these schools in nearly all the Southern States," he said, "I did not hear of the white people taking any interest in them." With rare exceptions, he continued, "I never saw or heard of a Southern citizen, male or female, entering one of those humble school-rooms." Whites who deplored violence and recognized the validity of education for blacks might still regard freedmen's schools as symbols of Radical Reconstruction, resent them as instruments of Republicanism, Northern interference, and black insolence, and resist taxation for their support.[80]

One way Southerners could manifest hostility to the whole process of Reconstruction was by ostracizing Northern teachers. The latter found white society closed to them and board and lodging available, in many communities, only from blacks. Two Yankee teachers in the public school at Warrenton, North Carolina, although acknowledged to be "educated, well-dressed, and modest women," were shunned by the white population because, as a resident explained, "the citizens did not approve of their work or of their coming." Margaret Newbold Thorpe, one of the teachers involved, wrote her family: "You can't imagine how strange it seems never to speak to a white person, and have no social life, not one visitor. The Southern women will not notice us at all, and we will not allow the men to call on us."[81] In northeastern Mississippi a group of men who paid an uninvited call on a teacher from Illinois put the message Warrenton communicated silently into blunt language. The teacher summarized it in testimony to a congressional committee: "They did not want radicals there in the South; did not want northern people teaching there; they thought the colored people could educate themselves if they needed any education; they advised me to go home."[82]

---

[80] Trowbridge: *A Picture of the Desolated States*, p. 336; for discussions of Southern attitudes toward freedmen's education see Abbott: *Freedmen's Bureau in South Carolina*, pp. 93–95; White: *Freedmen's Bureau in Louisiana*, pp. 182–87; John Hope Franklin: *Reconstruction: After the Civil War* (Chicago, 1961), pp. 52–53; William Preston Vaughn: *Schools for All: The Blacks and Public Education in the South, 1865–1877* (Lexington, Ky., 1974), pp. 44–47.

[81] Morton, ed.: "A 'Yankee Teacher' in North Carolina," pp. 566, 570.

[82] Testimony of Sarah E. Allen, November 11, 1871, in *Ku Klux Conspiracy, Testimony Taken by the Joint Select Committee to Inquire into the Condition of Affairs in the Late Insurrectionary States* (13 vols., Washington, D.C. 1872), vol. XII, p. 778.

In view of the difficulties Northern teachers faced, and because they were always in short supply, bureau leaders early
indicated interest in setting up schools to train black teachers.
Alvord's first semiannual report sketched the outlines of what he
described as "a systematic plan" to prepare 15,000 freedmen as
teachers "in a very few months."[83] In the spring of 1867 Howard
recommended that the newly created Peabody Fund use its resources to assist in training teachers in the South and called on
the benevolent associations to develop plans for normal schools
and colleges for blacks. During the next year and a half, the
bureau attempted to exercise some control over the quality of the
institutions by using the power of the purse to limit the number
established. By autumn 1869, Howard could report that at least
one normal school had been organized in each Southern state
and that several colleges for freed people were in operation.[84]

Howard later asserted that public officials rather than private donors "led the way" in establishing higher education for
Southern blacks. His objective as commissioner of the Freedmen's Bureau, he said, was to lay the institutional foundations
and build on them as rapidly as possible in order to produce "as
many good teachers, professional men, and leaders to the rising
generation as we could, during the few years of Governmental
control." Between 1867 and 1870 the Freedmen's Bureau granted
approximately $450,000 to twenty institutions, including How-
ard, Fisk, and Atlanta universities, Berea College, and Hampton
Institute in the South, as well as Oberlin, Wilberforce, and others
in the North, that supplied teachers for freedmen. Grants to
Howard University were the largest ($180,000) and the most con-
troversial, since critics viewed that institution as the general's
monument to himself. General Howard justified the bureau's
generosity to the university on the grounds that it was intended
to offer both complete college courses and professional training
in law, medicine, and theology. When he objected to its name,
the committee told him that " 'there are other Howards.' "[85]

83 Alvord to Howard, January 1, 1866, p. 118.

84 Bentley: History of the Freedmen's Bureau, pp. 175–76; Howard:
"Report . . . Nov. 20, 1869," in U.S. War Department: Annual Report, 1869
(2 vols., Washington, D.C., 1869), vol. I, p. 506.

85 E.g., John Howard (1726–1790), the English prison reformer:
Howard: Autobiography, vol. II, pp. 395–97, 402; for charges of corruption
in construction of Howard University buildings see Bentley: History of the
Freedmen's Bureau, pp. 203–09.

Most students concur in the judgment of George R. Bentley, historian of the Freedmen's Bureau, that getting the colleges, universities, and normal schools started was the agency's most permanent contribution to education.[86]

The educational and bounty divisions of the bureau and its supervision of three hospitals and asylums continued after other operations ended on January 1, 1869. By July 1870, however, the agency's funds for education had been spent or promised, and Howard had nothing to give applicants for assistance except words of advice and encouragement. In the space of five years the bureau had allocated $5,200,000 to education. These funds were the nucleus around which clustered the sums raised by freedmen's aid and benevolent societies, churches, state and local authorities, and the freedmen themselves. In the opinion of R. M. Manly, the bureau's superintendent of education in Virginia, "Christian charity and Government aid" had never been "more wisely or profitably expended." Howard took satisfaction in 1868 in knowledge that "We are no longer obliged to argue 'ability to learn' on the part of the negro race. A great process is going on, not of experiment but unceasingly productive results."[87] As the bureau's resources, activities, and personnel dwindled, however, its officials became less confident of the permanence of its achievements. Superintendent Edward L. Deane of South Carolina, skeptical of the ability of county school officials and doubtful of the legislature's interest in educational matters, wrote Howard in 1870: "I . . . close my connection with this work with gloomy forebodings."[88] Alvord, depressed by educational reverses in Tennessee in 1870, predicted that similar conditions would prevail in freedmen's education throughout the South when the bureau closed: "drooping, discouraged; teachers with blasted hopes, working hard, desperately, but pulling only against the current."[89]

No one was more aware than Howard of the limited achieve-

[86] *History of the Freedmen's Bureau*, p. 176; Robert Stanley Bahney: "Generals and Negroes: Education of Negroes by the Union Army, 1861–1865" (unpublished Ph.D. dissertation, University of Michigan, 1965), pp. 270–71.

[87] Manly is quoted in Alderson: "Freedmen's Bureau and Negro Education in Virginia," p. 75; Howard: "Report . . . October 14, 1868," in U.S. War Department: *Annual Report, 1867–68*, vol. I, p. 1031.

[88] Quoted in Abbott: *Freedmen's Bureau in South Carolina*, p. 96.

[89] Alvord: *Letters from the South*, p. 32.

ments and remaining needs. In 1868 he noted that only one-seventh of the children of freedmen had as yet received any formal education. A year later his report showed that no more than one-tenth of the school-age population was attending school. He recommended that the educational functions of the Freedmen's Bureau be transferred to the federal Department (later Office) of Education so that the work under way could be continued and expanded. Nothing came of Howard's recommendation or of the efforts of Representative George F. Hoar of Massachusetts to obtain congressional approval of a national system of aid to education. By law the Freedmen's Bureau educational division was supposed to function until each Southern state had made "suitable provision" for the education of freedmen, but at the end of 1870, when the bureau was all but defunct, Howard reported "no Southern State is fully prepared with buildings, teachers, funds, and intelligent officers to set in operation and sustain a free school system."[90] Fortunately, through the combined efforts of the bureau and voluntary agencies, a cadre of young people like George Stephens and Benjamin Holmes had received enough training and inspiration to serve as the teachers of the first generation of blacks born into freedom.

The last clients of the bureau were 250 patients and 100 outpatients of the Freedmen's Hospital and 101 inmates (52 boys, 24 girls, 24 old women, and 1 old man) of the Colored Orphan Asylum, both in Washington. Some of them, former slaves on the Custis-Lee Arlington estate, had been wards of the federal government since the outbreak of hostilities; the rest had drifted into Washington or other Union-controlled areas during the war. Howard warned that most of the hospital patients were so helpless from infirmity or extreme old age that they would probably need to be supported for the rest of their lives. District of Columbia authorities denied they were legal residents of the District and "no town, city, county, or State could be found which would assume the care and support of them." Hence, when Congress terminated the Freedmen's Bureau in 1872, it provided for the continuance of the Freedmen's Hospital and Asylum, under supervision first of the Secretary of War and later

[90] Howard: "Report . . . October 20, 1870," in U.S. War Department: *Annual Report, 1870* (2 vols., Washington, D.C., 1870), vol. I, p. 317.

of the Secretary of Interior. The hospital was still in operation more than a century after the bureau went out of existence.[91]

[91] *Ibid.*, pp. 318–19; Howard: "Report . . . October 20, 1871," in U.S. War Department: *Annual Report, 1871* (2 vols., Washington, D.C., 1871), vol. I, pp. 452–53; *U.S. Statutes at Large*, vol. XVII (1871–1873), p. 366; Thomas Holt *et al.: A Special Mission, The Story of the Freedmen's Hospital, 1862–1962* (Washington, D.C., 1975), pp. 13–17; in 1975 the institution became the Howard University Hospital.

Chapter 7

Public Charities

After the War

T he most moving passage of Lincoln's Second Inaugural
Address, "With malice toward none, with charity for all,"
was the opening part of a sentence bidding the nation to bind up
the wounds of war and "care for him who shall have borne the
battle and for his widow and his orphan." Some of the wounds
were beyond healing. The battles, accidents, diseases, and other
hazards of war cost the lives of more than 600,000 men, sons
and husbands who were actual or potential breadwinners and
fathers of families. South Carolina sacrificed the lives of 23
percent of its military population, North Carolina 17 percent.
Of the men who marched to war from Vermont, New Hampshire,
and Maine, less than half returned to those states as permanent
residents. The North escaped the physical devastation experienced by portions of the South, but the disruption and unsettle-
ment of the war years left it with a permanent unemployed
population of about 1,000,000.[1]

Binding up the wounds of war in the sense of restoring or
reconstructing the nation's political, constitutional, social, and
economic fabric was a difficult and time-consuming process, but
it was accomplished long before the work and expense of caring

[1] J. G. Randall and David Donald: *The Civil War and Reconstruction*
(Boston, 1961), p. 531; William F. Fox: *Regimental Losses in the Amer-
ican Civil War, 1861–1865* (Albany, N.Y., 1889), p. 555; Harold Fisher
Wilson: *The Hill Country of New England* (New York, 1936), pp. 72–73;
Fred A. Shannon: "The Homestead Act and the Labor Surplus," *American
Historical Review*, vol. XLI (1936), pp. 650–51.

for veterans, widows, and orphans of the conflict was well begun. Although invalid veterans and widows, orphans, and dependents of Union soldiers and sailors began receiving pensions during the war, annual appropriations for pensions ($15,000,000 in 1866) did not reach their peak of approximately $174,000,000 until 1913. The total cost of Civil War pensions awarded by 1885, twenty years after the end of the war, was $700,000,000, a modest figure compared to the $5 billion reached in 1916. By 1932 sums paid out in pensions over the preceding seventy years amounted to twice the cost of the war to the North. The last Union veteran survived until 1956; the last Confederate, until 1959. In the late 1970s, 280 widows and children of men who had fought for the Union remained on federal pension rolls.[2]

Hostilities had scarcely begun in the summer of 1861, when Congress enacted the first measure providing invalid pensions for Union volunteers wounded or disabled in service and payments to widows or heirs of those who died. A year later, on July 14, 1862, President Lincoln approved an act which became the basis for all subsequent pension legislation until 1890. Under its provisions payments to men totally disabled, or the widows of those killed, ranged from $8 a month to enlisted men to $30 a month to officers of or above the rank of lieutenant colonel. Before the end of the war Congress adopted additional legislation granting higher monthly payments to veterans suffering specific disabilities of a serious character, such as loss of both hands ($25), sight of both eyes ($25), loss of both feet ($20), or loss of one hand and one foot ($20). Postwar legislation expanded and elaborated the list of specific disabilities and increased rates of payment to victims.[3]

In addition to inaugurating a liberal pension policy, Congress authorized a nationwide system of institutional care for disabled veterans. The latter action was prompted by a petition submitted in December 1864 by William Cullen Bryant, Henry Wadsworth Longfellow, Horace Greeley, Clara Barton, P. T. Barnum, and others, calling for the founding of a National Home

[2] E. H. Hall: "Civil War Pensions," *Proceedings* of the Massachusetts Historical Society, vol. XLII (1908–09), p. 115; William H. Glasson: *Federal Military Pensions in the United States* (New York, 1918), pp. 123–24; Talcott Powers: *Tattered Banners* (New York, 1933), p. 127; U.S. Veterans Administration: *Annual Report*, 1977 (Washington, D.C., 1977), p. 66.

[3] Glasson: *Federal Military Pensions*, pp. 124–29; Powers: *Tattered Banners*, pp. 141–42.

for Disabled Volunteer Soldiers. The home went into operation between 1867 and 1870, not as a single centralized institution, but with four (ultimately fifteen, some founded as late as 1933) branches located in different sections of the country.[4]

The soldiers' home movement met vigorous and vocal opposition from Sanitary Commission leaders. As early as 1862 Bellows advised against "any general scheme for herding the invalids of the war into State or National Institutions. . . . We don't want a vast net-work of soldiers' poor-houses scattered through the land, in which these brave fellows will languish away dull and wretched lives," he wrote. "Nor do we want petty State asylums, to be quarrelled about and made the subject of party politics."[5] Surveying the wants of and provision for sick and invalid veterans in December 1865, Bellows asserted reports from correspondents around the country showed only 2,000 of 1,830,000 Union veterans were "so homeless, so helpless, so utterly disabled by sickness or wounds" as to require public support in asylums or soldiers' homes. He agreed they needed "prompt temporary provision," but in his opinion it would be "a wicked waste of money, and time, and wisdom" to erect "slow, expensive palaces" or permanent institutions. Much more deserving of public concern than the few needing institutional care were the vast number of veterans and their families reduced to poverty by slow settlement of pension claims and insufficiency of authorized awards. To ease their wants, Bellows proposed a simple solution: "Pensions ought to be paid promptly and doubled in amount."[6]

Samuel Gridley Howe scorned soldiers' homes as products of shallow, popular sentiment rather than intelligent policy. "The warmer is the public heart, the more need of right direction for its impulses," he observed in his first report as chairman of the Massachusetts Board of State Charities (1866). This position, which he held from 1865 to 1874, gave Howe both an opportunity and an obligation to turn those impulses in the anti-institutional direction he favored not only for veterans but for all subjects of public charity. "Many of our soldiers need *homes*," he

[4] "Petition of William C. Bryant . . . and others," *Senate Miscellaneous Documents*, 38 Cong., 2 Sess., No. 3 (1865), pp. 1–3 (serial 1210); *U.S. Statutes at Large*, vol. XIII (1863–65), p. 509.

[5] U.S. Sanitary Commission, Document No. 95, "Provision Required for the Relief and Support of Disabled Soldiers and Sailors and Their Dependents," in U.S. Sanitary Commission: *Documents* (New York, 1866), vol. II, pp. 22–29.

[6] U.S. Sanitary Commission: *Documents*, vol. II, pp. 9, 12–13, 19–21.

wrote in 1866, "but such homes as we ourselves need; and a great institution . . . never was and never can be such a home as our . . . veterans ought to have." "Better the poorest hut in a retired hamlet, . . . than a showy building, set upon a hill, with its corps of officials, parade of charity, and its clockwork and steam for domestic work. . . . Better have 500 maimed veterans stumping about the towns and villages of Massachusetts, living partly on their pension and partly by their work, than shut up in the costliest and best structures that art could plan or money build." Simply giving the money to the soldiers "to be spent, or saved, or even wasted," Howe concluded, would be better than sinking it in expensive institutional buildings that would have to be staffed and maintained.[7]

For a number of years after the war observers noted and deplored the abundance of "one-armed, one-legged, scarred-faced veterans" begging on streets, ferries, and trains or trying to make a living as crossing sweepers or organ grinders. A correspondent of *The Soldiers' Friend*, taking issue with Howe, regretted that the money spent on purchasing Alaska—"sterile Russian lands" in the Arctic Circle—had not been used to build more homes for deserving ex-soldiers.[8]

Union veterans began the transition to civilian life in better financial condition and with brighter prospects than Confederates. The former received $250, on the average, in final pay, undrawn pay, unpaid bounties, and other claims. Some used the money to go to college, and at least one state, Ohio, granted tuition-free education at public institutions to honorably discharged servicemen who had enlisted as minors. Confederate veterans, on the other hand, arrived home penniless with nothing to look forward to except artificial limbs—if needed—provided by state governments and voluntary associations. They had to wait until the end of Reconstruction for Southern states to enact pension laws and establish homes for the wounded and indigent. In Missouri, which had provided soldiers for both sides, private groups founded separate institutions for Confederate and Union

---

[7] Howe's report is reprinted in Sophonisba P. Breckinridge: *Public Welfare Administration in the United States, Select Documents* (Chicago, 1938), pp. 305–09.

[8] Nathan D. Urner: "Street Children of New York," *Packard's Monthly*, vol. I (1869), p. 22; J.M.S., in *The Soldier's Friend* (March 1868), quoted in Dixon Wecter: *When Johnny Comes Marching Home* (Boston, 1944), p. 189.

veterans, both of which came under state control about thirty years after the war.[9]

In both North and South the plight of war orphans roused keen sympathy. In July 1865 newspapers reported—erroneously, as it turned out—that Rear Admiral Samuel Francis Du Pont had bequeathed "a noble gift," $175,000 of his prize money gained during the war, to found a national asylum in Washington for orphans of soldiers and sailors.[10] In an appeal for Confederate orphans the Ladies' Southern Relief Association of Baltimore estimated that Alabama alone had 4,800 needy children and quoted a Tuscaloosa woman, "We are all too poor to help each other." In Illinois, "Mother" Mary Ann Bickerdyke urged members of soldiers' aid societies to keep their organizations alive in order to serve children of soldiers comforted in their dying hours by confidence that "the same benevolence which led you to work for them would lead you to work for their children." The Cincinnati branch of the Sanitary Commission, continuing in existence until 1880, used part of its balance at the end of the war to contribute to the support of 200 war orphans in local asylums.[11]

Bellows, who opposed institutionalizing orphans as much as veterans, acknowledged that there might be a temporary need for shelters to hold children for brief periods pending their "dispersion" in private households, preferably farmers' families. "There is a real demand for these children," he asserted in December 1865.

> Even infants are readily disposed of to trustworthy families ready to adopt them. Girls specially are wanted to rear as domestic helpers. Boys are without trouble placed in farmer's families, if they have not been picked up in the

[9] Carl Russell Fish: "Back to Peace in 1865," *American Historical Review*, vol. XXIV (1918–19), pp. 435–37; Wecter: *When Johnny Comes Marching Home*, pp. 119–20; Thomas W. Hoover: *A History of Ohio University* (Athens, Ohio, 1954), pp. 124–25; Fern Boan: *A History of Poor Relief Legislation and Administration in Missouri* (Chicago, 1941), pp. 108–09.

[10] *New York Times*, July 7, 1865; *Ohio State Journal*, July 10, 1865; John D. Hayes, ed.: *Samuel Francis Du Pont, A Selection from His Civil War Letters* (3 vols., Ithaca, N.Y., 1969), vol. II, p. 380.

[11] Ladies' Southern Relief Association: *Report, 1866*, p. 12; Bickerdyke to Ladies of the Soldiers' Aid Societies of Illinois, 1865, Lincoln Clark Family Papers, Huntington Library; William J. Jacobs: "Quiet Crusaders, A History of the Cincinnati Branch of the U.S. Sanitary Commission" (unpublished M.A. thesis, University of Cincinnati, 1956), pp. 87–88.

streets, or have not been trained to vice by bad companion-
ship in crime, whether in public Refuges or elsewhere.[12]

When Bellows wrote, a dozen homes or schools for soldiers'
and sailors' orphans were already in operation, and more were
projected. Pennsylvania took the lead in making war orphans
wards of the state. Rejecting an alternative proposal to make
local authorities responsible for finding homes for the children in
their own communities and binding them out as apprentices
(girls at eleven, boys at thirteen), the legislature allowed the
governor to use a grant of $50,000 from the Pennsylvania Rail-
road to inaugurate a contract plan. Approved orphanages received $100 a year for the care of each child under eleven, and
selected boarding schools $150 a year per student aged eleven
to sixteen. In 1866, when it seemed likely that rather than appropriate $300,000 requested for continuation of the contracts, the
legislature would revert to the so-called pauper or binding-out
plan, the orphans saved the day for the institutions. "Neatly and
uniformly clothed," girls in brown and black, boys in blue and
gray, the children appeared before both houses of the legislature and by songs, poems, and orations won approval for the
appropriation.[13]

In 1866 Congress increased pensions to widows with dependent children by $2 a month for each child under sixteen; in case
the mother died or remarried, the children were permitted to
receive a pension of the same amount she would have collected.
An act of 1868 specifically authorized payments to widows or
guardians of dependent children being cared for in charitable
institutions.[14] Whether in spite of or because of the pension laws
the need for soldiers' orphan homes persisted, and legislators continued to receive reports of homeless, friendless children with no
place to go except the poorhouse. Thus, in 1869, trustees of the
Indiana Soldiers' Home advised members of the General Assembly that there were 500 destitute war orphans in the state.

New Jersey was able to close its Soldiers' Children's Home
(financed by the state but managed by a private association) in
1876 after a decade of operation, but institutions in other states

[12] U.S. Sanitary Commission: *Documents*, vol. II, p. 20.
[13] James L. Paul: *Pennsylvania Soldiers' Orphan Schools* (Harrisburg,
1877), pp. 33, 50–52, 62–73.
[14] *U.S. Statutes at Large*, vol. XIV, p. 230 (July 25, 1866), vol. XV, pp.
235–37 (July 27, 1868).

survived into the twentieth century. In 1910, forty-five years after Appomattox, Hastings Hart of the Russell Sage Foundation found seven states still maintaining homes for Civil War orphans. They were, in fact, free boarding schools for children of indigent veterans, since school-age children of men who had fought in the Civil War were scarce. In 1910 Maine proposed opening its institution to grandchildren of the veterans. Kansas, Iowa, Illinois, and Indiana admitted poor children who were not soldiers' orphans.[15]

Special provisions for needy veterans and their families were intended to spare them the disgrace and discomfort of public poor relief. Advocates described a liberal military pension policy as not a charity, but a business investment, comparable to insurance against risks in a hazardous occupation.[16] Congress was never too busy to devote attention, or at least to adopt, general and special pension legislation, and states vied with each other to demonstrate gratitude and generosity to disabled servicemen and widows and children of fallen warriors. Relief of the ordinary, nonmilitary poor, on the other hand, remained largely a local responsibility, a burdensome obligation that was evaded when possible and discharged in a mean and grudging spirit. Disputes between one town and another, between different counties, and even between a town and the county in which it was located, were common as each tried to establish that a given pauper was a resident, and hence the responsibility, of the other.

As before the war, local officials ordinarily adopted either the New England system of contracting out the care of the poor or providing for them in publicly owned poorhouses, poor farms, homes, or infirmaries. Under the former plan individuals, often needy themselves, bid for the job of housing and feeding some or all of the paupers, the contract going to the person offering to undertake the task for the least amount of money. "SALE OF PAUPERS!" announced a notice posted in central Ohio in 1866:

[15] James Leiby: *Charities and Correction in New Jersey* (New Brunswick, N.J., 1967), p. 76; Robert H. Bremner, ed.: *Children and Youth in America, A Documentary History* (3 vols., Cambridge, Mass., 1970–74), vol. II, pp. 261–63.

[16] A. O. Wright: "Pensions and Soldiers' Homes," *Proceedings of the National Conference of Charities and Corrections, 1895* (Boston, 1895), p. 303.

There will be sold on Wednesday, May 16th, 1866. Mary Houk and Della Hengst, Paupers of Polk Township, Crawford County, O., to the lowest responsible bidders for one year. Terms of pay for keeping said Paupers, half in six months, from day of sale, and the remainder at the experation of the year. Proposals will be received from one to four o'clock P.M.

> Samuel Shunk,
> Daniel Hoover, Trustees.
> John Lemon.

May 1st, 1866.

In practice, the contract system and poorhouse were often combined, as in Barry County, Missouri, where in the early 1870s the county bought an eighty-acre farm, erected a building of hewn logs, and thereafter rented the property to the person who agreed to keep the poor at the lowest figure.[17]

Poorhouses, once hailed by reformers as humane alternatives to the contract system, had fallen into disrepute both because they were so often wretchedly managed and maintained and because of the concentration of misery within them. The Madison County (Ohio) Home, probably no worse and no better than most, was a catchall for the misfortune, sorrow, and neglect of a reasonably prosperous rural area. In its register for the years 1866–1868 infirm old age and dependent childhood ("orphan," "widow's child," "father eloped," "father deserted," "illegitimate") appear most frequently as the "Cause of Infirmity." Other causes listed on the register for females were: "partial idiot," "sick in jail," "insanity," "deaf and dumb," "sick and destitute," "masturbation," "fits and idiotic," "pregnant," "big neck," "had two illegitimate children"; and for males: "fell threw Grieby's mow," "sick with asthma," "blind," "partial insanity," "fitz," "lost left arm on RR. April 30, 1867," "idiot and crazy," "weak minded," "lazy old age." The youngest person admitted, a "widow's child," nine days old when he came to the home, died of strangulation two weeks later, aged twenty-three days.[18]

Conglomerate poorhouses holding people ranging in age from infancy to extreme old age, families and single persons, and individuals of all degrees of mental and physical health or in-

---

[17] "SALE OF PAUPERS!" broadside is in Audio-Visual Collection, Ohio Historical Society, Columbus; Boan: *Relief Legislation and Administration in Missouri*, p. 195.

[18] Madison County Home Register, 1868–85, Ohio Historical Society.

firmity required routine and regimentation. At the Marion County, Ohio, Infirmary in the 1860s the getting-up bell rang at 5 A.M. Breakfast came at 6 A.M., dinner at 11:30 A.M., and supper at 5:30 P.M. Rules of the house specified:

> Retire to Bed Rooms at Nine o'clock—or dusk, the men to thair rooms and the woman to thair rooms. No going through the House after Nine oclock only in case of sickness.
>   No smoking while clensing or sweeping the House. No Spitting Tobacco Juce on the floor of the rooms. No profain language or swearing or fighting or quarreling amongst each other and no lying on each other.[19]

Cheapness was the principal justification for such institutions. Francis A. Walker, who prepared the statistics of pauperism and crime for the federal census of 1870, concluded that a poor farm employing one salaried worker, the overseer, and using the labor of paupers was the most economical method of keeping the poor. The cost per pauper could be held to $50 to $60 a year, considerably less than the general range of $75 to $90 for poor relief in rural areas and $90 to $125 in cities.[20]

Conditions in poorhouses were among the concerns of state boards of charities established in about a dozen of the more populous and progressive states in the postwar years. Even before the war legislators in New York and Massachusetts acknowledged the need for some central agency to oversee the growing number of state-supported hospitals, reformatories, and asylums, each established by separate act of the legislature, governed by its own board, and operating independently of the others. Massachusetts, with six state-subsidized and eleven state-administered institutions, including three asylums for state paupers —indigents who could not meet the requirements for "settlement" in any of the commonwealth's 300 cities and towns—was the first to act. John A. Andrew, governor when the Massachusetts board was established, was a critic not of abuses in the town

[19] Marion County Infirmary Record, Ohio Historical Society.
[20] Francis A. Walker: "Remarks on the Statistics of Pauperism and Crime," in U.S. Census Office: *Ninth Census, 1870* (3 vols., Washington, D.C., 1872), vol. I, p. 565.

poorhouses, but of the state pauper system, particularly the three "great pens" or almshouses at Bridgewater, Tewksbury, and Monson. In a letter to Samuel Gridley Howe, Andrew observed:

> I think the State pauper institution more expensive than it would be to leave the State paupers—where they once were—to the towns—compensating the towns reasonably with board money. Moreover, we should then have three hundred, instead of three, sets of officers, whose duty it would be to be on the lookout for employment for the paupers. And the paupers would be nearer to the places where, being known, they would be in the way of opportunity.[21]

The duties assigned to the Massachusetts board, although for the most part supervisory—i.e., to investigate, report, recommend changes to promote efficiency and economy—rather than administrative, included authority to transfer pauper inmates from one institution to another. Andrew's appointees, notably Franklin B. Sanborn, first secretary, and Samuel Gridley Howe, chairman of the board from 1865 to 1874, converted the three state almshouses into a workhouse, an asylum for the chronic insane, and a children's home and obtained changes in the settlement laws permitting former state paupers to be relieved in their own towns and cities.[22]

New York and Ohio in 1867, Pennsylvania, Rhode Island, Illinois, and North Carolina in 1869, and several more states in the 1870s established boards of charities, most of which were patterned after the Massachusetts model. The boards visited and inspected charitable and correctional institutions, gathered statistics and conducted inquiries, and published reports of their findings and recommendations but exercised no control over such politically sensitive matters as hiring, firing, and purchasing. Like the Sanitary Commission during the war, the boards had the meddlesome task of criticizing and counseling those officially responsible for running the institutions in order to make them discharge their responsibilities fully and properly. The hope was that free of administrative and political pressures, the boards

---

[21] Andrew to Howe, December 15, 1862, in Henry Greenleaf Pearson: *The Life of John A. Andrew* (2 vols., Boston and New York, 1906), vol. II, p. 231.

[22] F. B. Sanborn: *The Public Charities of Massachusetts During the Century Ending Jan. 1, 1876* (Boston, 1876), pp. CCIV–CCV.

could concentrate on policy and planning issues. In practice shortage of staff, lack of funds, and official indifference or hostility limited the influence of many of the boards. The boards came into conflict not only with politicians and county officeholders but also with superintendents of state hospitals for the insane. These proud professionals resented "supernumerary functionaries" armed with "the privilege of scrutinizing the management of the hospital" and offering "stringent advice" the superintendents had no desire to hear and no intention of heeding.[23]

While establishment of the Massachusetts board was under discussion, Howe suggested to Governor Andrew that one of its duties should be "to protect the rights of paupers" and pointed out the "justice and necessity" of having the treatment of pauperism "looked at a little from the *pauper standpoint*."[24] Neither the Massachusetts nor the other state boards became advocates of the poor, but their investigations and reports publicized innumerable instances of indignities, neglect, and abuse inflicted on inmates of poorhouses and jails. Frederick H. Wines, longtime secretary of the Illinois Board of Public Charities, spelled out his philosophy in an early report:

> Great care ought to be taken in the admission of inmates, not to exclude any who are actually in need of assistance, nor on the other hand to allow lazy and vicious persons to become pensioners upon public bounty. Thoroughness in the discipline, and employment at hard labor, in proportion to their strength, will prevent serious imposition, because able bodied beggars will not submit to it. Those who do, and whose misfortunes are irremediable, are entitled to sympathy, and should not be permitted to suffer, because they are poor and unfortunate. They should be made thoroughly comfortable, and the small expense necessary to accomplish this ought not be grudgingly bestowed.[25]

[23] Gerald N. Grob: *Mental Institutions in America, Social Policy to 1875* (New York, 1973), pp. 295–96, quoting resolutions adopted in 1875 by the Association of Medical Superintendents of American Institutions for the Insane.

[24] Howe to Andrew, December 21, 1862, in Laura E. Richards, ed.: *Letters and Journals of Samuel Gridley Howe* (2 vols., Boston, 1906–09), vol. II, p. 511.

[25] Illinois Board of Public Charities: *Second Biennial Report, 1872* (Springfield, Ill., 1873), pp. 188–89.

Wines, son of the prison reformer Enoch Cobb Wines, was a laconic reporter. He described life in the ordinary Illinois almshouse as "that of a family in the country, rather poorly clothed and fed, and bearing the marks of a listless poverty." Of a log-and-frame poorhouse in White County he said: "It is evident, without argument, that the keeper's family and thirty-two paupers cannot be properly and well cared for in nine rooms." In this case the keeper had the use of the farm rent-free as an inducement to charge a low rate (14½ cents per person per day) for the care of the paupers. Of another poorhouse the discomforts of which he had previously detailed, Wines said he had "nothing to add" and "nothing to take back." The only change in the condition of the Winnebago County almshouse since an earlier visit was "the successful invasion of the main building by that foe to human repose known in science by the name of *cimex lectularius*" (bedbug).[26]

Wines and officials of the other state boards were particularly critical of the systems of letting the care of paupers to the lowest bidder. C. T. Murphy, chairman of the North Carolina State Board of Charities, asserted that under this system overseers were "either imbeciles or soulless mercenaries, taking the position at prices so ruinously low as to preclude the possibility of fair dealing or honest provision for the inmates." But no matter how low the price was set, "some heartless, soulless man, without energy, industry or character will always be found to accept the situation at a little less than his predecessor, expecting by hook or by crook to make up his losses out of the helpless paupers under his control." The "true" method, according to Wines, was for the county to hire the best man and wife (the latter to head the "domestic department") available, pay them a fixed salary, and work the farm in the interest of the county rather than the keeper, "the object not being to make money, but to secure proper attention to the paupers."[27]

Albert G. Byers, chaplain of the Ohio Penitentiary, who served as secretary of the Ohio Board of State Charities—the act establishing the agency having made no provision for payment of members or staff—conscientiously visited jails and infirmaries (almshouses) and respectfully but unsparingly reported his find-

---

[26] *Ibid.*, p. 186; *Sixth Biennial Report, 1880* (Springfield, Ill., 1880), pp. 260, 266–68.

[27] Murphy's report for 1872 is quoted in Roy M. Brown: *Public Poor Relief in North Carolina* (Chapel Hill, N.C., 1928), pp. 77, 80; Illinois Board of Public Charities: *Second Biennial Report, 1872*, p. 188.

ings. "General confusion seems to prevail here," he wrote of one infirmary, the superintendent of which was absent at the time of the visit. "Fierce disputes and terrible threatenings among the inmates characterized the hour or so which we spent in our inspection of the place."[28] When the legislature abolished the board in 1872, Byers attempted to continue his inspections and reports as agent of a voluntary organization, the Prison Reform and Children's Aid Association of Ohio. "I thought," he wrote in 1875, "it would be better to have the work carried forward by voluntary benevolent enterprise—thus the politicians could be set at defiance and a popular sympathy awakened that ordinarily does not respond to work however charitable done by law." In practice he found it difficult to obtain private contributions not because of lack of interest, but because "many good people insist that the state ought to provide for the work."[29] In 1876 the administration of Governor Rutherford B. Hayes reestablished the board, this time with provision for a paid secretary, a position Byers held until his death in 1890.

In contrast with Byers' short-lived Ohio society, the New York State Charities Aid Association became a powerful voluntary adjunct of the New York State board. Its founder and guiding spirit, Louisa Lee Schuyler, spent several years recuperating from her strenuous labors for the Women's Central and the Sanitary Commission before fastening on "Reform in the public institutions" as a means of rousing the sense of responsibility and patriotic zeal which seemed to have gone to sleep since the war. In 1869 she wrote her old chief, Frederick Law Olmsted, of her intention to organize committees to visit county farms, asylums, jails, insane asylums, and other public institutions. "I think there is a great deal of misdirected benevolence in this country, a great waste of power," she told Olmsted, "and I think something might be done about it by means of thorough organization and a general system."[30]

Schuyler's own visits to the Westchester County Poorhouse began in 1871; in January 1872 she organized visiting committees

[28] Ohio Board of State Charities: *First Annual Report, 1867* (Columbus, Ohio, 1868), p. 25.

[29] Albert G. Byers to Rutherford B. Hayes, November 12, 1875, Hayes Papers, Hayes Memorial Library, Fremont, Ohio.

[30] Schuyler to Olmsted, August 27, 1869, November 8, 1869, Olmsted Papers, LC; Sheila M. Rothman: *Woman's Proper Place, A History of Changing Ideals and Practices, 1870 to the Present* (New York, 1978), pp. 71–72.

for both the Westchester Poorhouse and Bellevue Hospital in New York City. While the state board's official report on the Westchester Poorhouse was bland and uncritical, Schuyler's committee found much that needed correction: "an absence of classification which led to gross immorality, a want of enlightened treatment of the insane, no nursing for the sick; children badly fed, badly clothed, badly taken care of. . . ."[31] Its first reaction to Bellevue was surprise:

> We could not believe that this was the celebrated Bellevue Hospital, of American and European fame. This old building, of three and four stories high, with wards opening one into the other, with closets ventilated only into the wards; with operating room at the top of the house, and patients carried to and fro on stretchers; without elevators; with kitchen and laundry that were simply disgraceful as compared with the improvements of the day, with a violation of all scientific principles of hospital construction; was this the building so well-known through the reputation of its medical college, as the celebrated Bellevue Hospital of the City of New York? Could it be true that America, at the close of our late war, was the acknowledged foremost country in the world in the construction of its hospitals; and yet the largest public hospital of her metropolis was allowed to stand as a monument of bygone days of ignorance!

After several months of visiting, the committee concluded that the condition of the hospital was such that a patient undergoing even minor surgery—say, the amputation of a finger—risked being "poisoned to death by the poisoned walls of the building itself."[32]

From the start, Schuyler determined to involve both men and women in the association and have them work together at all levels of its activities. Among early officers were Theodore W. Dwight of the Columbia Law School, who was a member of the State Board of Charities; Charles Loring Brace, secretary of the New York Children's Aid Society; John Crosby Brown and

[31] New York Board of State Commissioners of Public Charities: *Fourth Annual Report, 1871* (Albany, N.Y., 1871), p. 80; State Charities Aid Association: *First Annual Report, 1873* (New York, 1873), pp. 15–17.

[32] State Charities Aid Association: *Second Annual Report, 1874* (New York, 1874), pp. 15–17.

Howard Potter, of the Brown Brothers banking firm; Dorman B. Eaton, lawyer and civil service reformer who headed the association's committee on legislation; Laura Wolcott Gibbs D'Oremieux, society leader; Josephine Shaw Lowell, a member of the State Board of Charities after the mid-1870s; and Ellen Collins and Abby Woolsey, who, like Mrs. Lowell, were hardworking and reliable veterans of the Women's Central. In 1874 John Ordronaux, a lawyer-physician who was the State Commissioner in Lunacy, 1872–82, prepared a handbook, *Questions Relating to Poorhouses, Hospitals and Insane Asylums*, for the use of the visiting committees; three years later the association published separate handbooks for visitors to poorhouses and hospitals written respectively by Olmsted and Abby Woolsey. All three were reminiscent of Sanitary Commission questionnaires, seeking detailed information on construction, drainage, and cleanliness and offering practical suggestions for improving ventilation, heating, sanitation, and—in Woolsey's book—instructions for making soap and washing woolens. Olmsted advised visitors that "penurious economy in providing food, clothing and attendants" was not wise economy. "A want of wisdom in saving often defeats its ends," he warned, "and is as bad a fault as careless expenditure." In 1873 and, in stronger fashion, in 1881 the legislature confirmed the legal right of State Charities Aid Association visitors to enter and inspect all the public charitable institutions of the state. "The Association desires only to see, and to speak of what it sees," Schuyler told the International Conference of Charities, Corrections and Philanthropy in 1893. "This is power enough, in a country where the press is free and where public opinion is all powerful."[33]

Both the state boards and voluntary agencies like the SCAA deplored the presence of children in poorhouses and repeatedly urged their removal. Byers devoted a portion of his first (1867) report to an account of the condition of 220 children found in thirteen of Ohio's county infirmaries, some of them afflicted in mind or body, many "as pretty and smart as little boys and girls

[33] State Charities Aid Association: *Handbook for Visitors to the Poorhouse* (New York, 1877), p. 27; Louisa Lee Schuyler: "The State Charities Aid Association of New York, 1872–1893," in International Congress of Charities, Corrections and Philanthropy: *The Organization of Charities* (Baltimore and London, 1894), p. 58.

can be," but all growing up "amid the loathsome moral corruption so common to our poorhouses." On a representative—or at least unexceptional—Illinois poor farm, Wines recorded seven children among twenty-four inmates. "Four of them were born in the poor house. . . . None of them attend school."[34] Even before establishment of the state board Ohio passed a law authorizing counties to open homes for children under sixteen who would otherwise be sent to infirmaries. The act was permissive rather than mandatory, and by the early 1880s only fourteen of the state's eighty-eight counties had established such homes. New York, which in 1868 had more than 2,000 children in almshouses, took more stringent action. In 1875, under prodding by the State Board of Charities and the State Charities Aid Association, the legislature ordered the removal from and prohibited the commitment to poorhouses of normal children aged three to sixteen.[35] Prudential as well as humanitarian considerations figured in the removal effort. "What can be more dreary than the future prospects of a pauper child?" asked Wines. "Alas! we know only too well what becomes of children who live and grow up in the poorhouse," exclaimed Louisa Lee Schuyler. Olmsted's handbook spelled out the reformers' view of the matter: poorhouse children, acquiring their ideas of life, society, and social duties from pauper associates, and habituated to dependence on charity, inevitably met problems and discouragements as adults, leading them to fall back on the poorhouse as a refuge, often bringing with them their own young children "to repeat their degrading experience and again reproduce their kind." Hence, as William Letchworth of the New York State Board pointed out, "aside from the moral benefits [of removal] immense pecuniary benefits would result to the public."[36]

Removing children from poorhouses sometimes meant separating them from their parents. Overseers, even when legally empowered to bind out children of paupers, were often reluctant to break up families. Letchworth, a childless bachelor, argued

[34] Ohio Board of State Charities: *First Annual Report*, pp. 34–36; Illinois Board of Public Charities: *Sixth Biennial Report*, p. 267.

[35] For the New York Children's Law of 1875 and its antecedents, see David M. Schneider and Albert Deutsch: *The History of Public Welfare in New York State, 1867–1940* (Chicago, 1941), pp. 60–71.

[36] Illinois Board of Public Charities: *Second Biennial Report, 1872*, p. 189; State Charities Aid Association: *First Annual Report*, p. 17, and *Handbook for Visitors to the Poorhouse*, pp. 53–54; New York State Board of Charities: *Eighth Annual Report, 1875* (Albany, 1875), p. 177.

against this misplaced tenderness. He acknowledged that when a family entered a poorhouse for a few months, over the winter, perhaps, it seemed harsh to take children from parents, but he was convinced that even a short stay could breed moral corruption in children and destroy energy and self-respect. "Looking to the best and permanent welfare of the children," he wrote in 1874, "is it not due them that they should be taken from those who have been legally proved incompetent to provide even for their bodily comforts? Beyond the well-being of the child has not society a right to charge this much for its own protection?" Martin B. Anderson, president of the University of Rochester and also a member of the New York State Board, was even more emphatic: "When parents fail utterly to discharge their duties to children, their right of possession terminates. . . . Society, when obliged to provide for the support of the children of the vicious and idle, has the right to make its present and prospective burden as light as possible."[37]

Wines, who prepared the statistics on *Defective, Dependent and Delinquent Classes* for the 1880 census, reported that in the country as a whole 9,172 children under sixteen remained in almshouses; they constituted about 14 percent of the total almshouse population and ranked second in number to the 16,000 persons classified insane. Yet even in 1880 many more dependent children were maintained in "institutions of a benevolent or beneficent character" than in almshouses. By 1890, according to Wines's *Report on Crime, Pauperism and Benevolence* for the eleventh census, removal had made such progress that the ratio of children under sixteen in almshouses to those in benevolent institutions was 1 to 13: fewer than 6,000 were in almshouses; slightly more than 68,000 in orphanages and children's homes.[38]

As of 1881, according to the report of John Eaton, United States Commissioner of Education, there were 354 institutional homes and asylums for orphan and dependent children in the United States. They operated under the auspices of state, county, and municipal government and sectarian and nonsectarian

[37] New York State Board of Charities: *Eighth Annual Report*, pp. 125, 176.

[38] Frederick H. Wines: *Report on the Defective, Dependent and Delinquent Classes of the Population of the United States as Returned at the Tenth Census (June 1, 1880)* (Washington, D.C., 1888), pp. XXVIII, 443, 465; Frederick H. Wines: *Report on Crime, Pauperism, and Benevolence in the United States at the Eleventh Census, 1890*, part I (Washington, D.C., 1896), pp. 116, 308, 363.

benevolent associations. One of the best known and most highly regarded of the state institutions was the Michigan State Public School at Coldwater, characterized by Eaton as "justly famous for its beneficent purpose, methods and results." The school, which opened in 1874, received children between the ages of four and sixteen, housed them in cottage "families" of twenty-five or thirty, and retained them only until they could be placed in private homes. One of the cardinal tenets of the school's administration was: "No child is admitted because it has become delinquent. Poverty is the only cause." The other was that admission to the school meant forfeiture of all parental rights. Knowing this, said the author of the bill establishing the school, parents "make a more serious effort to keep their children and often succeed. This is one important cause of decrease of child dependence."[39]

A more specialized state institution was New York's Thomas Asylum for Orphans and Destitute Indian Children. It was located on an Indian reservation, and five of its ten managers were Indians. The object of the school was to impart "a plain elementary education," instruct the children in home and domestic industries, and thus enable them not only to become self-supporting" but (in the words of Letchworth) "to carry with them into Indian families the elements of civilization." Letchworth approvingly recorded the rigorous daily regimen of study, worship, housework, farm chores, broom making, needlework, and other tasks performed at prescribed hours, commencing at 5 A.M., every day. The routine was broken only by a weekly meeting of the Band of Hope, a temperance organization, on Friday evenings and "bathing and recreation" on Saturday afternoons.[40]

In most states provision for children removed from almshouses remained a responsibility of county rather than state government. One method of disposing of them was to send them to and pay for their keep in private institutions. This was the method followed by most counties in New York after passage of the Children's Act of 1875; some counties, however, objecting to the increased cost, established public homes in the hope of doing the job more cheaply. Ohio, Indiana, Pennsylvania, and other

[39] U.S. Bureau of Education, *Report of the Commissioner of Education for the Year 1881* (Washington, D.C., 1883), pp. CCXXIV, CCXXIX–XI; C. D. Randall, quoted in Bremner, ed.: *Children and Youth in America, A Documentary History*, vol. II, pp. 263–64.

[40] Bremner, ed.: *Children and Youth in America*, vol. II, pp. 265–66.

states opted for county homes. Ohio, after having mandated the removal of children from infirmaries to county homes in 1883, softened the blow in 1884 by exempting counties that established separate facilities for children in their infirmaries. Everywhere the watchword was economy. Josephine Shaw Lowell, first woman appointed to the New York State board, contended that lax commitment policies allowed irresponsible parents to flood institutions with children, shifting the cost of their care to the public. Albert G. Byers, secretary of the Ohio board and a supporter of the county home system, complained that buildings used for the homes were poorly suited to the purpose and worried lest the institutions might be "so managed as to become burdensome to the people without accomplishing a corresponding benefit to the children." In contrast with the "wise economy" advocated by reformers, hard-pressed or hard-fisted overseers and superintendents might seek to cut costs by skimping on services, amenities, and even necessities. An official of a county home that was without grounds and scarcely a playground, unable to furnish statistical data requested by the Ohio board, reassured Byers: "We have a cheap home. It don't cost much to run it."[41]

Justly or not, private institutions for dependent children enjoyed a better reputation than public ones. Letchworth attributed the superiority of private asylums (which, in fact, were often heavily subsidized by public funds) to the "benevolent ladies" who managed them. "However well-intentioned and faithful may be the efforts of a public official, he has not the same experience in the work as ladies connected with asylums," Letchworth observed in 1886.[42] Lowell, a more critical observer, grouped twenty-eight private child-caring institutions in New York City into three categories: those supported by private charity and invested funds (three); those receiving up to half their support from public funds (eight); and those receiving more than half and sometimes practically all their support from public resources (seventeen). The reason for the popularity of such institutions, and the cause of increase in the number of children served, according to Lowell, was that they provided "exactly the

---

[41] Ibid., pp. 266–67; Schneider and Deutsch: *Public Welfare in New York State*, pp. 66–67; Ohio Board of State Charities: *Ninth Annual Report, 1884* (Columbus, Ohio, 1885), pp. 47–50.

[42] "The Children of the State," *Proceedings of the National Conference of Charities and Correction, 1886* (Boston, 1886), pp. 143–44.

care which parents desired for their children, that of persons of their own religious faith," at public expense but in privately managed institutions and hence without "the stigma which fortunately attaches to public relief."[43] Some of the asylums she visited sheltered boys fourteen or fifteen years of age who had spent years in the institution without receiving any industrial training. Of one such institution she observed that "as a machine for keeping 700 boys alive and in moderately good physical condition" much could be said in its favor, but as a means of educating future citizens there was little to recommend it. "The only present object seems to be to collect as many [boys] as possible together, and maintain them at the expense of private charity and public money and educate them as good Catholics."[44]

Lowell's distrust of institutions and dislike of institutional life was so widely shared that both public and private asylums emphasized their role as temporary shelters through which children passed on their way to placement, by adoption, indenture, or verbal agreement, in families. Even an esteemed and useful institution like the Cincinnati Children's Home felt compelled to announce: "Asylum life, at its best, costs heavily, uselessly, and in the end unfits its 'inmates' for self-dependence." The method the Children's Home recommended, and said it followed, was to place children

> in good Christian families; see that a fair definite contract is made for the child, and duly performed by both child and foster parents; which contract includes that the child should be reared as a member of the family, suitably educated and fitted to engage creditably in the pursuits of life. The institution retains a prior guardianship, and continues to look after the child with paternal solicitude until it comes of legal age.[45]

The advice was easier to preach than to practice. Institutional pride, religious considerations, profits derived from the subsidy system, and hard-to-place children—all contributed to what Letchworth called "the tendency of all asylums . . . to retain their

[43] Quoted in Bremner, ed.: *Children and Youth in America*, vol. II, p. 281.

[44] New York State Board of Charities: *Nineteenth Annual Report, 1885* (Albany, N.Y., 1886), p. 212.

[45] *Twenty-fifth Annual Report of the Children's Home, 1885* (Cincinnati, 1886), p. 9.

children too long." On the other hand, the boast of an officer of a deplorable county institution, "We find homes for many children," might simply mean that the local government was all too ready to get rid of the burden of their support. Putting children in families without adequate investigation before placement or careful follow-up, as many children learned by bitter experience, resulted in exploitation and mistreatment as shocking as those suffered in poorhouses.[46]

Aside from children, the group whose removal from poorhouses seemed most needed was the insane. Theodore W. Dwight asserted in 1870 that abuses in the treatment of the insane pointed out by Dorothea Dix a quarter of a century earlier were still to be found in New York's county institutions. In one poorhouse, the secretary of the board discovered an insane man who had been confined in an outbuilding for nearly seventeen years. "He was entirely nude, filthy and destructive, and, apparently, hopelessly crippled by the long confinement."[47] Byers, reporting instances of neglect "pitiable beyond description" in Ohio infirmaries, also argued that the presence of the mentally ill added to the strain and discomfort of other inmates. In the Scioto County Infirmary

> the insane are kept up stairs, and when, as is often the case, their rooms require scrubbing, all the filth must be washed down the stairway. . . . There are no pipes or sewers, no escape for filth save as carried or washed out, so that the bad odor of one filthy cell is of necessity diffused throughout the premises.[48]

In Illinois, Wines found 150 insane inmates of county asylums held "in seclusion," i.e., shut up in rooms, cells, or pens in solitary

[46] "The Children of the State," p. 144; Bremner, ed.: *Children and Youth in America*, vol. II, p. 267; Schneider and Deutsch: *Public Welfare in New York State*, pp. 78–79.

[47] "The Public Charities of New York," *Journal of Social Sciences*, vol. II (1870), p. 87; New York State Board of Charities: *Fourth Annual Report, 1871* (Albany, N.Y., 1871), p. 67.

[48] Ohio State Board of Charities: *First Annual Report*, p. 31; Illinois Board of Public Charities: *Sixth Biennial Report, 1880* (Springfield, Ill., 1880), pp. 114–15.

confinement. "These people rarely, if ever, are allowed their personal liberty; they are virtually imprisoned for life with absolutely nothing to relieve the monotony of their existence."

Dwight's indignation at New York for permitting the "unnecessary and preventable evils of squalor, filth and utter destitution" to be heaped on "the dreadful misfortune of want of reason" was tempered by his hope that the newly opened Willard Asylum would alleviate the problem. This huge institution, taking its name from Dr. Sylvester Willard, who had investigated and exposed the condition of the insane in poorhouses in 1855, was authorized by the New York legislature in 1865 and opened in 1869. It was intended to provide custodial care for the "chronic" or incurable insane, and the act establishing it directed counties to transfer such persons from almshouses to the new institution. "Acute," potentially curable cases were to be sent to the Utica State Hospital for therapeutic treatment. Dwight, writing in 1869, announced that Willard had begun to receive patients, many of whom arrived bound with chains and ropes.

> Soon the day of chains and noisome dungeons will be passed [he exulted], and we may hope that the pauper bereft of reason will live in well-lighted and ventilated rooms, with kind and considerate treatment; and though his reason remains forever darkened, there will be nothing to cause him needless irritation, suffering, or disease, or to offend the sense of humanity in those who look with sorrow upon his condition.[49]

Unfortunately, although Willard Asylum was the largest institution of its kind in the country, its capacity (1,500 patients) was not adequate to hold all of New York's long-term pauper insane. During the 1870s the State Board of Charities was forced to grant numerous counties authorization to keep the chronic insane in asylums that were, in fact, merely annexes of the poorhouses. Whether authorized or not, many counties preferred to use poorhouses for the confinement of the insane because care in them cost approximately $1.50 per week per patient while the rate at Willard, chargeable to the counties, was $2.75. By 1881, although the number of state hospitals had increased to six, including a second for the care of chronic patients, the num-

[49] "The Public Charities of New York," pp. 72–73.

ber cared for in them was little more than half that in local institutions.[50]

The problem was by no means peculiar to New York, and judging by figures compiled for the 1880 census, New York's record was better than the national average. Only three states— California, New Jersey, and Massachusetts—had a higher percentage of insane in institutions specifically intended for their care; New York, with 57 percent in this category, ranked well above the national average. Of the approximately 92,000 insane persons in the country as a whole, 41,000 were in hospitals or insane asylums, an equal number "at home," and 10,000 in almshouses and jails. Despite great activity and heavy expenditures for hospital construction and expansion since 1865, resulting in buildings so ornate and showy they were sometimes called Cathedrals of Lunacy, the universal complaint was of overcrowding. In order to make room for new, acute cases, some state hospitals returned long-term patients deemed harmless and incurable to their home communities for such care as their families and overburdened poor law officials could devise.[51]

For insane Negroes the problem was not removal from poorhouses but release from jails or, in many cases, provision of shelter and care of any kind. In 1866 directors of Longview Insane Asylum, an institution serving Hamilton County (Cincinnati), Ohio, refused to admit a black woman duly committed by the probate court on the grounds that the asylum had no suitable accommodations separate from white inmates. Under pressure from state authorities, the directors purchased a building adjacent to the institution to serve as a "colored asylum" and admitted "two female patients from the jail." Albert Byers's 1867 report as secretary of the Ohio Board of State Charities referred to "the *colored insane*" as a "strangely neglected class," to whom the state of Ohio extended no help.[52]

During the late 1860s, Virginia, Kentucky, Tennessee, and

[50] Schneider and Deutsch: *History of Public Welfare in New York, 1867–1940*, p. 90; local institutions included large asylums for the insane in New York City, Brooklyn, and Rochester.

[51] Wines: *Report on the Defective, Dependent and Delinquent Classes*, pp. XXIII–IV; Albert Deutsch: *The Mentally Ill in America* (Garden City, N.Y., 1937), pp. 142 n., 263; John L. Gillin: *History of Poor Relief Legislation in Iowa* (Iowa City, 1914), p. 178.

[52] Trustee Minutes, Longview Insane Asylum, Cincinnati, Ohio, May 26, July 13, August 29, 1866, Ohio Historical Society; Ohio Board of State Charities: *First Annual Report*, p. 12.

Texas established separate institutions or buildings for insane freedmen, and in some states, such as North Carolina, the Freedmen's Bureau provided for their support in segregated wards. The common practice, however, was to put blacks considered dangerously insane in jail while allowing those thought harmless to wander at large. "That crazy negro woman is still permitted to go about the streets, to the annoyance of the public," complained a Natchez, Mississippi, newspaper in 1867. "She is becoming an unbearable nuisance." In 1870, Mississippi authorized admission of both races to its state asylum, but blacks were housed in an abandoned bowling alley without ventilation in summer or heat in winter. For better or worse, most of the black insane of the state remained in jail—a newspaper editor suggested that one who was especially disruptive might be disposed of by lynching —until 1890, when the legislature appropriated funds for construction of more wards for Negroes at the state asylum in Jackson.[53] In the 1890s, Southern states like Virginia drastically reduced appropriations for charitable institutions, necessitating the closing of facilities for blacks, release of black patients to their counties of residence—and in some cases, for want of other accommodations, their return to jail.[54]

"The mere enumeration of our deficiencies is almost enough to paralyze the effort necessary to remove them," declared the superintendent of the New York City Lunatic Asylum in 1866. Over the years many persons concerned with the care of the insane must have felt—and no doubt still feel—the same sense of frustration and hopelessness. Dorothea Dix, before her death in 1887, is reported to have been saddened by the knowledge that the same kind of abuse and suffering she had witnessed in jails and poorhouses and had brought to light in her *Memorials* in the 1840s could be found in state hospitals established through her labors. Frederick Wines, reviewing progress in the half century since 1830, took comfort in numbers: 92 hospitals in 1880 as compared to 8 in 1830; a total of $150,000,000 spent on institutions for the insane over the fifty-year period; and a great increase in average per capita expenditure for maintenance (he estimated $200 per annum in 1880) caused not only by the in-

[53] Vernon Lane Wharton: *The Negro in Mississippi, 1865–1890* (Chapel Hill, N.C., 1947), pp. 266–67.
[54] Morton Keller: *Affairs of State, Public Life in Late Nineteenth Century America* (Cambridge, Mass., 1977), p. 501.

creascd cost of living but also by more liberal standards of care.[55]

In the 1870s and 1880s, reformers and reform-minded office-holders in a number of states obtained important changes not so much in the treatment of mental illness as in responsibility for the cost of caring for its victims. Michigan in 1877 adopted a law looking toward the eventual prohibition of confinement of the insane in poorhouses and providing for the assumption by the state of the cost of their cases if the illness persisted for more than two years. Between 1878 and 1881 Wisconsin worked out a system of assigning chronic cases to county asylums and acute ones to state hospitals, and dividing the cost of care for both categories between state and counties. In New York, Louisa Lee Schuyler of the State Charities Aid Association, Dr. Stephen Smith, State Commissioner in Lunacy (an ex officio member of the State Board of Charities), and the state board itself championed the idea of making the state responsible for the care of all the insane, chronic as well as acute. A bill providing for this change, first introduced into the legislature in 1887, was adopted in 1890. Like the Willard Act of 1865, it called for the removal of the insane from poorhouses to state hospitals, but now the state relieved counties of the cost of care of indigent patients and required hospitals to admit all the insane from their districts without distinction between chronic and acute cases.[56]

Samuel Gridley Howe, America's foremost educator of the blind and leading theorist of public welfare, chose the dedication of a new state school for the blind at Batavia, New York, in 1866 as the occasion for an attack on institutionalization as a means of dealing with social ills. "Our people have rather a passion for public institutions, and whenever their attention is attracted to any suffering class, they make haste to organize one for its benefit. . . . Hence," said Howe, "we sometimes have follies of the people as well as of individuals—many stories high, too—and so strongly built and richly endowed that they cannot be got rid of

[55] Dr. Parsons, superintendent of Blackwell Island Asylum, New York City, in *American Journal of Insanity*, vol. XXIII (1866–67), p. 487; Deutsch: *Mentally Ill in America*, p. 183; Wines: *Report on the Defective, Dependent and Delinquent Classes*, p. XLIV.

[56] Deutsch: *Mentally Ill in America*, pp. 256–67; Schuyler: "The State Charities Aid Association of New York, 1872–1893," pp. 65–67.

easily." In Howe's opinion, instead of gathering a crowd of persons of like condition or infirmity behind the walls of a showy building, society should diffuse them among sound and normal people. "Separation and not congregation should be the law of their treatment."[57]

Howe's dislike of congregate institutions, which went back to his prewar dispute with advocates of the Auburn, as opposed to the Pennsylvania, system of prison discipline, may have led him to overemphasize Americans' readiness to establish institutions for the afflicted. As late as 1880 only ten (out of the then thirty-eight) states had training institutions for the mentally retarded; sixteen states and the District of Columbia had no school for the blind, and thirteen had none for the deaf. Generally speaking, more liberal provision was made for the deaf than for the blind, and for the blind than for the retarded, but only one-third of the deaf children of school age, one-fifth of the blind, and one-sixteenth of the retarded were in training schools. The percentage of black children in such schools was so small as to be barely measurable.[58]

Although Howe believed blind and other afflicted children should receive education from the state "not as a charity but as a right," he opposed public institutions except as a last resort and urged the state to make use of the services and facilities of voluntary organizations. As a case in point, the Perkins Institution and Massachusetts School for the Blind, which Howe had founded in 1832, was a chartered corporation, with the state represented on its board of directors; it was supported by payment of tuition and board ($300 per annum in the 1870s) as well as appropriations from Massachusetts and other New England states which sent indigent blind children to it. Around the time of Howe's death in 1876 the ratio of support was approximately 60 percent private, 40 percent public.

In his Batavia speech, Howe said that common politeness in our dealings with the blind tells us we should not dwell on their affliction but act as if they had none. The object of education for a blind child should be to put him or her on the road to self-help, "trained to consider the dangers, difficulties and obstacles aris-

[57] *Ceremonies at Laying the Cornerstone of the New State Institution for the Blind at Batavia, New York* (Batavia, N.Y., 1866), pp. 19, 40; Richards, ed.: *Letters and Journals of Howe*, vol. II, p. 520.

[58] Wines: *Report on the Defective, Dependent and Delinquent Classes*, pp. XXVII–III.

ing from his condition as things to be met and overcome, by sharpened senses, by hard study, by muscular strength and activity, by courage and presence of mind, by self confidence and resolution. . . ." In practice the Perkins Institution trained students for occupations such as piano tuning. The superintendent of the Ohio Institution for the Education of the Blind boasted of his school's success in turning out self-supporting broom-makers.[59]

For deaf children Howe advocated training in lip reading and articulation rather than in sign language. As the dominant figure of the Massachusetts State Board of Charity he withdrew his state's support from the Hartford Asylum, a school committed to traditional methods of instruction, and rallied private benevolence and public aid for the new Clarke Institute in Northampton, Massachusetts, which pioneered in instructing students in lip reading and articulation. Theodore Dwight, discussing experiments with articulation methods in New York, was eloquent on the joys that mastering of "the divine gift of language" might impart to child and parent. He did not hesitate, however, to point out more utilitarian considerations: "How much will be added to his means of support if in after years his employers can communicate with him with the swiftness and ease of speech rather than the slower and more studied methods of the hand or of the pen!"[60]

One who shared Howe's stand on education as a right for any youth who could benefit from it was John Eaton, former superintendent of freedmen's affairs in the Mississippi Valley, Freedmen's Bureau official, and United States Commissioner of Education, 1870–1886. The federal Bureau of Education, which Eaton headed, was organized in 1867 to perform functions similar to those assigned to state boards of charities—not to run the nation's schools, but to collect and disseminate information about them, what they were doing, and the results of research relating to education, including education of children disadvantaged by physical or mental handicaps and those held in reformatories for

[59] George E. Waring, Jr.: *Report on the Social Statistics of Cities* (2 vols., Washington, D.C., 1886), vol. I, p. 143; *Ceremonies at . . . Batavia, New York*, pp. 18, 38; "Twenty-eighth Annual Report of the Ohio Institution for the Education of the Blind," *Ohio Executive Documents, 1864*, part I (Columbus, 1865), p. 334.

[60] F. B. Sanborn: "Poverty and Public Charity," *North American Review*, vol. CX (1870), p. 345; Dwight: "Public Charities of New York," p. 76.

juvenile delinquents. In 1879 Congress authorized annual subsidies to the American Printing House for the Blind to allow it to donate books and learning apparatus to state schools for the blind. The national government assisted education for the deaf by offering scholarships to qualified students, usually graduates of state schools, to Gallaudet College, a federally supported institution in Washington, D.C., that trained teachers for state institutions.[61]

Since juvenile reformatories, in name and theory, were curative and preventive rather than punitve institutions, their academic and industrial training programs were matters of no small significance. "All the boys work on the farm or in the shops half of the day, the other half is spent in the school room" was a typical sentence in superintendents' reports. Eaton, noting "severe criticism of reform schools," devoted considerable space to these institutions in his 1881 report as U.S. Commissioner of Education. "It should be remembered," he commented at the start, "that the treatment of juvenile delinquents is attended with a multitude of difficulties and imposes a task much easier to criticize than to perform." Eaton's survey gave little attention to academic programs except to note that in reformatories for girls (where the emphasis was on training for domestic service and homemaking) only elementary or common school subjects were attempted. Carefully avoiding criticism, Eaton commended such hopeful developments as "instruction in music and the organization of brass bands; the general practice of using single beds and separating younger from older inmates; and the economy of having boys and girls in the same establishment, so that the labor of the girls can be utilized for the genuine good of the school."[62]

Unlike Eaton, Samuel Gridley Howe, who had been a director of the Boston House of Reformation, one of the earliest reform schools, had little confidence in the "artificially organized moral machinery" of such institutions. Howe had once proposed a reformatory for girls in which "there would be *no pupils to be seen!*" They all were to be boarded out with private families, who would be paid for taking care of them, and visited frequently by assistants, who would counsel both the children and foster families. With "no great building, no great congregation of girls, and

---

[61] U.S. Commissioner of Education: *Report for the Year 1881* (Washington, D.C., 1883), pp. CCVIII, CCXVII.
[62] *Ibid.*, pp. CCXXIII–IV, CCXXVIII.

no display," each girl would still be "vigilantly watched and under constant control." Would not such a system have a greater chance of reforming girls than if several hundred of them were shut up in a single building? Which would a wise parent choose for a perverse child: "Residence in the bosom of a family, or in a community of vicious girls, though ever so well regulated . . . ?"[63]

Howe's proposal had been rejected. The reality for both boy and girl delinquents was large institutions: the New York Catholic Protectory with almost 1,700 "pupils," the New York House of Refuge with nearly 700, the Ohio Industrial School for Boys with about 550, organized into "families" of 40 to 60. Some of the boys and many of the girls shut up in these institutions had been committed for status offenses such as truancy, incorrigibility, or sexual promiscuity, or because the conduct of their parents—crime, drunkenness, or neglect—seemed likely to predispose them to delinquency. Each institution had its own method or "moral machinery," usually described as unique, of reclaiming and educating "wayward, vicious, and criminal" boys or girls and making them independent, self-reliant, law-abiding, devout, and employable. Massachusetts had a much-admired Nautical Branch of the State Reform School which took the older and rougher boys from the parent school and prepared them for service on whaling ships. In the years just after the war the ship school's population also included Negro youths who had wandered to the North and, without relatives or employment, had been arrested for vagrancy. The Ohio Industrial School for Boys, in addition to its vaunted family plan, under which an "elder brother" acted *in loco parentis* for each cottage, took pride in its work-your-way-out system. On entering the institution, boys received a number of demerits according to the seriousness of the offense for which they had been committed; by conduct in the family, school, farm, or shop they wiped out demerits until each won his release. The process took from eighteen months to four years. Except for a gift of $10 and a new suit, the state gave discharged youths no help in finding homes, work, or a place in society. B. W. Chidlaw, a missionary of the American Sunday School Union who was associated with the school for more than thirty years estimated that 75 percent of its graduates became

[63] For Howe's proposal, made in 1854, see Bremner, ed.: *Children and Youth in America*, vol. I, pp. 701–02.

decent, self-supporting citizens. Some, he acknowledged, drifted into evil lives or became "drones"; "and of others," he concluded, "we must say, as of many a gallant vessel, she left port and was never heard from."[64]

When reformers praised the family as the best preventive of delinquency, the model for its treatment, and an economical substitute for institutions, they had in mind an ideal version— Howe called it "the virtuous, industrious family," "the simple, honest family." In 1875 Richard Dugdale, secretary of the New York Prison Association, presented an account of a very different kind of family, the Jukes. The care of this degenerate and dissolute family, generation after generation, in poorhouses, jails, prisons, and insane asylums, said Dugdale, had cost New York taxpayers vast sums of money.[65]

The Jukes were the kind of family whose proliferation charity reforms were committed to preventing. Josephine Shaw Lowell, first woman member of the New York State Board of Charities, was firmly convinced that "unrestrained liberty allowed to vagrant and degraded women" was among the most important and dangerous causes of the increase of crime, pauperism, and insanity. Early in her thirteen-year tenure on the board (1876–1889), on the theory that "vicious and pauper women" became mothers of "vicious and pauper children," she directed her efforts to the removal of girls and women of childbearing age from poorhouses to state asylums and reformatories staffed by women officers. Although hopeful that education, steady work, and kind influences would reclaim some victims of "moral insanity," she was willing to have the incurable incarcerated for life in order to "cut off the line of hereditary pauperism, crime and insanity now transmitted mainly through them." As a result of Lowell's determined work, New York established two asylums for

[64] "Eighth Annual Report of the Massachusetts Nautical School, October 1867," *Massachusetts Public Document No. 14, 1867* (Boston, 1868), p. 32; B. W. Chidlaw: *The Story of My Life* (Philadelphia, 1890), pp. 270–71.

[65] Massachusetts Board of State Charities: *Second Annual Report, January 1866* (Boston, 1866), p. XLIV, and *Fourth Annual Report, 1867* (Boston, 1868), p. XXIX; Richard L. Dugdale: "Special Study of the Crime and Pauperism of the Jukes," Prison Association of New York: *Thirtieth Annual Report, 1874* (Albany, N.Y., 1875), pp. 139–91; James Leiby: *History of Social Welfare and Social Work in the United States* (New York, 1978), pp. 107–09.

"idiotic and weak-minded young women who have not sufficient intellect to protect themselves from the baser of the opposite sex" and three reformatories for women offenders formerly sent to jails and prisons.[66]

The census of 1880, the first whose figures on the prison population are deemed reliable, showed 58,600 persons (not counting 11,500 children and youth in reform schools) in confinement as of June 1, 1880. They included 1,600 in station houses, 12,600 held for some reason in city and county jails, 8,000 petty offenders in houses of correction or workhouses, 30,600 prisoners in penitentiaries, and about 5,000 at work under lessees or county officials away from prisons or jails. The prisoners were predominantly male, and their average age was twenty-nine and a half years. One-fourth were under twenty-three, one-third under twenty-five, and half under twenty-eight. "Their youth is a very striking fact," commented Frederick Wines. "It indicates that even under our imperfect prison system, a very large number of criminals, after reaching middle life, either abandon a career of crime as unprofitable," become more cautious, "or their lives are cut short by habits of vicious self-indulgence." Wines did not suggest that some of them might have been reformed by prison discipline, but he pointed to their comparative youth as "an incentive and an inspiration to more earnest efforts for their reformation."[67]

Station house lodgings, the least punitive or corrective of institutions, operated for the most part without legal sanction or requirements. In New York City the practice of giving free shelter to the homeless and transient poor went back to the days of watchhouses and continued after organization of the Metropolitan Police in 1845 and establishment of station houses in each ward. By the time of the panic of 1857, usage had given vagrants and other needy persons the right to a free lodging, and by the late 1860s the newer station houses contained two bare rooms, one for men, one for women, where the homeless could sleep on

[66] William Rhinelander Stewart: *The Philanthropic Work of Josephine Shaw Lowell* (New York, 1911), p. 61; William P. Letchworth: "President's Address," *Proceedings of the National Conference of Charities and Correction, 1884* (Boston, 1885), p. 17.

[67] Wines: *Report on the Defective, Dependent and Delinquent Classes,* pp. XXVIII, XLVIII.

the floor or on an inclined plane against the wall. In 1880 female lodgers outnumbered male.[68]

In the depression years of the 1870s, small inland cities such as Leavenworth, Kansas, and villages like Oberlin, Ohio, offered free shelter to tramps and jobless wanderers, presumably viewing the practice as a lesser evil than allowing them to freeze or tempting them to steal. Some communities added a free meal of cheese and crackers or tea. Charity reformers deplored such indulgences as encouragements to vagrancy, and in response to complaints of this sort, officials might require lodgers to perform a few hours of labor at sawing wood or similar tasks. The New York Tramp Act of 1880, which Louisa Lee Schuyler cited as one of the achievements of the State Charities Aid Association, disallowed payments from county funds to overseers of the poor in reimbursement for lodgings given to casuals. "Since the enactment of this deterrent measure," said Schuyler, "the State of New York has been less attractive to tramps."[69]

County jails were among the most frequently and severely criticized parts of the prison system. Albert Byers characterized those of Ohio as "little better than seminaries of crime," and Eliot of St. Louis called the county jail in Jefferson City "the black hole of Calcutta, repeated with aggravation." Students in an early course in criminology at Cornell University, after weekly visits to the Tompkins County jail, concluded that it would be better for all concerned, society as well as the criminals, if the latter were discharged upon conviction. "Another Howard is needed to go from jail to jail throughout the length and breadth of this land," exclaimed Enoch Wines, corresponding secretary of the New York Prison Association and the best-known prison reformer of the postwar period. "A new 'State of Prisons' is wanted in which every jail in the United States would be minutely described."[70]

---

[68] Edward Crapsey: "Public Lodgers," *Harper's New Monthly Magazine*, vol. XXXIX (1869), pp. 753–59; Waring: *Report on the Social Statistics of Cities*, vol. I, p. 592.

[69] Waring: *Report on the Social Statistics of Cities*, vol. I, pp. 69, 119–20, 268, 379, vol. II, pp. 484, 765; Schuyler: "State Charities Aid Association of New York, 1872–1893," p. 64.

[70] Ohio State Board of Charities: *First Annual Report*, p. 11; Prison Association of New York: *Twenty-ninth Annual Report, 1873* (Albany, N.Y., 1874), p. 61; Enoch C. Wines and Theodore Dwight: *Report on the Prisons and Reformatories of the United States and Canada, Made to the Legislature of New York, January 1867* (Albany, N.Y., 1867), pp. 317, 332.

Wines's comments appeared in a report he and Theodore Dwight prepared on their inspection of prisons and jails of the northern and eastern parts of the United States and Canada in the summer of 1865. They made the tour on behalf of the New York Prison Association, a voluntary organization in which former Sanitary Commission workers were active and which had rights to visit, inspect, and report on conditions in New York prisons similar to those later granted to the State Charities Aid Association in regard to poorhouses. Wines and Dwight's report contained detailed information of the kind John Howard had collected a century earlier on English prisons: ventilation, sanitary facilities, heat, light, food, and clothing. Their chief complaint respecting county jails was want of classification. Jails, in much the same way as poorhouses, brought together "a commingled assemblage of petty convicts of misdemeanors, revelling drunkards recovering sobriety, children and vagrants, and all grades of accused persons detained for further examination or for trial." Josephine Shaw Lowell, a member of the Prison Association visiting committee for Richmond County, who believed jails *should* be "a terror to offenders, a punishment for crime, a school of reform" believed—like Howard before her—that the heart of the problem was the sheriff. He received no salary but collected fees for various services and made what he could by skimping on the prisoners' board. "In fact," said Lowell, "he keeps a cheap boarding house."[71]

Frederick Wines, in his capacity as secretary of the Illinois Board of Public Charities, reported jails that were, literally, tanks and others that were iron cages without light, heat, or ventilation. Of one of the more abominable he commented that "the prisoner who escaped during the last year, by knocking down the jailer when he entered to clean the cell, can hardly be blamed for his conduct." Fortunately, such conditions were the exception; Wines's major criticism was "the universal reign of idleness in county prisons. . . . Multitudes of men commit larceny every autumn, simply to secure, free of cost to themselves, comfortable board and lodgings with agreeable company, through the winter months."[72]

[71] Prison Association of New York: *Twenty-ninth Annual Report*, pp. 47, 56.
[72] Illinois Board of Public Charities: *Second Biennial Report, 1872* (Springfield, Ill., 1873), p. 209, and *Sixth Biennial Report, 1880* (Springfield, Ill., 1880), pp. 301–02, 307.

Idleness was not a problem at most state penitentiaries, where the object, according to a veteran Sing Sing officer, was "to make the prison pay its own way!" Some states, such as Maine and Wisconsin, provided raw materials and capital for prison industries; the majority, however, relied on the system of letting the labor of convicts to contractors at so much per day for periods of up to five years. Contractors ordinarily paid about one-third the going rate for free labor—prison labor being reckoned only two-thirds or three-fourths as productive as free—and received use of shops and grounds without charge for rent. Under the contract system prisoners in the Northern states worked for a variety of mining, manufacturing, handicraft, and agricultural enterprises, some of which were reputed to be highly profitable to the contractors. Only a fourth of the prisons, however, made a profit, and some, like those in Maryland, Pennsylvania, and New York, lost money because the amount received for the prisoners' labor did not amount to the cost, estimated at $80 per person per year, of their keep.[73]

The convict lease system, which continued in use in the South throughout the nineteenth century, was even more exploitative of prisoners than the contract plan. To relieve themselves of the responsibility and trouble of caring for convicts—a heavy proportion of whom were black—Southern states, pleading poverty, assigned the labor and the entire control and management of prisoners to private individuals and companies, which undertook to profit not only from the prisoners' labor but from economies in providing for their shelter, food, and clothing. Midwestern and border states, like Illinois, Indiana, Kentucky, and Missouri, had used the convict lease system before 1865; Kentucky retained it after the war, and Missouri escaped its restoration in 1875 through the determined opposition of William Greenleaf Eliot and other prison reformers.[74]

In 1880 Florida and Georgia had no penitentiaries, leasing all state prisoners to contractors. Texas had as many convicts leased out as in its state prison. Mississippi had a prison, but many of those sentenced to it were kept in county jails and hired

[73] Wines and Dwight: *Report*, pp. 248–65; Enoch C. Wines: *Report on the International Penitentiary Congress of London, 1872* (Washington, D.C., 1873), pp. 74–75.

[74] *Transactions of the National Prison Reform Congress, 1873* (Washington, D.C., 1873), pp. 476–77; Charlotte C. Eliot: *William Greenleaf Eliot* (Boston and New York, 1904), pp. 314–17.

out to work on plantations and railroads. Frederick Wines enlivened his summary of prison statistics for the compendium of the 1880 census with the story of a convicted murderer who was leased to his own wife and returned home—an occurrence Wines thought improbable but not impossible.[75]

In 1873 inspectors of the Michigan State Prison scoffed at "mawkish sentiment" opposing enforced labor in prison and stoutly defended a literal and stern interpretation of the hard-labor part of prisoners' sentences. Keeping convicts at work, the inspectors asserted, "promotes health, secures discipline and subordination, diminishes the expense of maintaining the Prison, and promotes economy." Enoch Wines and Theodore Dwight, in their 1867 report, did not question the value and necessity of labor in prison discipline but contended that the contract system, combined with the use of prison appointments for political patronage, nullified the theory of prisons as reformatory institutions. Not only was there not a single state prison in America wholeheartedly committed to reformation as its major objective, but Wines and Dwight saw little hope for the future. "Inspection may correct isolated abuses; philanthropy may relieve isolated cases of distress; and religion may effect isolated moral cures; but genuine, radical, comprehensive, systematic improvement is impossible."[76]

It was a bleak prospect. Notwithstanding prison reform conferences and congresses and isolated successes with educational programs in prisons and reformatories, better classification of prisoners, and commutation of sentences for good behavior, Wines and Dwight's report accurately forecast the disappointments and frustrations that lay ahead. Fortunately the record of postwar philanthropic activity and achievement among the non-deviant population affords a more genial story.

[75] Frederick H. Wines: "Defective, Dependent and Delinquent Classes," *Compendium of the Tenth Census* (Washington, D.C., 1888), p. 1667.

[76] Michigan, Inspectors of the State Prison: *Annual Report for the Year 1873* (Lansing, Mich., 1873), p. 7; Wines and Dwight: *Report*, pp. 265, 287–88.

Chapter 8

Private Philanthropy

and Public Need

F ranklin B. Sanborn, comparing the state of philanthropy in
Europe and America in 1867, regretfully concluded that
primacy in such matters as "relief of the poor, the interests of
labor, the discipline of prisons, [and] the amelioration of the
criminal law" had passed from the United States to England,
France, and Belgium. The reason advanced by Sanborn, who was
the founder and leading spirit of the American Social Science
Association as well as the secretary of the Massachusetts Board
of State Charities, was that the task of transforming European
peasants and Negro slaves into "equal orders of accordant citizens"
had diverted American attention from "the more external forms
of philanthropy." Yet even as Sanborn wrote, his friend Samuel
Gridley Howe was in Greece supervising distribution of American
relief supplies to refugees from Crete who had fled their homes
after an unsuccessful uprising against Turkish rule. Howe was
eager to direct aid "to the cause of freedom and of humanity" but
uncertain whether to adminster it so as to encourage or dis-
courage an exodus from the island. Meanwhile, at the Paris
Universal Exposition, which opened in April 1867, the Sanitary
Commission was awarded a grand prize for an exhibit of ambu-
lances, medical wagons, hospital tents, mobile kitchens, clothing,
food, bandages, amputating apparatus, crutches, artificial limbs—
"everything necessary," according to an official report "for the
comfort and convenience of the sick and wounded soldier." The
exhibit, organized by Dr. Thomas W. Evans, an American dentist
practicing in Paris, also included a coffee wagon for dispensing

hot drinks to soldiers "on the march or in battle"; the one displayed had been used by the Christian Commission at Appomattox to serve the sick and wounded of both Union and Confederate armies.[1]

Philanthropy of a somewhat different kind was the subject of a lawsuit, decided in 1867, that strained relations among Boston's old radical abolitionists. The case, *Jackson* v. *Phillips and Others,* involved disposition of three trust funds established by Francis Jackson, a Boston merchant who died in 1861: one provided $10,000 to oppose slavery, a second $2,000 to assist fugitive slaves, and the third $5,000 to promote woman suffrage. Jackson gave the money for the last cause to Wendell Phillips, Lucy Stone, and Susan B. Anthony before his death ("without waiting for my exit," as he said); funds for the other two did not become available to trustees until after the war and passage of the Thirteenth Amendment had put an end to both slavery and the problems of fugitives. In the circumstances one faction of the trustees, led by Phillips, favored using the money to support efforts by Phillips and the *National Anti-Slavery Standard* to promote political equality for Negroes; the other, headed by William Lloyd Garrison, who had given up agitation and suspended publication of *The Liberator*, advocated turning the money over to the American Freedmen's Union Commission for its educational activities. The master in chancery to whom the Massachusetts Supreme Court referred the case sided with the Garrisonian view that education was the more appropriate use of the fund.[2]

The case of *Jackson* v. *Phillips* is remembered today because of an oft-cited definition of charity contained in Justice Horace Gray's opinion. In the legal sense, said Gray, a charity is "a gift, to be applied consistently with existing laws, for the benefit of an indefinite number of persons" for one or more of the following purposes:

[1] Franklin B. Sanborn: "Philanthropy in America and Europe," *The Nation*, vol. IV (1867), pp. 309–10; Laura E. Richards, ed.: *Letters and Journals of Samuel Gridley Howe* (2 vols., Boston, 1906–09), vol. II, pp. 540–62; William P. Blake, ed.: *Reports of the United States Commissioners to the Paris Universal Exposition, 1867* (6 vols., Washington, D.C., 1870), vol. I, pp. 311–14.

[2] *Jackson* v. *Phillips and Others*, 96 Mass. 539–40, 596–99; James M. McPherson: *The Struggle for Equality, Abolitionists and the Negro in the Civil War and Reconstruction* (Princeton, N.J., 1964), pp. 400–01.

bringing their minds or hearts under the influence of education or religion, . . .

relieving their bodies from disease, suffering or constraint, . . .

assisting them to establish themselves in life, . . .

erecting or maintaining public buildings or works, or otherwise lessening the burdens of government.[3]

In applying this definition to the case in hand, Justice Gray ruled that Jackson's bequests for antislavery propaganda and aid to fugitive slaves were valid charities but that the bequest for promoting woman suffrage, being intended to secure a change in the law, was not a charity and not entitled to any special protection from the courts.[4] More than a century later vestiges of this doctrine survived in Internal Revenue Service regulations denying charitable tax deductibility to gifts made to organizations seeking to influence legislation.[5]

It is impossible to state how much money Americans contributed to the various aspects of charity included in Justice Gray's definition. Sanborn, who was as well informed on the subject as anyone in the country, estimated in 1869 that of the $60,000,000 the United States spent annually on the care of the poor, prisoners, and delinquents, $40,000,000 came from public taxation, $20,000,000 from private sources, including churches. The total of private philanthropic giving was undoubtedly larger since Sanborn's figure did not cover gifts for education, religious concerns other than aid to the poor, hospitals, scientific research,

---

[3] 96 Mass. 556.

[4] *Ibid.*, 539–40. In 1881, in a will drafted by Wendell Phillips, Eliza Eddy, Jackson's daughter, bequeathed $50,000 to Susan B. Anthony and Lucy Stone. Although contested, the will was upheld. Anthony's biographer called Eddy's gift "the only instance where a woman had bequeathed a large amount of money to the cause of equal rights. . . . " Anthony used her share of the bequest to meet publication costs of Elizabeth Cady Stanton, ed., *History of Woman Suffrage* (3 vols., Rochester, N.Y., 1881–86), and to give copies of it to libraries in the United States, Canada, Europe, and Australia. Ida H. Harper: *Life and Work of Susan B. Anthony* (3 vols., Indianapolis, 1898–1908), vol. II, pp. 539, 598, 614.

[5] John P. Persons *et al.*: "Criteria for Exemption Under Section 501 (c) (3)," *Research Papers Sponsored by the Commission on Private Philanthropy and Public Needs* (6 vols., Washington, D.C., 1977), vol. IV, pp. 1929–30.

cultural activities, patriotic monuments, and a host of other causes appealing to promoters or donors. Thus, during and after the Franco-Prussian War society women and religious and business leaders, including Henry W. Bellows, William E. Dodge, and A. T. Stewart collected and donated funds for the sick and wounded of both armies, relief of French civilians, and aid to flood victims in Silesia.[6]

Much of the charitable activity of the postwar era had "lessening the burden of government" as its object. Philanthropy, which had played a major role in the establishment of hospitals and insane asylums, was sometimes directed to state hospitals. Dr. William Fisher's gift of $3,750, for example, enabled the Maryland Hospital for the Insane to install gas, running water, and bathrooms. In New Hampshire a legacy from Moody Kent was expected to yield the state hospital $9,000 a year to supplement public appropriations for the indigent insane, buy curative appliances, improve buildings and grounds, and obtain comfort articles and kindly attentions for patients the hospital's regular income could not provide. Encouraged by such donations, the board of trustees of the Wisconsin State Hospital adopted a resolution appealing to the charity of the wealthier citizens of the state for funds the legislature failed to appropriate.[7]

More common than direct gifts to public agencies were indirect efforts, usually made by associations rather than individuals, to ease the burden by caring for the poor, orphaned, sick, and aged, especially those of particular occupational, ethnic, or religious groups, so that they would not have to resort to county or state institutions. In this category were seventy homes for the aged, seventy-five orphan asylums, thirty dispensaries, and seventy-five hospitals established in the 1860s by churches and nonprofit corporations. Beneficiaries of some of the institutions were strictly defined: "aged members of the church," "aged Episcopalian women," "Scandinavian orphan children," "German

---

[6] "The Supervision of Public Charities," *Journal of Social Science*, vol. I (1869), p. 74; *Frank Leslie's Illustrated Newspaper*, vol. XXXI (1870), pp. 119, 187; Bellows: "To the Ministers of Religion in the United States," March 8, 1871, Bellows Papers, MHS; Carlos Martyn: *William E. Dodge, The Christian Merchant* (New York, 1890), pp. 275–76; William O. Stoddard: *Men of Business* (New York, 1893), p. 195.

[7] *American Journal of Insanity*, vol. XXIV (1867–68), pp. 431–32, 450–51, 461–62.

Lutheran orphan children," and "foreign missionaries and their children." Other institutions opened their doors wider to accept "aged or erring women, fallen girls and their infants," "orphan, defective, delinquent and homeless boys," "homeless men and women," and "destitute aged incurables." Most of the hospitals and dispensaries received Negroes as well as whites, but the majority of homes for orphans and the aged did not.[8]

Such institutions derived their funds from legacies, interest on endowments, donations, and membership subscriptions. The cost of membership in New York City's St. John's Guild, which operated a floating hospital and excursion steamer and maintained a seaside nursery for "sick children and weary mothers," ranged from $3 for an ordinary annual subscription to $50 for life and $100 for perpetual membership. The guild also solicited gifts of $250 for the expense of one day's operation of the hospital and $100 for endowment of a crib at the nursery. At the Episcopalian Church Industrial Community of St. Johnland, an ambitious project founded on the north shore of Long Island in 1866 by William Augustus Muhlenberg, annual memberships cost $10; $130 supported a destitute old man for a year; $125 provided food, clothing, and shelter for a child; $3,000 endowed an alcove for an old man, $2,500 a cot for a child. In some cases, sales of publications (as by the American Tract Society) or payments for hospital services, from those who could afford them, augmented charitable revenues. The Newsboys' Lodging House of the Children's Aid Society of New York made a point of charging its young clients 4 cents for supper and 5 cents for bed, with use of gymnasium and library free. The boys' payments, although intended primarily to build character rather than raise revenue, amounted to more than one-fourth of the institution's cost in its first dozen years of operation. As before the war, balls, fairs, lotteries (when permitted), and lectures continued as standard methods of charitable fund raising. A function intended for the benefit of the Gilbert Library and Prisoners' Aid Society ended in disarray and without a collection when, scheduled speakers failing to appear, Henry Bergh of the Society for the Prevention of Cruelty to Animals delivered an impromptu address proposing

[8] Information on the institutions is taken from U.S. Bureau of the Census: *Benevolent Institutions* (Washington, D.C., 1910).

restoration of the whipping post and wider use of capital punishment as alternatives to prison reform.[9]

Many voluntary associations, although privately managed and jealous of their autonomy, received aid from the public treasury. The state, county, and city of New York contributed to the Nursery and Children's Hospital of New York City, which also benefited from charitable donations, annual subscriptions, grants from Calvary Church, and proceeds of a Grand Charity Ball. Not infrequently the purpose of charitable enterprises such as balls and fairs was to raise money to match public appropriations granted to a hospital, foundling home, or dispensary on condition that an equal amount be obtained from private sources.[10] The Children's Aid Society of New York, like a number of other institutions serving children, received annual subsidies from New York City's public school fund. Charles Loring Brace, founder of the society, was an eloquent advocate of mixed public-private funding. "The best course for the permanency and efficiency of a charity," he wrote in 1872, "seems to be, to make it depend in part on the state, that it may have a solid foundation of support, and be under official supervision, and in part on private aid, so that it may feel the enthusiasm and activity and responsibility of individual effort."[11] The New York Association for Improving the Condition of the Poor, a nonsectarian but predominantly Protestant organization, the Roman Catholic Society of St. Vincent de Paul, and the United Hebrew Charities, along with more than 100 other voluntary charitable organizations, accepted a portion of New York City's excise fund obtained from taxes on sales of liquor and tobacco. In 1878 the fund amounted to slightly more than $100,000 and was divided among 109 charities in sums ranging from $150 to $5,000. One of the recipients, the German Society of New York, which assisted

[9] George P. Rowell: *New York Charities Directory* (New York, 1888), pp. 478–79; "The News-Boys Lodging-House," *Harper's Weekly*, vol. XI (1867), p. 318; *New York Times*, December 1, 1880. On the Gilbert Library and Prisoners' Aid Fund see Carol L. Urness: "Gilbert, Linda," in Edward T. James, ed.: *Notable American Women* (3 vols., Cambridge, Mass., 1971), vol. II, pp. 31–32.

[10] *Frank Leslie's Illustrated Newspaper*, vol. XXXI (1870–71), pp. 182, 331; Henry J. Cammann and Hugh N. Camp: *The Charities of New York, Brooklyn, and Staten Island* (New York, 1868), pp. 124–30.

[11] Charles Loring Brace: *The Dangerous Classes of New York and Twenty Years' Work Among Them* (New York, 1872), quoted in Robert H. Bremner, ed.: *Children and Youth in America, A Documentary History* (3 vols., Cambridge, Mass., 1970–74), vol. II, p. 275.

needy German immigrants with a battery of medical, welfare, and legal services, also received donations from the Emperor of Germany, the King of Bavaria, the senates of Bremen and Hamburg, and the government of the Grand Duchy of Baden.[12]

Dorothea Dix was a philanthropist in the John Howard mold, not a great money giver but "one who from love of her fellow-men exerted herself for their well-being." She remained in her wartime post as superintendent of army nurses through the first half of 1866, devoting her last months in office to collecting funds for a memorial to Union soldiers buried in the national cemetery at Fortress Monroe, Virginia. Thereafter she resumed what admirers called her "mission to the insane," visiting hospitals, corresponding with superintendents, and helping them get books, magazine subscriptions, musical instruments, and pictures and mottoes for the institutions. "I recognized the hand before I broke the seal," wrote Peter Bryce, superintendent of the Alabama Insane Hospital, in reply to his first postwar letter from Dix. "In seasons of gloom and despondency, when destruction to the very existence of our hospital seemed imminent, I have longed for your sustaining aid and encouragement, and when success seemed to crown my efforts, I have so eagerly desired your approval and congratulations."[13] *Appleton's Annual Cyclopaedia*, recording Dix's death in 1887, observed: "She defrayed her entire expenses from her private means, never received a cent of pay, and died among her wards in the New Jersey State Asylum for the Insane at Trenton." In her will she left to Harvard University a stand of flags presented to her by the U.S. government, and bequests of $500 to the Boston Society for the Prevention of Cruelty to Animals, $400 to the Home for Aged Colored Women in Boston, $500 each to the Women's Hospital and the Perkins Institution, also in Boston, and $100 each to Hampton Institute and the institution for the deaf at Hartford.[14]

George Peabody (1795–1869) was a philanthropist of a different kind and on a grander monetary scale than Dorothea

[12] *New York Times*, December 27, 1878, p. 3; The German Society of the City of New York: *Annual Report for the Year 1883* (New York, 1884), p. 65.

[13] Peter Bryce to Miss Dix, April 23, 1868, Dix Papers, HLHU.

[14] *Appleton's Annual Cyclopaedia*, vol. XXVII (1887), p. 582; *New York Times*, September 16, 1887, p. 4.

Dix. Peabody, a poor boy from Massachusetts who won success as a merchant in Baltimore and even greater fame and riches as an international banker in London, was hailed at the time of his death as "the most liberal philanthropist of ancient or modern times."[15] According to Peabody's own testimony, he was by nature parsimonious and inclined toward hoarding, tendencies which may have been strengthened by his poverty and trials in youth. J. L. M. Curry, an early biographer, acknowledged that Peabody "loved to accumulate, and was not free from pride at his gains and financial standing." During Peabody's years in London he employed lavish hospitality to advance his career. In the last two decades of his life, in Curry's words, Peabody "acquired habits of premeditated benevolence." After making benevolence his business, Peabody applied the same systematic and prudent methods to disposition of his wealth that he had earlier employed in acquiring it. "His generosity," said Curry, "was not a sudden impulse, the gush of a momentary sensibility, but the outcome of thoughtful inquiry and premeditation as to the best method of accomplishing a superior good."[16]

Quantitatively, Peabody's benefactions (totaling about $7,000,000) have been overshadowed by giant contributions of later donors; qualitatively, they set an example for and established the pattern followed by Carnegie, Rockefeller, and other practitioners of wholesale philanthropy. Peabody gave, as he said, not to relieve pauperism, but to prevent it; to encourage scientific research and discovery, to promote social welfare, to diffuse culture, and to stimulate education. He donated money to Yale for a museum of natural history and to Harvard for a museum of archeology and ethnography.[17] By his two largest philanthropic enterprises, the Peabody Donation Fund (1862) and the Peabody Education Fund (1867), he sought to serve even broader public needs than the announced purposes of the funds. The first, for construction of improved dwellings for the poor of London, was intended to foster Anglo-American friendship at a time when diplomatic relations were strained by the

[15] *American Annual Cyclopaedia*, vol. IX (1869), p. 557.

[16] J. L. M. Curry: *A Brief Sketch of George Peabody, and a History of the Peabody Education Fund Through Thirty Years* (New York, 1969, originally published in 1898), pp. 14, 16–17.

[17] For an analysis of Peabody's contributions to philanthropy see Franklin Parker: *George Peabody, A Biography* (Nashville, Tenn., 1971), pp. 206–10.

Civil War; the second, for education in the South, was Peabody's contribution to sectional reconciliation after the war.[18] Trustees of the two funds, in discharging their responsibilities, adopted a consciously businesslike attitude. Perhaps even more than Peabody himself, the trustees shared E. L. Godkin's conviction: "Philanthropy needs in our day, in order not to be mischievous, to have a good deal of the hard and cold and incredulous countinghouse spirit infused into it, and needs, like commerce, to get the worth of its money."[19]

The Peabody Education Fund was instituted by a letter, dated February 7, 1867, from Peabody to Robert C. Winthrop of Massachusetts, Charles P. McIlvaine, Episcopalian Bishop of Ohio, General U. S. Grant, and a dozen other distinguished men representing both North and South. The letter called attention to the educational needs of the South and the likelihood that the impoverishment of the Southern people would make it impossible for them, by "unaided effort," to make necessary advances in education for many years to come. Peabody's gift of $1,000,000 (subsequently increased to $2,000,000) was to be held in trust and the income used by the trustees "for promotion and encouragement of intellectual, moral, or industrial education among the young of the more destitute portions of the Southern and Southwestern States of our Union . . . without other distinction than their needs and the opportunities of usefulness to them."[20]

Robert C. Winthrop (1809–1894), a descendant of the Puritan leader John Winthrop and a staunch conservative in social and racial attitudes, advised Peabody on many of his donations, including the Education Fund, helped select the original trustees, and served as chairman of the board for twenty-seven years. In meetings held in the winter and spring of 1867, while Congress considered the Reconstruction Act and measures for Southern famine relief, Winthrop and his fellow trustees accepted donations of spellers, readers, and arithmetic, geography, and grammar books from textbook publishers. As general agent of the fund they appointed Barnas Sears, president of Brown University and Horace Mann's successor as superintendent of public education in Massachusetts.

18 On the Peabody Donation Fund see Robert H. Bremner: "The Business Spirit in Philanthropy," *The Business History Conference, 1962, America as a Business Civilization* (East Lansing, Mich., 1962), pp. 43–44.

19 "The Unemployed Rich," *The Nation*, vol. XXVI (1878), p. 354.

20 Curry: *Brief Sketch of George Peabody*, pp. 19–22.

In his first report, Sears outlined the operating principles which he proposed to follow and which, except in one important respect, determined policies of the fund in its formative years: support of public rather than private schools; concentration on aid to schools in towns and cities "where large numbers can be gathered, and where a model system can be organized," thus exerting "the widest possible influence upon the surrounding country"; and encouragement of state systems of education, state normal schools, and the training of female teachers.[21]

These principles were intended to give maximum effect to the limited income—$90,000 to $130,000 a year—available to the trustees. Equally divided among all schools, such amounts would have had no impact; wisely distributed, so Sears believed, they could widen acceptance of and stimulate apppropriations for public education. In 1871, when the fund was in full operation, it made grants to school districts on the basis of attendance ($300 to a school with 100 pupils, $1,000 to one with 300 pupils) on condition that the district provided at least twice as much money as the fund, supplied one teacher for every fifty pupils, and assigned students to grades.[22]

For policy reasons the Peabody Fund not only neglected rural schools in favor of urban ones but devoted more of its resources to fostering education of white children than black. In order to avoid antagonizing Southern white sentiment, the fund acquiesced in segregation and routinely aided schools for blacks at two-thirds the rate for whites, e.g., $200 for 100 black children compared to $300 for the same number of whites. Sears assisted Freedmen's Bureau schools for blacks in Virginia but rejected a request for help from the bureau superintendent in Texas on the ground that his schools were not state-supported. In Louisiana, where a Reconstruction government had instituted a system of desegregated schools, boycotted by whites, Sears reversed the fund's policy of aiding only public schools in order to assist the private academies attended by whites. When the Civil Rights Act of 1875 was under consideration, Sears opposed inclusion of a provision prohibiting segregated schools because he believed it

[21] *Ibid.*, p. 39.

[22] The largest donation the Peabody Fund made to any state in one year was $37,975 to Virginia in 1874; Henry J. Perkinson: *The Imperfect Panacea, American Faith in Education, 1865–1965* (New York, 1968), p. 28.

would destroy the start made toward public education in the South and leave both blacks and whites destitute of schools.[23]

In the opinion of J. L. M. Curry, who succeeded Sears as general agent in 1881, schools established with the assistance of grants-in-aid from the Peabody Education Fund, by "showing the people what a good graded school was, did more to enlighten the people, disarm opposition, and create a sound public educational sentiment, than all the verbal argument that could have been used. The chief benefit did not arise from what the fund gave, but from what it induced others to give and to do." Curry described the policy adopted by the fund of making grants only on condition that the community raise a larger sum by taxes or from other contributions as "the homely rule of helping those who help themselves." He estimated that application of this self-help principle had resulted in a fourfold increase in the modest sums donated by the Peabody Fund.[24]

Sears and Curry were aware of the severe limitations on what the impoverished South could "give and do" for public education, and both were vigorous advocates of federal aid to education, especially for Negroes. "The want of good schools in any quarter of the Union is an injury to the whole Union," Sears observed in his 1877 report. By the latter 1870s, ten years after the Peabody Fund had been established, Sears estimated that at least 2,000,000 children in Southern states—more than half of whom were black—were without means of education. In 1880 the trustees sent a memorial to Congress emphasizing the necessity of national aid (in the form of land grants) "for the education of the colored population of the Southern States, and especially of the great masses of colored children who are growing up to be voters under the Constitution of the United States." The memorial concluded:

> For twelve years the members of this Board have endeavored faithfully to discharge the duties of the trust reposed in them. The Board have the satisfaction of knowing that with the limited means at their disposal they have been able to accomplish much good. But these means are entirely

[23] *Ibid.*, pp. 28–29; William Preston Vaughn: *Schools for All, The Blacks and Public Education in the South, 1865–1877* (Lexington, Ky., 1974), pp. 145–56.

[24] Curry: *Brief Sketch of George Peabody*, pp. 14–15.

disproportionate to the end. Where millions of citizens
are growing up in the grossest ignorance, it is obvious
that neither individual charity nor the resources of impoverished States will be sufficient to meet the emergency.
Nothing short of the wealth and power of the Federal
Government will suffice to overcome the evil.[25]

Congress took no action on the memorial. During the 1880s the
Blair Bill, providing for federal aid, passed the Senate three times
but was never voted on in the House. Curry, an ex-Confederate,
commented in 1902: "Congress has appropriated money and sent
teachers to Alaska, Hawaii, Puerto Rico and the Philippines, but
in the Southern states the white man's burden has to be borne
unaided."[26]

In its later years the Peabody Fund gave increasing attention and support to normal schools and summer or week-long
training institutions for teachers. Its last major gift, an endowment of $1,500,000 for the George Peabody College for Teachers
in Nashville, was intended to provide a continuing center for
improvement of teacher education in the South. The fund was
dissolved in 1914, transferring its final balance to the John F.
Slater Fund and leaving a set of operational patterns for the
guidance of subsequent foundations.[27]

In a country as large and physically diverse as the United States
natural disasters, such as floods and tornadoes, could hardly be
avoided. Man-made ones, such as fires and explosions, were no
less common. Every year, some town or city won notoriety for a
catastrophe of epic proportions. In March 1865 the Genesee
River flooded Rochester, New York, sweeping down railroad
bridges, upending paving stones, and carrying off iron safes.

[25] The memorial is reprinted in its entirety in Alexander F. Robertson:
Alexander Hugh Holmes Stuart, 1807–1891, A Biography (Richmond, Va.,
1925), pp. 462–78. The quoted passages are on pp. 477–78.

[26] Quoted in Raymond B. Fosdick: *Adventure in Giving, The Story of the
General Education Board, A Foundation Established by John D. Rockefeller* (New York, 1962), p. 83.

[27] Daniel C. Gilman: "Five Great Gifts," *The Outlook*, vol. LXXXVI
(1907), pp. 648–57; Joseph C. Kiger: "The Large Foundation in Southern
Education," *Journal of Higher Education*, vol. XXVII (1956), pp. 125–32,
172; Parker: *George Peabody*, p. 208. On the Slater Fund, founded in 1882,
see Horace Mann Bond: *The Education of the Negro in the American Social
Order* (New York, 1934), pp. 133–35.

Later that year Augusta, Maine, lost banks, stores, and hotels in a fire started by a peddler angered by the failure of city police to stop soldiers from stealing lobsters from his cart. On July 4, 1866, a fire caused by a carelessly thrown firecracker in Portland, Maine, destroyed 1,500 buildings and left 10,000 persons—one-third of the city's population—homeless. All these and similar disasters were dwarfed by Chicago's fire of October 8–10, 1871, which cost 300 lives and $200,000,000 in property damage and left three-and-a-half square miles in the heart of the city in ruins and 100,000 people without homes.[28]

While the fire was still raging, Cincinnati and St. Louis tele-graphed offers of money or anything needed, and trains bearing food and clothing, donated by sympathizers and carried free by the railroads, began to converge on the city. On the day after the fire burned itself out, George Templeton Strong exclaimed in wonderment at "the great torrent of money and matériel that is spouting and gushing into Chicago from every quarter." Within a short time, merchants like A. T. Stewart, who sent $50,000, bank-ers, including J. S. Morgan and Company of London, stock and produce exchanges, chambers of commerce, church congrega-tions in New York City and villages like Worthington, Ohio, city councils, school classes, and individual donors all over the coun-try and around the world contributed $5,000,000 in cash as well as quantities of supplies for relief and rebuilding, the monetary value of which could not yet be established. Cincinnati's relief committee, early on the scene, staffed and supplied a soup kitchen for a month after the fire. Queen Victoria sent a gift of books that helped found the Chicago Public Library, opened in a church basement soon after the fire. George H. Stuart collected money from former Christian Commission supporters to rebuild the church and Sunday school of evangelist Dwight L. Moody. Dorothea Dix, like thousands of other Americans, packed a box for friends in Chicago. The recipient, in her letter of thanks, said the box contained items "one would not purchase immediately but would wait for": children's books, snowshoes, an apron, a duster, mop, and stereoscope.[29]

[28] George E. Waring: *Report on the Social Statistics of Cities* (2 vols., Washington, D.C., 1886), vol. I, pp. 6, 32, 616; vol. II, pp. 491–92.
[29] *New York Times*, October 10–12, 1871; *Chicago Tribune*, October 11, 19, 1871; George Templeton Strong: *Diary*, ed. by Allan Nevins and Mil-ton Halsey Thomas (4 vols., New York, 1952), vol. IV, pp. 391, 398; Robert Ellis Thompson, ed.: *The Life of George H. Stuart, Written by Him-*

Mayor Roswell B. Mason assigned the tasks of receiving and dispensing contributions for fire sufferers to the Relief and Aid Society, a voluntary association organized and incorporated in the 1850s but not very active until 1868. The society, dominated by lawyers and businessmen, was committed to the proposition that *"indiscriminate alms giving"* encouraged "indolence and beggary" and was so cautious in supplying assistance to the poor, sick, and aged that in 1869–70, a year of high unemployment in Chicago, its treasury had a comfortable unexpended balance. Under the leadership of Wirt Dexter, a lawyer who took a year off from his practice to superintend relief efforts, the society formed committees headed by prominent businessmen and civic leaders to oversee receipt and storage of supplies, shelter, employment, transportation, distribution of aid, and medical, hospital, and sanitary matters.

A mixture of conservatism and innovation marked the society's administration of relief operations. After the first few days, when fire victims found shelter in schools and churches and received food and clothing on request, the distribution committee systematized dispensation of relief, employed a large corps of visitors to investigate applicants, and applied a work test to the able-bodied. On the other hand, aided by churches, it made a special effort to locate and help persons "formerly in comfortable circumstances" who were thought to be "the keenest sufferers of all." The shelter committee erected a few temporary barracks but concentrated efforts on building and furnishing small frame cottages, at a cost of $125 each, which it presented to applicants without charge. These houses were intended for "mechanics and the better class of working people"; many of them were still standing in the 1930s, when Edith Abbott called them "part of the housing problem of Chicago." The committee on hospital and sanitary measures required persons receiving aid to be vaccinated for smallpox, enforced strict sanitary standards in temporary housing, and made grants totaling almost $500,000 to Chicago hospitals and dispensaries.[30]

When the Relief and Aid Society closed its books on the

self (Philadelphia, 1890), pp. 257–58; Mary E. Blatchford to Miss Dix, January 13, 1872, Dix Papers, HLHU.

[30] Otto M. Nelson: "The Chicago Relief and Aid Society, 1850–1874," *Journal* of the Illinois State Historical Society, vol. LIX (1966), pp. 57–62; Edith Abbott *et al.*: *The Tenements of Chicago, 1908–1935* (Chicago, 1936), pp. 19–21.

Great Fire in April 1874, the record showed $4,400,000 spent and a balance of almost $600,000 on hand; 157,000 persons had received "general aid," at first in kind—food, clothing, fuel, bedding, or stoves—and after 1873 in cash. The society had found work for 20,000 and provided tools to workmen, sewing machines to seamstresses, instruments to doctors and dentists, and legal books to lawyers. In autumn 1873, although unemployed workers were already feeling the consequences of the panic of 1873, the Relief and Aid Society announced a return to its prefire policy of giving no aid to able-bodied single men and women and helping only the aged, the sick, and widows with children.[31]

On November 9 and 10, 1872, not quite a year after the Chicago disaster, Boston suffered a fire that destroyed stores, warehouses, factories, and merchandise in the central business district. Many cities, including Chicago, which proposed to return $100,000 of the $450,000 Boston had raised for Chicago fire sufferers, sent offers of help. Boston's officials rejected or returned outside assistance on the ground that the city's own charitable resources were adequate to meet all legitimate needs. Under the captions "Pecuniary Aid Will Probably Be Declined with Thanks" and "Opposition to Any Unusual Legislation or Relief Measures" the *New York Times* ran a news item stating that not more than $100,000 would be required to make the few families burned out richer than before the fire. "The losers," asserted a Boston paper, "are not turned homeless into the street, and there is a sufficiency of necessities and comforts of life. The loss falls mainly on trade and investments." According to its president, Charles W. Eliot, Harvard, which lost investment property, was one of the greatest sufferers; by the end of November alumni and well-wishers had contributed more than $100,000 to the college's "Immediate Exigency" fund. Estimates, or impressions, of the extent of suffering and need for assistance among mechanics and laborers differed; newspapers warned against impostors, while the Citizen's Relief Committee and its Subcommittee on Temporary Relief to the Destitute and Poorer Sufferers emphasized the gravity of the problem. As in Chicago, the consensus was that the working classes needed tools and jobs more than profuse relief. The amount eventually raised for fire sufferers was $345,000, most of which went to injured firemen, families of firemen killed in the fire, and individuals or families left homeless or unem-

[31] Nelson: "Chicago Relief and Aid Society," pp. 63–64.

ployed as a result of it. "The rich people have taken it upon themselves to provide for the poor," commented the *New York Times* on November 28, "and they are doing it pretty effectively although . . . it would have been better had they consented to allow the benevolent elsewhere to share the burden with them."[32]

Not flames but ravenous grasshoppers were the agents of destruction in the mid-1870s in an area stretching from Dakota Territory through Kansas and Nebraska to northern Texas and eastward into central Missouri. In a memorable passage, the historian Fred A. Shannon described the onslaught of the plague of 1874, the worst of its kind yet known:

> With the crops half grown, the grasshoppers, borne in by the wind, descended in a cloud that so darkened the sun as to cause the chickens to go to roost. The weight of the insects broke the limbs from trees. They started in on the wheat and corn, progressing across the fields and mowing it to the ground. They ate everything green except native grasses, castor beans, and the foliage of some kinds of trees. They so loved onions that they ate them clear down in the ground to the roots, and, as one observer declared, "till their breath was rank with the odor." They also had a fondness for tobacco and red peppers. They killed trees by denuding them of the tender bark of the twigs and limbs. They ate the mosquito bar off the windows, then entered the house, ate the curtains (if any), and started in on the bed covers. Relishing the taste of sweat and grease, they ate into the sideboards of the wagons, the plow handles, and even so roughened hickory pitchfork handles as to ruin them. They covered the railroad tracks so heavily that they stopped the trains, the locomotive wheels spinning with insufficient friction to draw the cars through the slithering mass. Turkeys and chickens ate themselves sick. The insects polluted the streams with their dead bodies till the cattle were loath to drink.[33]

[32] Justin Winsor, ed.: *The Memorial History of Boston, Including Suffolk County, Massachusetts, 1630–1880* (4 vols., Boston, 1881), vol IV, p. 665; *New York Times*, November 11, 1872 (quoting *Boston Daily Advertiser*), November 13, 16, 21, 28, 1872; *Boston Evening Transcript*, November 20, 1872.

[33] Fred A. Shannon: *The Farmer's Last Frontier, Agriculture 1860–1897* (New York, 1945), p. 152.

When the grasshoppers moved on, after a stay of from two days to two weeks, the farmers, many of whom were homesteaders, were not absolutely destitute. They still had roofs over their heads, their land, possibly some cash or savings, implements, and livestock. But their crops were gone; they had nothing to feed livestock, no seeds for a new planting, and, unlike Boston, no local resources to sustain them. Hence they not only accepted but sought help from outside their communities, including state and federal governments. "Private relief has been bounteous, but inadequate," Congressman Stephen A. Cobb of Kansas told the House of Representatives. In January 1875 Congress approved distribution by the Commissioner of Agriculture of seeds to "sufferers by grasshoppers," and the following month it authorized the President, acting through army officers, to distribute food and surplus army clothing to the sufferers. Both the Kansas and the Nebraska legislatures voted bond issues to provide money for relief, seed, and feed for livestock.[34]

In human costs, the worst disaster of the postwar years was the yellow fever epidemic of 1878, which caused 13,911 deaths in twelve states, mainly in the deep South, but extending as far north as Illinois, Ohio, Pennsylvania, and New York. Memphis, with 5,000 victims, and New Orleans with almost 4,000, had the largest number of fatalities, but in ratio of death to population, small towns like Grenada and Holly Springs, Mississippi, each with more than 300 dead in a population of about 2,000, were probably hardest hit. Neither New Orleans nor Memphis was unfamiliar with calamity. The epidemic of 1878 was the sixth to strike New Orleans in thirty-one years. Memphis had suffered so many catastrophes during and since the war that anyone aware of her "wayward and untoward history," said John M. Keating, editor of the *Memphis Appeal*, could only wonder at her survival. "In any other country, and by any other people, she would long since have been abandoned and given over to decay and ruin."[35]

Both New Orleans and Memphis had Howard associations,

---

[34] *Ibid.*, p. 153; *Congressional Record*, vol. III (1875), p. 887; *U.S. Statutes at Large*, vol. XVIII, part 3 (1875), pp. 303, 314. On the "seed and feed cases" resulting from state disaster relief legislation, see Edith Abbott: *Public Assistance, American Principles and Practices* (Chicago, 1940), vol. I, pp. 73–96.

[35] *Appleton's Annual Cyclopaedia*, vol. XVIII (1878), p. 319; John M. Keating: *A History of Yellow Fever, The Yellow Fever Epidemic of 1878, in Memphis, Tenn.* (Memphis, Tenn., 1879), p. 102.

"a time-honored body of good Samaritans" in New Orleans, in Memphis a group organized during the epidemic of 1867 to follow the example of "the immortal philanthropist" John Howard and devote themselves "to the succor of the sick, the relief of the suffering, and the burial of the dead." A similar organization in Mobile called itself the Can't Get Away Club. The Howards reported cases of sickness in an assigned ward, gave out medicine, notified physicians, filled prescriptions, provided supplies for convalescents, hired nurses, and recruited doctors. In Memphis they were assisted by men and women from other parts of the country, who flocked to the city in much the same way some of them had hastened to battlefields during the war.

As in 1853, the Howards solicited and served as the principal channels of aid sent to Memphis, New Orleans, and other communities. Because of the cessation of normal economic activity, people in stricken communities needed everything from medicine and coffins to food and drink. In response to appeals from the Howards, church congregations, lodges, benevolent societies, and boards of trade in cities large and small in all parts of the country made special collections and sent contributions, as did concerned groups and individuals in England, France, Germany, India, Australia, Cuba, and South America. New York put ballot boxes in saloons, post offices, and other places to collect donations from workmen, bootblacks, newsboys, and washerwomen. In terms of amount collected, the most effective fund-raiser for yellow fever sufferers was the Southern Relief Committee of the New York City Chamber of Commerce, J. P. Morgan treasurer.[36]

"We are the most remarkable people in the world for taking pains to find out, after epidemics or disasters, how they might have been averted and we are the slowest in guarding against those which are plainly impending," exclaimed a Cincinnati clergyman in 1879. "We sent $70,000, and much more than that to the stricken cities in the South, but you can't imagine the difficulty with which an appropriation of $1000 is passed . . . for improvement at home." George W. Cable, after noting the outbursts of benevolence that accompanied yellow fever epidemics in New

[36] Keating: *History of Yellow Fever*, pp. 115–16, 135; *Appleton's Annual Cyclopaedia*, vol. XVIII (1878), pp. 317–18; *New York Daily Tribune*, September 9, pp. 1, 5, and October 22, p. 5, 1878.

Orleans, wryly observed that orphan asylums were "indifferent substitutes for sanitation." Between 1865 and 1870, repeated epidemics of cholera, smallpox, and scarlet and yellow fever acted like "dreadful but patient sanitary inspectors," challenging official inertia and public apathy and producing what the sanitary engineer George E. Waring called "an unwonted interest throughout the United States in measures of prevention."[37] If the man-made and natural disasters of the 1870s resulted in significant advances in public hygiene, their philanthropic legacy was the founding of the American Red Cross.

Clara Barton was not one of the volunteers who traveled to Memphis in 1878 to offer service as nurses, but in a pamphlet published that year she cited the need for organized voluntary action in times of domestic disaster as one of the reasons for adherence by the United States to the Geneva Convention and organization of an American Red Cross society. "Our Southern coasts," she wrote, "are periodically visited by the scourge of yellow fever; the valleys of the Mississippi are subject to destructive inundations; the plains of the West are devastated by insects and drought, and our cities and country are swept by consuming fires." Returning to the subject in 1881 in an "Address to the President, Congress, and People of the United States," Barton argued that in most disasters "our gifts fall short of their best, being hastily bestowed, irresponsibly received and wastefully applied." The American Red Cross, as she envisaged and described it, would be not another demanding relief agency, but an organization designed "to save the people's means, to economize their charities, to make their gifts do more by the prevention of needless waste and extravagance." Its function would be to lessen the burden of disaster relief by making "previous, calm preparation," thus doing away with the "strain and confusion of unexpected necessities and haste."[38]

In 1882 Barton succeeded, where Bellows and former

[37] Dudley W. Rhodes: *Creed and Greed* (Cincinnati, 1879), p. 117; Elisha Harris: "Health Laws and Their Administration," *Journal of Social Science*, vol. II (1870), pp. 176–87; Waring: *Social Statistics of Cities*, vol. II, pp. 259–87.

[38] Clara Barton: *The Red Cross of the Geneva Convention: What It Is* (1878), quoted in Foster Rhea Dulles: *The America Red Cross, A History* (New York, 1950), p. 14; Clara Barton: *The Red Cross, A History of This Remarkable Movement in the Interest of Humanity* (Washington, 1898), pp. 67–68, quoting Barton: "Address to the President, Congress, and People of the United States" (1881).

Sanitary Commission leaders had failed, in securing American ratification of the Geneva Convention, which provided for neutralization of aid to the wounded in time of war. Her conception of the Red Cross as an agency for rendering assistance in peace as well as war contrasted sharply with the limited program of the American Association for Relief of Misery on the Battlefield, organized by Bellows in 1866 as the proposed American affiliate of the International Red Cross. At that time the war-weary nation showed little interest in an organization intended solely for battlefield relief, and the association went out of existence in 1871.[39]

Clara Barton was sixty years old in 1881, when she organized the American Association of the Red Cross (later the American National Red Cross) "for the relief of suffering by war, pestilence, famine, flood, fires, and other calamities of sufficient magnitude to be deemed national in extent." She remained the dominant figure in the society for twenty-five years, administering relief in person and on the spot in domestic and overseas disasters as well as in the Spanish-American War. Despite her earlier criticism of disaster relief as wasteful, she enjoyed playing the role of Lady Bountiful. During an early and characteristic operation, the Mississippi flood of 1884, she presided over the Red Cross steamer *Mattie Bell* on its voyage from St. Louis to Vicksburg with periodic stops to put ashore supplies "for man and beast." On numerous occasions, Congress had approved distribution of army rations and clothing to flood sufferers, but according to an admiring account in the *New York Tribune*, "The work done by the Red Cross is different in important respects from that done by the government. It is unhampered by red tape or other restrictions which prevent its ministering to every case of suffering that may appear."[40]

For many Americans the gravest disaster of the postwar years was the economic depression that began in autumn 1873 and lasted, in most communities, until 1878 and, in some, until 1880. Not only in duration but in severity and destructiveness—bank and business failures, wage cuts, and unemployment—the de-

[39] Clyde E. Buckingham: *Red Cross Disaster Relief, Its Origin and Development* (Washington, D.C., 1956), pp. 7–9.

[40] Robert H. Bremner: *American Philanthropy* (Chicago, 1960), pp. 93–94; *New York Daily Tribune*, April 12, 1884.

pression was the most serious the country had yet experienced. Among the banks that failed was the Freedmen's Savings and Trust Company, with its numerous and far-flung branches in Southern cities. The bank was a victim not only of the times but of the neglect of some of its trustees, the cupidity and recklessness of the rest, and the dishonesty of some of its officers. Scholars disagree on the economic and psychological consequences of its failure. Throughout most of the nine years of its life the bank was a useful and successful institution, and only 2 percent of the total amount deposited in it over the years was lost. But that must have been cold comfort to blacks whose life's savings constituted the seemingly tiny percentage. One of them was an old woman who had once "made a good living" selling eggs and chickens, cleaning bachelors' rooms, and taking in laundry. Her granddaughter, Susie King Taylor, a former slave and volunteer teacher in Higginson's black regiment, recalled the old woman's plight and reaction to the closing:

> The hardest blow to her was the failure of the Freedmen's Savings Bank in Savannah, for in that bank she had placed her savings, about three thousand dollars, the result of her hard labor and self-denial before the war, and which, by dint of shrewdness and care, she kept together all through the war. She felt it more keenly, coming as it did in her old age, when her life was too far spent to begin anew; but she took a practical view of the matter, for she said, "I will leave it all in God's hand. If the Yankees did take all our money, they freed my race; God will take care of us."[41]

In the winter of 1873–74, more or less in the spirit of disaster relief, individuals and groups in hard-hit industrial cities acted to feed the hungry and shelter the homeless. "We must not desert the poor even while we pray Heaven to help the rich," declared the *New York Herald*; as if to prove the point its publisher, James Gordon Bennett, donated $30,000 to set up free soup counters in firehouses, where applicants who had obtained

[41] Susie King Taylor: *Reminiscences of My Life in Camp* (Boston, 1902), p. 3; James McPherson: *The Abolitionist Legacy, from Reconstruction to the NAACP* (Princeton, N.J., 1975), pp. 74–75; Carl R. Osthaus: *Freedmen, Philanthropy, and Fraud: A History of the Freedmen's Savings Bank* (Urbana, Ill., 1976), pp. 201–25.

tickets at police stations received a pint of soup prepared under the supervision of restaurateur Lorenzo Delmonico and chef Charles Ranshoffer.[42]

Journalists and reformers who rejoiced in state intervention to promote public health took an entirely different attitude toward official action to combat the depression or counteract its effects. "Things," explained the *New York Times*, "must regulate themselves." City officials, supported by the press, rejected appeals and agitation by the unemployed for public works instead of charity and relief in the form of police station lodgings and doles of food and coal. Even modest and makeshift efforts at public relief for the unemployed came under attack by reformers on the grounds that they were corruptly and wastefully administered, and pauperizing in their effect on recipients. "The first duty of a community like the American is not to feed the hungry and clothe the naked," said a speaker at a conference on charities sponsored by the American Social Science Association in spring 1874, "but to prevent people from being hungry and naked" by inculcating habits of self-help and self-support. After an investigation of public relief in New York City during the winter of 1873–74 Louisa Lee Schuyler, speaking for the State Charities Aid Association, advised the State Board of Charities that the larger the sums appropriated for public relief, the greater the inducement for outsiders to crowd into the city, thus increasing the "pauper element" of the population. "The wisest and safest course," she asserted, "would be ultimately to abolish all official out-door relief, to improve and enlarge the accommodations in the institutions, and to throw the responsibility of providing for the wants of the poor entirely on existing private charity."[43]

During the winter of 1875–76, volunteer visitors to the poor, organized by a citizen's group, took over the task of investigating applicants for relief in New York City. Of the 14,000 cases investigated, the visitors rejected almost 10 percent as "totally unworthy"; according to an approving observer, the mere knowledge

[42] Herbert G. Gutman: "The Failure of the Movement by the Unemployed for Public Works in 1873," *Political Science Quarterly*, vol. LXXX (1965), p. 255; *Harper's Weekly*, vol. XVIII (1874), pp. 213, 222.

[43] Gutman: "The Failure of the Movement by the Unemployed for Public Works in 1873," p. 260; R. T. Davis: "Pauperism in the City of New York," *Proceedings of the Conference of Charities, 1874* (Boston, 1874,) p. 24; State Charities Aid Association: "Out-door Relief in New York County," in New York State Board of Charities: *Ninth Annual Report, 1874–75* (Albany, N.Y., 1876), p. 133.

that all cases were carefully scrutinized was enough to deter many worthless people from applying. Before the end of the depression, not only New York City but Brooklyn, Buffalo, Indianapolis, and Philadelphia had joined Chicago and other cities in refusing to grant public relief outside of almshouses.[44]

Ending public outdoor relief meant that communities delegated the task of helping the poor who were not so forlorn as to require poorhouse care to charitable organizations, many of which, as previously noted, were themselves subsidized by public funds. The assumption was that aid received from a private society was more effective and less dangerous in consequences than that obtained directly from a public agency. "We help families over hard places that, but for us and this timely aid, would become burdens to the taxpayers," said the superintendent of a Protestant mission in New York. "Were they obliged to go to 'the Island' [the poorhouse on Blackwell's Island], they would become hopeless paupers." In practice, private charities could be as careless and unfeeling as public relief agencies were reputed to be. While Schuyler denounced "soup kitchen" charities, which, in her opinion, fostered crime and pauperism without serving the deserving poor, journalists decried the employment of paid agents by charitable societies. The *New York Daily Graphic* defended Bennett's soup houses, often condemned by reformers, as providing "all soup and no salary," whereas "professional philanthropy" offered "all salary and no soup."[45]

Despite such gibes, professional philanthropists persisted throughout the depression in efforts to introduce a more business-like spirit into the haphazard operations of private charity and to combine, to federate, or at least to secure some degree of cooperation between separate and sometimes rival charitable organizations. In a number of cities the work of the London Charity Organization Society, founded in 1869, provided a model for American reformers seeking to restrict "the great stream of char-

[44] Henry E. Pellew: "Out-Door Relief Administration in New York City, 1878," *Proceedings of the Conference of Charities, 1878* (Boston, 1878), pp. 60–61; Charles D. Kellogg: "Charity Organization in the United States," *Proceedings of the National Conference of Charities and Correction, 1893* (Boston, 1893), p. 60.

[45] William D. Clegg, superintendent of the Howard Mission and Home for Little Wanderers, quoted in William P. Letchworth: *Homes of Homeless Children* (New York, 1974, first published in 1876), p. 254; State Charities Aid Association: "Out-Door Relief in New York County," p. 113; *New York Daily Graphic*, vol. III (February 20, 1874), p. 749.

ity to its legitimate object of assisting without pauperizing the deserving poor." Between 1873 and 1883, organizations patterned directly or indirectly after the London society were established in twenty-five American cities, including Buffalo, Philadelphia, Boston, and New York. In most cases the new societies were not intended to function as relief associations. With some exceptions, they furnished no material aid to the poor from their own funds but acted simply as bureaus of information, registration, and investigation, referring "helpable" applicants to the appropriate relief-dispensing agencies. Their motto was: "Not alms but a friend." When a prospective donor asked Josephine Shaw Lowell, founder and guiding spirit of the New York Charity Organization Society, how much of his donation would go to the poor, she firmly replied: "Not one cent."[46]

Charity organization and the "scientific philanthropy" it exemplified had both a kindly and a stern aspect. Its aim was to husband the charitable responses of a community so that aid would be available in sufficient quantity to provide adequate assistance for all deserving cases. Robert Treat Paine counseled friendly visitors of the Boston Associated Charities: "You are to give—what is far more precious than gold or silver—your own sympathy, and thought, and time, and labor." In its first few years of operation the pioneer Buffalo Charity Organization Society founded a day nursery for children of workingwomen, established a provident wood yard and coal saving fund—the latter to enable poor families to buy fuel at a low price—founded a dispensary, hospital, labor bureau, and training school for nursemaids, and surveyed the sanitary condition of homes of the poor, recommending and securing improved housing ordinances. But in the COS creed, guarding against what Lowell called "pauperism, imposture, etc." was no less important than helping the poor. "Nothing is taken for granted, but all cases are thoroughly investigated," reported the president of the Associated Charities of Columbus, Ohio. Instead of personally assisting applicants, citizens referred them to the association. "There it was ascertained" —seemingly without difficulty—"first, whether they were deserving; second, if deserving, what kind of assistance they needed;

---

[46] Leah Feder: *Unemployment Relief in Periods of Depression* (New York, 1936), pp. 59–61; Pellew: "Out-Door Relief Administration in New York City, 1878," p. 68; Robert H. Bremner: " 'Scientific Philanthropy,' 1873–93," *The Social Service Review*, vol. XXX (1956), pp. 169–70.

third, if unworthy, they were warned against further imposing on the benevolence of the people."[47]

Charity organization spokesmen saved their harshest strictures for thoughtless philanthropists whose misguided benevolence turned the poor into paupers. "We must reform those mild, well-meaning, tender-hearted, sweet-voiced criminals who insist on indulging in indiscriminate charity," asserted H. L. Wayland, founder of the New Haven COS. His brother, Francis Wayland, dean of the Yale Law School, was even more emphatic:

> Do not be deceived. Do not say that a piece of bread, an old coat, a pair of cast-off shoes, a hat of archaic pattern, can do no harm. If the person so helped is able-bodied, and he received the article without having earned it, positive mischief has been done. Because the very moment that any man, woman, or child has taken the first lesson in the art of living without labor, that moment the first step is taken in a downward career. For he who has discovered how to live, without labor, on the labor of other people is on the direct road to living by appropriating to himself the property of others, and graduating from the pauper class into the criminal class.[48]

Admirers of scientific philanthropy had no doubt of its superiority to traditional charity. Mrs. James T. Fields explained the difference in *How to Help the Poor*, a handbook prepared for the Boston Associated Charities: "The old method of working for the poor always left the man in the swamp but threw him biscuits to keep him from starving. The new method is to throw him a plank. He cannot eat the plank but he can scramble out upon it, and have his share of the labors and rewards which the experience of life brings both to high and low." Herbert Baxter Adams put nineteenth-century movements in social science and organized charities in historical perspective. "For eighteen centuries," he told a conference on charities in 1887, "the charitable

[47] Bremner: " 'Scientific Philanthropy,' 1873–93," pp. 169–71; Mrs. Lowell to Charles S. Fairchild, November 28, 1881, Fairchild Collection, NYHS; "Columbus Associated Charities," *The International Record of Charities and Correction*, vol. II (1887–88), p. 169.

[48] H. L. Wayland quoted in Bremner: " 'Scientific Philanthropy,' 1873–93," p. 170; Francis Wayland quoted in Frederick H. Wines: "The Baltimore Conference," *The International Record of Charities and Correction*, vol. II (1887–88), p. 128.

and legislative efforts of society have been pauperizing instead of elevating men." It has remained for the nineteenth century to undertake "the great work of organizing charity into self-help."[49]

To balance self-praise, charity organization had its share of critics inside and outside the movement. Lyman Abbott, formerly secretary of the American Freedmen's Union Commission and Henry Ward Beecher's successor as pastor of Plymouth Church in Brooklyn, objected:

> If the Good Samaritan had been a Yankee, he would not have stopped and picked up that sore and wounded traveller, and put him on his own beast, and taken him to an inn. He would have hurried on to Jerusalem and organized a society for the relief of sick and wounded travellers, with a president, vice-president, treasurer, half a dozen secretaries, a board of managers, and a collecting agent in every district of Palestine.

Bellows acknowledged in 1880 that he was well over his "fit of sympathy with economical science." His counsel now was to avoid "too much suspicion of the sentiment of pity and mercy." Shortly before his death, he advised his congregation to "break many politico-economic maxims by filling . . . the mouths of the hungry with a plenty they have not earned, [any] more than you have earned your right to live and think and feel—a pure gift of your creator and Father in Heaven."[50]

In the president's address at the 1883 meeting of the National Conference of Charities and Corrections Frederick Wines scoffed at the "romantic nonsense" uttered by "political and social doctrinaires" who denied the need for public relief and insisted that private charity was the proper way of dealing with the needy. Wines acknowledged that the objects, extent, form, and mode of relief were subject to debate but maintained that in

[49] Mrs. James T. Fields: *How to Help the Poor* (Boston, 1883), p. 122; Herbert Baxter Adams: "Notes on the Literature of Charities," in *Johns Hopkins University Studies in History and Political Science*, vol. V (1887), p. 320.

[50] Abbott quoted in Wines: "The Baltimore Conference," p. 128; Bellows: "Patriotism and Piety" (1880), quoted in Clifford E. Clark: "Religious Beliefs and Social Reforms in the Gilded Age: The Case of Henry Whitney Bellows," *The New England Quarterly*, vol. XLIII (1970), p. 77.

certain cases—e.g., support for paupers with "legal settlement" (i.e., having a right to assistance because of birth or established residence in a community), or education for deaf and blind children—relief was a right, not a boon to be bestowed or withheld at the whim of philanthropists. The audience Wines addressed included men and women representing both the public and the private sectors of charities and corrections. Not all of them shared and some bitterly opposed his view of relief as a right. But the point to be noted is that Wines spoke at a national organization the annual meetings of which served as a clearinghouse for the exchange of information and experience about social welfare and a forum for the expression of ideas and opinions concerning it. Nothing like the national conference, with its ranks of officers, state corresponding secretaries, and standing committees on subjects ranging from child saving and charity organization to management of poorhouses and administration of police systems, existed before 1860. Organized in 1874 by members of the state boards of charities and the American Social Science Association, the conference was a product of the encouragement and opportunity the war gave responsible and high-minded men and women to apply their idealism, professional skills, and managerial talent to public need.[51]

At the 1890 meeting, Franklin B. Sanborn, one of the founders of the NCCC, referred to able-bodied paupers, a frequent target of charity reformers, as "that mythical class" and vigorously defended "family aid"—his name for outdoor relief—as a more economical, humane, and practical method of caring for many of the poor than institutionalization.[52] Josephine Shaw Lowell, rigorous advocate of scientific philanthropy and charity organization, took Sanborn to task for failing to distinguish between public relief and private charity. "Because certain persons think that certain other persons need help is no doubt the best reason why they should help them," she observed, "but not a good reason why they should require the community to help them." Her sympathies, like those of William Graham Sumner,

---

[51] Wines's address is in *Proceedings of the National Conference of Charities and Corrections, 1883* (Madison, Wis., 1884), pp. 12–13; on the founding of the NCCC see Frank J. Bruno: *Trends in Social Work, 1874–1956, A History Based on Proceedings of the National Conference of Social Work* (New York, 1957), pp. 3–9.

[52] Sanborn: "Indoor and Outdoor Relief," *Proceedings of the National Conference of Charities and Corrections, 1890* (Boston, 1890), pp. 75–78.

were with "the forgotten man," the hardworking, self-supporting taxpayer:

> Every dollar raised by taxation comes out of the pocket of some individual, usually a poor individual, and makes him so much the poorer, and therefore the question is between the man who earned the dollar by hard work, and needs it to buy himself and his family a day's food, and the man who, however worthy and suffering, did not earn it, but wants it to be given to him to buy himself and his family a day's food. If the man who earned it wishes to divide it with the other man, it is usually a desirable thing that he should do so, and at any rate it is more or less his own business, but that the law, by the hand of a public officer, should take it from him and hand it over to the other man, seems to be an act of gross tyranny and injustice. . . .

Lowell had a pessimistic view both of human nature (very few people will work if someone else will support them in idleness) and of society's resources (finite and easily exhaustible) for maintaining its nonproductive members. "The less that is given," she said of public relief, "the better for everyone, the giver and the receiver."[53]

In public, at least, no one called Lowell doctrinaire or accused her of speaking romantic nonsense. Instead, her contemporaries seem to have regarded her as a saint, above controversy and beyond reproach. The respect and deference accorded her were inspired not so much by her well-recognized ability and industry as by something in her presence that conveyed a feeling of absolute devotion and dedication to a sacred cause. As the widow of one war hero and the sister of another Josephine Shaw Lowell embodied the treasury of virtue the North gained as a legacy of the Civil War. "One could not be with her—I never could—" recalled Louisa Lee Schuyler, "without feeling through her silence, the ever present background of war; without a sense of reverence for that supreme sacrifice for country, so nobly accepted; without seeing the halo upon her brow."[54]

[53] Lowell: "The Economic and Moral Effects of Public Outdoor Relief," *ibid.*, pp. 81–82.

[54] Schuyler is quoted in William Rhinelander Stewart: *The Philanthropic Work of Josephine Shaw Lowell* (New York, 1911), p. 544. On "the treasury of virtue" see Robert Penn Warren: *The Legacy of the Civil War, Meditations on the Centennial* (New York, 1961), pp. 54–59.

Philanthropy's role and achievements in the Civil War won voluntarism an aura of rectitude and sanctity similar to Lowell's halo. During the war everyone recognized that the expense, labor, and responsibility of government agencies vastly overshadowed the contributions of voluntary organizations like the Sanitary and Christian commissions. Quartermaster General Montgomery C. Meigs, defending the Union army's ambulance and hospital system against civilian criticism, asserted: "No nation has ever, I believe, made such large, such prodigious provision for its sick and wounded soldiers. It is the greatest charity on earth."[55] The efforts of the various commissions and aid associations, however, gave countless civilians a sense of participation in the struggle and ultimately a feeling of personal satisfaction and fulfillment in its outcome. After the war critics were less likely than before to scorn charitable work, particularly when practiced by women, as silly and ineffectual. On the other hand, postwar defenders and advocates of voluntarism were more firmly convinced than ever of private charity's moral and practical superiority to public relief.

The impact of the Civil War on philanthropy and welfare, therefore, was to enhance the prestige of voluntary efforts and to encourage reliance on them for solutions to social problems. For good or ill, depending on circumstances and point of view, this influence was to be felt for many years to come.

[55] Meigs to Henry I. Bowditch, M.D., October 30, 1862, in U.S. War Department: *War of the Rebellion: A Compilation of the Official Records of the Union and Confederate Armies* (70 vols., Washington, D.C., 1890–1901), Series 3, vol. II (1899), p. 702.

Chapter 9

Ladders for the Aspiring

P ostwar philanthropy, when not directed to the relief of poverty, and therefore less inhibited by fear of inducing pauperism, expressed itself in generous and positive ways. In *The
American Commonwealth* (1888) James Bryce observed: "In
works of active beneficence no country has surpassed, perhaps
none has equalled the United States." Nearly all American giving
and service, he thought, were done by religious people under a
religious impulse. As an earlier English visitor, James Shaw, had
noted, contributions to home and foreign missions quadrupled
during the war, and in 1866 members of Methodist churches
observed the centennial of their denomination's establishment
in America by making a thank offering of $5,000,000 to religious,
educational, and charitable causes.[1]

Despite the panic of 1873, average yearly giving to the various home and foreign mission societies of the Protestant churches
rose from about $3,300,000 in the 1860s to $5,200,000 in the
1870s and to $7,000,000 in the 1880s. According to Leonard
Woolsey Bacon, a church historian, the enormous demands of
missions, colportage work of the Bible and tract societies, Sunday
school expenses, construction of churches and parsonages in cities, towns, and villages, and maintenance of the myriad charities
clustering around local congregations eased "the perils of

---

[1] James Bryce: *The American Commonwealth* (2 vols., New York, 1888),
vol. II, p. 579; James Shaw: *Twelve Years in America* (Chicago, 1867),
pp. 140–41.

abounding wealth" that beset the church after the war. "The voluntary gifts of Christian people for Christ's sake in the promotion of such works," Bacon declared, "would make an amount that would overtax the ordinary imagination to conceive." Twice during the latter half of the 1860s Sunday school children raised funds for mission ships to replace the original *Morning Star* and its successor, *Morning Star II*, wrecked off the Caroline Islands. From a prewar prayer club and boardinghouse in New York City, the Young Women's Christian Association grew to twenty-three city societies in 1871. During the war the Young Men's Christian Association dwindled in numbers but gained prestige as a result of involvement with the Christian Commission. After 1865, under the guidance of business and religious leaders—William E. Dodge, Morris K. Jesup, and J. P. Morgan in New York, Dwight Moody and John V. Farwell in Chicago—YMCA's expanded in both membership and range of activities.[2]

The philanthropic career of "the Christian merchant," William E. Dodge (1805–1883), reproduced on a broader canvas the interests and activities of many less prominent businessmen of his generation. Dodge, whose giving to religious and educational causes was reputed at one time to approach $1,000 a day, had investments in mining, railroads, and timberlands; although active in the management of many enterprises, he refused to serve on any board of directors that caused railroads to run on Sunday or derived a profit from Sunday labor. He took such an active part in evangelical religious movements that he was once introduced to Lord Shaftesbury, the English social reformer, as "the Shaftesbury of America." In addition to the YMCA, he was a longtime officeholder in and large contributor to the Evangelical Alliance, the American Board of Commissioners for Foreign Missions, and the Presbyterian Board of Missions. An ardent advocate of total abstinence, he was also a faithful supporter of Negro colonization, serving as vice-president of the American Colonization Society for more than twenty years before the war and still active in the organization in 1882. Dodge sponsored Dwight Moody and Ira Sankey's evangelistic campaign in New York in

---

[2] Leonard Woolsey Bacon: *A History of American Christianity* (New York, 1918), pp. 358–61; William E. Strong: *The Story of the American Board, An Account of the First Hundred Years of the American Board of Commissioners for Foreign Missions* (Boston, 1910), p. 242; C. Howard Hopkins: *History of the YMCA in North America* (New York, 1951), pp. 105, 108.

1876; his support of Jerry McAuley's Water Street Mission made that institution a favorite object of religious giving in New York. Dodge's formal education ended at thirteen, but he contributed to Williams, Dartmouth, Amherst, Lafayette, Beloit, Marietta, Oberlin, Hamilton, and Maryville (Tennessee) colleges; to the University of Virginia; to theological seminaries at Princeton and Yale; to American missionary colleges in Hawaii, Syria, Turkey, Lebanon, Liberia, Japan, and Ceylon; and to a number of institutions for Negroes, including Lincoln University in Pennsylvania, Zion Wesley College in North Carolina, Hampton Institute, and Atlanta and Howard universities. He advised John F. Slater in the founding of the Slater Fund for Negro education (1882) and was a member of the fund's original board of trustees.[3]

The best-known woman philanthropist of the 1870s and 1880s was Catharine Lorillard Wolfe (1828–1887). Heiress of two large fortunes, "the richest unmarried lady in America," she was described by a contemporary as the embodiment of the American idea of a philanthropist: "rich, without the pride of wealth; and generous, without false sentiment." Her obituary in the *New York Times* put the matter bluntly: "Miss Wolfe will be remembered, as she was known, chiefly because of her enormous benefactions. For 15 years she has given away an average of fully $200,000 a year." To charitable institutions and associations that had relied on Wolfe for donations and subscriptions, her death, in the words of a mourner, "reached the importance of a public misfortune." Her gifts had been directed to agencies of the Protestant Episcopal Church, particularly Grace Church in Manhattan, but reached overseas to the American churches in Rome and Paris and extended at home from the St. Johnland Colony on Long Island to a theological seminary in Ohio and schools for girls in Denver and Topeka. She was a faithful supporter of institutions her father had aided, including Union College at Schenectady, the Shepherd's Fold (a children's home), and the Newsboys' Lodging House in New York City. According to the *New York Times*, "many a school was bolstered, many a missionary was started on his labors, and many a church was saved through her timely help." But Wolfe, like George Peabody and

[3] Richard Lowitt: *A Merchant Prince of the Nineteenth Century, William E. Dodge* (New York, 1954), pp. 199–201, 341–46, 354–55; Theodore Ledyard Cuyler: *Recollections of a Long Life, An Autobiography* (New York, 1902), pp. 56–57, 275.

an increasing number of philanthropists of later date, was interested in and gave support to artistic and scientific causes as well as religious and benevolent ones. She bequeathed her collection of paintings and an endowment fund of $200,000 to the Metropolitan Museum of Art, contributed to the American School of Classical Studies in Athens, and sponsored the first American expedition to conduct archeological research in ancient Babylonian sites.[4]

At a Fourth of July celebration in 1875, Frederick Douglass denounced "broken down ministers without churches" and "wandering teachers without schools" who professed to be concerned about the education of Negroes: "They say 'Please give something to help educate the poor black people but do, I pray, pay it to me,' and if it is $100, it is reduced to about 100 cents when it gets to the 'poor black people.' We do not want, we will not have these second-rate men begging for us." By 1875 the education of freedmen was no longer the popular cause it had been ten years earlier, and it is unlikely that mendicants of the sort Douglass mimicked would have gained much by their solicitations. A year later, Douglass acknowledged that his real aims in the speech had been "to inspire the colored people with a purpose of self-dependence" and to tell white Americans "we need justice, and the protection of the law, more than alms." But in the circumstances prevailing in the late 1870s, Douglass continued, "Where no provision is made for our education by state or nation; while we are persecuted and hunted, and our schools are burnt and our teachers beaten and driven off, I would not throw one straw in the way of the American Missionary Association, or of any other society honestly laboring to disseminate light and hope amongst us."[5]

[4] Daniel M. Fox: "Wolfe, Catharine Lorillard" in Edward T. James, ed.: *Notable American Women* (3 vols., Cambridge, Mass., 1971), vol. III, p. 641; "Miss Wolfe," *The International Record of Charities and Correction*, vol. II (1887), p. 53, citing as source "M.A.H.," in *The Orphan's Friend* (Louisville); *New York Times*, April 5, 1887; Calvin Tomkins: *Merchants and Masterpieces, The Story of the Metropolitan Museum of Art* (New York, 1970), pp. 71–72, comments on the Wolfe collection and use made of the income from the endowment fund.

[5] *New York Times*, July 7, 1875; *American Missionary* (September 1876), p. 208.

The major groups still laboring for freedmen's education in the mid-1870s were the American Missionary Association, which was predominantly Congregationalist, and associations of the Methodist, Baptist, and Presbyterian churches of the North. Unlike the defunct American Freedmen's Union Commission, which was nondenominational and committed to secular education, the denominational societies were regarded and supported by church members as missionary enterprises. James McPherson has pointed out that although the income of the AMA and the other associations declined during the depression years of the 1870s, it began to rise as economic conditions improved, and by the end of the 1880s the four societies collected more money than *all* the freedmen's aid organizations in 1866. With the gradual emergence of public education in the South missionary societies were able to concentrate on secondary schools and colleges to train black ministers and teachers. Between 1880 and 1915, largely as a result of steadfast support by church members, contributions of the Slater Fund, and Daniel Hand's record-setting gift (1888) to the AMA, the number of secondary schools for blacks quadrupled and the number of institutions offering college-level instruction tripled.[6]

Long before 1875, black students and their parents were practicing the self-dependence Douglass preached by contributing their labor to build and support schools and colleges. The most famous and successful of these efforts was a series of concert tours undertaken by the Fisk University Jubilee Singers "to sing the money out of the hearts and pockets of the people." The chorus donated the proceeds of the first paid concert in autumn 1871 to a fund for Chicago fire sufferers. When the singers returned to Nashville after warm receptions in New England and New York and an appearance at the White House, they brought their struggling institution $20,000. Subsequent tours, including two to England and the European continent, raised funds that

---

[6] James McPherson: *The Abolitionist Legacy, from Reconstruction to NAACP* (Princeton, N.J., 1975), pp. 143–48. In 1888, Daniel Hand (1801–1891), a Connecticut-born merchant who made a fortune before the war in Augusta, Georgia, and Charleston, South Carolina, gave securities valued at more than $1,000,000 to the AMA to establish the Daniel Hand Fund for Colored Education. It was the largest gift made up to that time by a living donor to an American benevolent society.

enabled Fisk to buy a new site, move out of dilapidated old army barracks, and erect a new building, Jubilee Hall.[7]

Following Fisk's example, Samuel C. Armstrong sent singers from the Hampton Institute in Virginia on a profitable fund-raising tour. In the long run, however, Armstrong himself and his approach to education of freedmen proved the crucial factors in winning confidence and support of donors. Armstrong's first report to trustees of the Hampton Institute (1870) set forth his conviction that not ignorance but "deficiencies of character" were the Negro's chief handicaps in meeting the challenge of freedom. Through a threefold program of manual, moral, and intellectual training (similar in many ways to the regimen he had experienced as a student at a missionary school in Hawaii) Armstrong proposed to overcome the faults he believed caused by slavery: improvidence and lack of energy, judgment, and foresight. The school, in his words, became "a drill-ground for the future work; it sends men and women rather than scholars into the world." In 1890, twenty-two years after Hampton's founding and when it was already on its way to becoming the best equipped and most richly endowed institution for Negroes, Armstrong could still boast that it held fast to the idea of education by self-help, asked nothing for students that they could provide by their own labor, and gave students nothing but opportunities to work their way.[8]

Neither presidents nor prospective donors imposed such stringent demands on students in predominatly white colleges and universities. Gifts to higher education, probably the most flourishing field of American philanthropy in the twenty-five years after the Civil War, resulted in the founding of major new institutions, including colleges for women, graduate schools, and technological institutes, enrichment and strengthening of existing institutions, and restoration of Southern colleges and universities shattered by the war. In an inaugural address (1868) as provost of the University of Pennsylvania, Charles J. Stillé cited recent contributions, estimated at $15,000,000, for the endowment and support of higher education as at once the most characteristic and most creditable aspects of American life. Most of these con-

---

[7] Horace Mann Bond: *The Education of the Negro in the American Social Order* (New York, 1934), p. 129; Hodding Carter: *The Angry Scar, The Story of Reconstruction* (Garden City, N.Y., 1959), pp. 193–94.

[8] *Twenty-two Years' Work of the Hampton Normal and Agricultural Institute* (Hampton, Va., 1892), pp. 526–31.

tributions, Stillé noted, had been made "not by men who have had the advantage of a classical training, by alumni of colleges, but almost wholly by self-made men . . . by capitalists who, in their prosperity, have felt that no amount of money can supply the defects of early training, and who have proved the sincerity of their belief by taking care that future generations shall not suffer from the same cause."[9]

Aside from respect for education as an elevating influence, morally, economically, intellectually, and socially, the motives of donors and purposes of their gifts defy generalization. While givers like John D. Rockefeller and William E. Dodge developed charitable habits early in their careers, others, notably Cornelius Vanderbilt, denied themselves the pleasures of philanthropy until late in life. Matthew Vassar attributed his decision to devote part of his fortune to charity to the discovery that an ancestor had founded Guy's Hospital in London; Leland Stanford and his wife established Stanford University as a memorial to a beloved son; Sophia Smith, an aged, deaf spinster who inherited a fortune from a bachelor brother, relied on the advice of her clergyman in bequeathing it for founding a college for women; Charles Pratt studied technological institutes in America and Europe and corresponded with Commissioner of Education John Eaton and other experts before establishing Pratt Institute in Brooklyn. Rockefeller preferred to strengthen endowments; friends of struggling schools like Hampden-Sydney College in Virginia gave to help meet operating expenses; a host of donors in all parts of the country immortalized themselves, spouses, children, or parents in names of buildings or professorships. James Lick left the University of California funds for a powerful telescope with the proviso that his body be buried beneath it. Daniel Drew, described in the *Dictionary of American Biography*, as "a mixture of piety and rascality," promised much but went bankrupt before meeting his pledges to Drew Theological Seminary and Wesleyan University. In 1889 Andrew Carnegie argued that Cooper, Pratt, and Stanford deserved as much

[9] Charles J. Stillé: *The Claims of Liberal Culture in Philadelphia* (Philadelphia, 1868), p. 23. The number of colleges and universities in the United States grew from 49 with 3,582 students in 1830 to 370 with 33,000 students in 1884. In both 1830 and 1884 denominational institutions outnumbered nondenominational ones (35 to 14 in 1830, 309 to 61 in 1884); Daniel Dorchester: *Christianity in the United States from the First Settlement to the Present Time* (New York, 1888), pp. 725–26.

credit and admiration "for the time and attention given during their lives, as for their expenditures, upon their respective monuments." Merle Curti and Roderick Nash, writing three-quarters of a century later and viewing the matter from the perspective of donee institutions rather than donors, concluded that over the years the optimum relationship between a philanthropist and a college or university was one "in which the donor gave little but his money."[10]

On the afternoon of July 13, 1865, a crowd of 30,000 people, sprinkled with pickpockets, watched in a carnival mood while P. T. Barnum's American Museum on Fulton Street and Broadway in lower Manhattan burned to the ground. According to newspaper accounts, the crowd responded with hilarity to the spectacle of animals trapped and dying in the building, some, like the "man-eater alligator," inert and listless, others, like the anacondas and pythons, desperately trying to escape.

> The whales [reported the *New York Times*] were, of course, burned alive. At an early stage of the conflagration, the large panes of glass in the great "whale tank" were broken to allow the heavy mass of water to flow upon the floor of the main saloon, and the leviathan natives of Labrador, when last seen, were floundering in mortal agony, to the inexpressible delight of the unfeeling boys, who demanded a share of the blubber.

George Templeton Strong, passing through the crowd late in the afternoon, remembered childhood visits to the museum and rejoiced that the "horrible brass band . . . always tooting in its balcony" had been stilled.[11]

The estimated value of the creatures and curiosities consumed in the fire was $500,000. Barnum had the museum insured for only $40,000 but recouped some of his losses by selling the lease of the property for $200,000. Barely a week after the disaster he was planning a new museum, stuffed like a sanitary fair with presents from famous people at home and abroad. The value of

[10] Merle Curti and Roderick Nash: *Philanthropy in the Shaping of Higher Education* (New Brunswick, N.J., 1965), p. 263.

[11] *New York Times*, July 14, 1865; *Diary of George Templeton Strong*, ed. by Allan Nevins and Milton Halsey Thomas (4 vols., New York, 1952), vol. IV, pp. 17–18.

the gifts was not important, he said. "The names of the donors would render them *very* attractive." Two weeks after the disaster he devised a scheme for "a *free museum* for the instruction and edification of the *Youth of America*": Barnum, the philanthropist, would erect a five-story building to house a national collection of treasures, presented by government agencies, foreign countries, and private donors. Next to the stately museum, Barnum, the showman, would operate a popular exhibition of freaks and spectacles, open from early morning to late at night. People purchasing tickets to the latter would be admitted to the "American British Museum" at all hours; others could visit the national collection free but only during the time it was officially open, a few hours a day a few days a week. Nothing came of Barnum's project, but just as he had popularized the museum idea before the war, so his conception of a museum as a joint private-public philanthropic venture, serving educational, aesthetic, and utilitarian purposes, prefigured museum developments after the war.[12]

While the war was still going on, the critic James Jackson Jarves pointed out that extraordinary prosperity in the North had made art fashionable. "Private galleries are becoming almost as common as private stables," he wrote in 1863. More significant, in Jarves's opinion, was "the zeal" he detected in a number of communities "to found institutions for the promotion of [art's] culture and the conservation of its works, foreign or national." The decade and a half after 1865 saw the founding of some of America's leading museums: the American Museum of Natural History (1869) and Metropolitan Museum of Art (1870) in New York, Boston Museum of Fine Arts (1870), Philadelphia Museum of Art (1876), Art Institute of Chicago (1879), and Cincinnati Art Museum (1881). These all were nonprofit institutions without the money-making appendage Barnum proposed. Their founders were convinced, like Jarves, that "the only security of the republic lies in the enlarged culture of all classes of citizens" and agreed that the real object of a museum was to develop public appreciation of the meaning and purpose of art. In a characteristically American way, however, many of the founders also felt obliged to justify the institutions on practical grounds,

---

[12] Neil Harris: *Humbug, The Art of P. T. Barnum* (Boston, Toronto, 1973), pp. 173–80; Barnum helped establish a museum of natural history at Tufts University.

e.g., their value for industrial design. By exposing students and artisans to masterpieces (if only in the form of reproductions and casts), museum collections would improve industrial design, elevate popular taste, and perhaps arouse native genius. Moreover, a good public art collection would attract tourists to a city. "Yes," said William C. Prime, vice-president of the Metropolitan Museum of Art, "there is *money* in teaching people to love beautiful objects."[13]

As a general rule, the museums were chartered corporations, privately managed, but with a few public representatives included on the self-perpetuating boards of trustees. Most of their support came from subscriptions, gifts, and bequests from private individuals, but they also received varying amounts of public assistance. In the early 1870s, even under the double handicap of the Boston fire and the panic of 1873, Boston's Museum of Fine Arts conducted a successful fund drive for money to erect an inexpensive fireproof building on a site contributed by the city (which had received the land from a donor with the stipulation it be used for a park or museum). Gifts and bequests enabled the Boston Museum to get through its first twenty years without spending for collections.[14] Trustees of the Metropolitan Museum boasted in 1879 that its collections had been attained "without a dollar of public aid," but the Metropolitan, like the American Museum of Natural History, received $15,000 (later $25,000) a year from the city government for rent and operating expenses. The city also provided both institutions with "suitable fireproof" buildings in Central Park.[15]

Hardworking trustees and officers, contributing heavily in time and, in some cases, money, tended to think of the museums as belonging to them and resented public interference in internal management. In New York City the question of opening the

[13] James Jackson Jarves: "Art in America, Its Condition and Prospects," *The Fine Arts Quarterly Review*, vol. I (1863), pp. 399–400; Neil Harris: "The Gilded Age Revisited: Boston and the Museum Movement," *American Quarterly*, vol. XIV (1962), pp. 553–55, 561; Prime quoted by Daniel Fox: *Engines of Culture, Philanthropy and Art Museums* (Madison, Wis., 1963), p. 16.

[14] Helen Lefkowitz Horowitz: *Culture and the City, Cultural Philanthropy in Chicago from the 1880s to 1917* (Lexington, Ky., 1976), p. 23; Harris, "The Gilded Age Revisited," pp. 549, 559.

[15] Leo Lerman: *The Museum, One Hundred Years of the Metropolitan Museum of Art* (New York, 1969), p. 44; Tomkins: *Merchants and Masterpieces*, p. 45.

Metropolitan and the Museum of Natural History on Sunday—a problem as old as the museums but especially heated in the late 1880s and early 1890s—raised issues of control as well as religion, morality, and underlying purpose of the institutions. Press and public clamored for Sunday openings so that workmen and their families could derive the promised benefits from the exhibits; public authorities threatened to reduce subsidies if the doors remained closed; Presbyterians, Methodists, and other religious groups condemned the threatened desecration of the "American Sabbath"; trustees found themselves divided on the rectitude, costs, and possible consequences of opening—or of staying closed. Morris K. Jesup, president of the Museum of Natural History, argued that opening would be costly because of added expense and loss of support from Sabbatarians. William C. Prime saw the issue as a threat to the power of the trustees. In 1885 he advised John Taylor Johnston, president of the Metropolitan:

> *Now* they think the Museum is a public institution, in the management of which the public has a voice. . . . They must be *forced* to think of it as a private institution. . . . They must stop thinking they support the Museum, and be compelled to see that *we* own and support the Museum and give it in pure charity for public education.

Prime resigned from the museum in 1891, when the board voted to open on Sunday afternoons. A disgruntled donor revoked proposed bequests of $50,000 each to the Metropolitan and the Museum of Natural History, but both institutions received substantial increases in the annual appropriation from the city government.[16]

Libraries, like museums, looked to both taxpayers and philanthropists for support. The catalyst in the founding of the Boston Public Library was Joshua Bates's offer of $50,000 for the purchase of books "if a building be provided and care taken of them." After the city met Bates's conditions, scarcely a year passed without additions to the library's collections and endowment by other donors. Before the fire of 1871 Chicago had no

---

[16] Tomkins: *Merchants and Masterpieces*, pp. 75–79 (Prime quotation on p. 77); see also Lerman: *The Museum*, pp. 69–71, and Winifred E. Howe: *A History of the Metropolitan Museum of Art* (2 vols., New York, 1913), vol. I, pp. 236–46.

public library; after the fire, to secure a home for the books and a use for the money sent by English sympathizers, the Illinois legislature passed an act allowing Chicago to establish a public library and to levy taxes to maintain it. Even in the 1870s free public libraries were scarce. A survey conducted by the federal Bureau of Education in 1875 listed more than 3,600 subscription, college, society, institutional, and professional libraries but found fewer than 350 in the country as a whole that were open to the general public without charge. Most of these were in New England and the older Midwest.[17]

Aside from considerations of expense, there were few objections to founding or assisting free libraries except prejudice against novel reading in general and "blood-and-thunder" stories in particular. Advocates disposed of the latter objections by asserting that librarians could and should exercise "reasonable censorship" in keeping sensational and trivial works off the shelves. On the positive side, the point was often made that libraries established and maintained on the same principles as free public schools were "the people's colleges," fulfilling for all the benefits that college libraries conferred on the fortunate few. "Unlike all other public charities," declared J. P. Quincy of Boston, "a free public library, serving rich and poor, is equally generous to those who have and those who lack." Best of all, libraries fostered self-development and self-help. "The fundamental advantage of a library," said Andrew Carnegie, "is that it gives nothing for nothing. Youths must acquire knowledge themselves."[18]

In his autobiography, Carnegie spoke with pride of an ancestor who was a "library-founding weaver"; as a "working boy, although not bound," he had successfully asserted his right to free use of a library for apprentices. As the recorder of Carnegie's philanthropies has pointed out, he did not give libraries. "He gave money for the erection of library buildings. The community receiving the gift for a building agreed to maintain from tax funds a free public library." Carnegie's first gift for this purpose was offered in 1879 to his birthplace, Dunfermline, Scotland. The community accepted the offer in 1880, and Carnegie and his

[17] United States Bureau of Education: *Public Libraries in the United States of America* (Washington, D.C., 1876), pp. 799, 863–64, 894.

[18] *Ibid.*, pp. 393–94, 402; *Autobiography of Andrew Carnegie* (Boston and New York, 1920), p. 47.

mother were present when the cornerstone of the building was laid in 1881. Over the next twenty-five years Carnegie gave $56,000,000 to build 2,500 library buildings in the United States, Canada, Great Britain and Ireland, the West Indies, Australia and New Zealand, South Africa, and islands as remote as Fiji and the Seychelles. He based the size of his gift on the population of the community, ordinarily giving $2 per capita and asking the city or town to pledge an annual appropriation for books and maintenance amounting to 10 percent of the gift. Thus, a town of 10,000 would receive $20,000 for a building and be expected to appropriate $2,000 a year for its support. He did not require the libraries to bear his name, but about one-third of them were called Carnegie libraries.[19]

Most of the libraries and his other major benefactions were still in the future in 1889, when Carnegie published two articles in the *North American Review*, "Wealth" in the June issue, "The Best Fields for Philanthropy" in December. For twenty-five years before 1889 he had been making private resolutions about the disposition of his own fortune. In 1868, when he was a rich young man of thirty-three, he had proposed, in a private memorandum, to limit his income to $50,000 a year, spend the surplus on benevolence, and, as soon as possible, "cast business aside forever except for others. . . . To continue much longer overwhelmed by business cares and with most of my thoughts wholly upon the way to make more money in the shortest time, must degrade me beyond hope of recovery. I will resign business at thirty-five. . . ."[20]

Of course, Carnegie did not retire at thirty-five. He was several years older than that when he embarked on a new career as a steelmaker. If he did not allow himself to become overwhelmed by business or devote his thoughts entirely to making money, he gave it enough serious attention and pushed hard enough so that by 1889 his income had grown from $50,000 to $1,850,000 a year.

"Wealth," which after publication in England became known as "The Gospel of Wealth," expresses or advocates not the worship of money or wealth but rather the idolization of persons, like

---

[19] Carnegie: *Autobiography*, p. 48; Robert M. Lester: *Forty Years of Carnegie Giving* (New York, 1941), pp. 92–93; Joseph Frazier Wall: *Andrew Carnegie* (New York, 1970), pp. 38, 106–07, 818.

[20] Wall: *Andrew Carnegie*, pp. 812–13; Burton J. Hendrick: *The Life of Andrew Carnegie* (2 vols., Garden City, N.Y., 1932), vol. I, p. 147.

Carnegie himself, who proved successful in amassing it in vast quantities. Carnegie maintained that such persons owed their success not to God, as Rockefeller and Dodge would have said, but to natural superiority in the economic struggle. Carnegie insisted that they must be left free to accumulate wealth according to the laws of economics, but having made or taken their pile, they had an obligation to dispose of it, during their lifetimes, for the benefit of society.[21]

In "The Best Fields for Philanthropy" Carnegie cited the successful lawsuit breaking Samuel Tilden's will as a lesson "for the rich who only bequeath." Even a lawyer as skilled as Tilden and with the expert legal advice available to him could not be sure that the benevolent intention expressed in his will (establishment of a free public library in New York City) would be carried out after his death. Carnegie's advice to millionaires who chose the better path of administering surplus wealth during their own lifetimes was to use the money to promote the "permanent good" of the community from which it had been gathered. They must avoid giving for purposes that had "a degrading, pauperizing tendency upon . . . recipients" and be on the alert for projects that would "stimulate the best and most aspiring poor of the community to further efforts for their own improvement." Among the causes Carnegie recommended to men of wealth as worthy of their generosity were colleges and universities, technological institutes, medical schools and medical research, astronomical and scientific investigations, and libraries, museums, music halls, parks, and other civic improvements. These were not pauperizing doles, but "ladders upon which the aspiring can rise."[22]

Carnegie's creed, although generally reflecting and expressing late-nineteenth-century attitudes toward philanthropy and welfare, was outdated in its idealization of the "individual administrator of surplus wealth." People like Carnegie who amassed huge fortunes were more likely to be heads of efficient

---

[21] Andrew Carnegie: "Wealth," *North American Review*, vol. CXLVIII (1889), pp. 653–64.

[22] Andrew Carnegie: "The Best Fields for Philanthropy," *North American Review*, vol. CXLIX (1889), p. 685; on the Tilden will case see Alexander C. Flick: *Samuel Jones Tilden, A Study in Political Sagacity* (New York, 1939), pp. 514–17, and Harry Miller Lydenberg, "A History of the New York Public Library, Part IV (The Tilden Trust)," *Bulletin* of the New York Public Library, vol. XXI (1917), pp. 71–80.

organizations than individual entrepreneurs. As a businessman Carnegie took pride in his ability to choose able assistants who managed details of day-to-day operations without his constant attention. It was impossible for him, in disposing of his vast surplus, to devote the amount of personal time and attention to each gift that he recommended to others. Just as persons of modest means used the Associated Charities or some other organization, as almoner Carnegie needed a more impersonal and objective agent than his own or his secretary's judgment. John D. Rockefeller dealt with the problem forthrightly in 1901 when he urged: "Let us erect a foundation, a Trust, and engage directors who will make it a life work, to manage, with our cooperation, this business of benevolence properly and effectively."[23] Early in the twentieth century both Rockefeller and Carnegie delegated their major philanthropic decisions to general purpose foundations the trustees of which received only very general instructions from the donors.

The objects, if not the method, Carnegie endorsed continued to find favor with twentieth-century philanthropists. The underlying assumption, which he did not hesitate to put into plain language, was that the philanthropist's responsibility extended only to the "industrious and ambitious," those "most anxious and able to help themselves"; attempting to reach and help "the irreclaimably destitute, shiftless, and worthless," "the inert, lazy, and hopelessly-poor" was the province of the state.[24] This division of labor was as much a matter of necessity as of choice. Experience during and after the Civil War had repeatedly demonstrated that philanthropy lacked the resources to assist more than a fraction of those in need, whether soldiers, freedmen, or victims of disaster or depression. Pejorative language aside, and even if reluctant to assume the burden, the state had to bear major responsibility for social welfare.

By the end of the 1880s, philanthropy had come to be regarded mainly as a way of using surplus wealth. It could be wasted or spent foolishly, but the counsel of prudence was to apply it to productive purposes, treat it like an investment, put it into programs that would pay off. Carnegie scorned philan-

[23] John D. Rockefeller: *Random Reminiscences of Men and Events* (Garden City, N.Y., 1933), p. 188.
[24] Carnegie: "Best Fields for Philanthropy," pp. 685–86, 690.

thropic efforts to "help those who cannot help themselves" as worse than useless.[25]

John Howard, John Augustus, Dorothea Dix, and members of the Howard associations and the Can't Get Away Club had thought otherwise. So did Jane Addams, who opened Hull House the same year Carnegie published "Wealth." A later age calls helping those who cannot help themselves "advocacy." Whether deemed the worst or the best field of philanthropy, it is always open to those who have the heart and will to enter.

[25] *Ibid.*, p. 690.

Acknowledgments
and Bibliographical Note

Research on this volume began at the Huntington Library, San Marino, California; I completed the last chapter during a period of residence at the Rockefeller Foundation Study and Conference Center, Bellagio, Italy. In the intervening period, research and writing, although carried out in less idyllic surroundings, were greatly assisted by fellowships from the Social Science Research Council and the National Endowment for the Humanities and grants from the Development Fund, Graduate School, and College of the Humanities of the Ohio State University. I am grateful to these organizations and institutions for support and encouragement. I would also like to express appreciation for assistance given me by the staffs of the following libraries and archives at which the bulk of my research was conducted: Library of Congress, National Archives, Huntington Library, Widener and Houghton libraries, Harvard University, New York Public Library, New-York Historical Society, Ohio Historical Society, Duke University Library, University of North Carolina Library, Ohio State University Library, and the U.S. Army Chaplains Archives.

Helen Bloomfield, Richard Thomas, J. Mark Stewart, Calvin Ruskaup, and John Weaver rendered valuable editorial and research assistance. Particular thanks go to Theresa Hirgelt, Sandra Lyman, Renée Grimm, the office staff of the Ohio State University Department of History, and Mrs. Charles Ott, who typed drafts of the manuscript. Family and friends showed patience and forbearance during the time the study was in preparation.

Merle Curti's pioneering studies—"American Philanthropy and the National Character," *American Quarterly*, X (1958), 420–37; *American Philanthropy Abroad* (1963); and (with Roderick Nash)

Philanthropy in the Shaping of American Higher Education (1965)—were helpful in all parts of the work; so, too, were Gerald Grob, *Mental Institutions in America, Social Policy to 1875* (1973); Walter Trattner, *From Poor Law to Welfare State, A History of Social Welfare in America* (1974); James Leiby, *History of Social Welfare and Social Work in the United States* (1978); and *The Diary of George Templeton Strong*, edited by Allan Nevins and Milton Halsey Thomas (4 vols., 1952).

Among, and in addition to works cited in the footnotes, the following books and articles contain data relating to topics dealt with in the indicated chapters.

Prologue and Chapter 1

Barbara J. Berg, *The Remembered Gate, Origins of American Feminism, the Woman and the City* (1978); Clifford S. Griffin, *Their Brothers' Keepers, Moral Stewardship in the United States, 1800–1865* (1960); David Grimsted, ed., *Notions of the Americans, 1820–1860* (1970); Neil Harris, *Humbug, The Art of P. T. Barnum* (1973); Carroll Smith Rosenberg, *Religion and the Rise of the American City, The New York Mission Movement, 1812–1870* (1971); David J. Rothman, *The Discovery of the Asylum, Social Order and Disorder in the New Republic* (1971); Lee Soltow, *Men and Wealth in the United States, 1850–1870* (1975); Mary Bosworth Treudley, "The 'Benevolent Fair,' A Study of Charitable Organizations Among America Women in the First Third of the Nineteenth Century," *The Social Service Review*, vol. XIV (1940), pp. 509–22.

Chapters 2, 3, 4

Daniel Aaron, *The Unwritten War, American Writers and the Civil War* (1973); Linus P. Brockett and Mary C. Vaughn, *Women's Work in the Civil War* (1867); John A. Carpenter, "The New York International Relief Committee, A Chapter in the Diplomatic History of the Civil War," *The New-York Historical Society Quarterly*, vol. LVI (1972), pp. 239–52; Paul D. Escott, " 'The Cry of the Sufferers,' The Problem of Welfare in the Confederacy," *Civil War History*, vol. XXIII (1977), pp. 228–40; George M. Frederickson, *The Inner Civil War, Northern Intellectuals and the Crisis of the Union* (1965); Mary Elizabeth Massey, *Bonnet Brigades* (1966); William Quentin Maxwell, *Lincoln's Fifth Wheel, The Political History of the United States Sanitary Commission* (1956); Charles Capen McLaughlin, *The Papers of Frederick Law Olmsted* (1 vol. to date, 1978–   ), vol. I; James

H. Moorehead, *American Apocalypse, Yankee Protestants and the Civil War, 1860–1869* (1978); Allan Nevins, "The United States Sanitary Commission and Secretary Stanton," *Massachusetts Historical Society Proceedings*, vol. LXVII (1941–44), pp. 402–19; Laura Wood Roper, *FLO, A Biography of Frederick Law Olmsted* (1973); Holland Thompson: "Private Agencies of Relief," in Francis Trevelyan Miller, ed.: *The Photographic History of the Civil War* (10 vols., 1911), vol. VII, pp. 321–44.

Chapters 5 and 6

Refugees and "Contrabands": Gaines M. Foster, "U.S. Army Medical Department Participation in Disaster Relief" (unpublished monograph, Medical History Division, Department of the Army, Fort Detrick, Maryland, 1977); Eugene Genovese: *Roll, Jordan, Roll, The World the Slaves Made* (1974); Louis Gerteis, *From Contraband to Freedmen, Federal Policy Toward Southern Blacks, 1861–1865* (1973); Leon F. Litwack: *Been in the Storm So Long, The Aftermath of Slavery* (1979); Peyton McCrary: *Abraham Lincoln and Reconstruction, The Louisiana Experiment* (1978); Jay R. Mandle: *The Roots of Black Poverty, The Southern Plantation Economy After the Civil War* (1978); Mary Elizabeth Massey, *Refugee Life in the Confederacy* (1964); Cam Walker, "Corinth, The Story of a Contraband Camp," *Civil War History*, vol. XX (1974), pp. 5–22.

Freedmen's Bureau: Martin Abbott, *The Freedmen's Bureau in South Carolina* (1967); George R. Bentley, *A History of the Freedmen's Bureau* (1955); John A. Carpenter, *Sword and Olive Branch, Oliver Otis Howard* (1964); John Hope Franklin: *Reconstruction: After the Civil War* (1961); William S. McFeely, *Yankee Step Father, O. O. Howard and the Freedmen* (1968); Victoria Olds, "The Freedmen's Bureau as a Social Agency" (unpublished DSW dissertation, Columbia University, 1966); Carl R. Osthaus, *Freedmen, Philanthropy and Fraud, A History of the Freedmen's Savings Bank* (1976); Howard A. White, *The Freedmen's Bureau in Louisiana* (1970).

Education of Freedmen: Robert Stanley Bahney, "Generals and Negroes, Education of Negroes by the Union Army, 1861–1865" (unpublished Ph.D. dissertation, University of Michigan, 1965); John W. Blassingame, "The Union Army as an Educational Institution for Negroes, 1862–1865," *The Journal of Negro Education*, vol. XXXIV (1965), pp. 152–59; Richard B. Drake, "The American Missionary Association and the Southern Negro, 1861–1888" (unpublished Ph.D. dissertation, Emory University 1957); John Hope Franklin, *From Slavery to Freedom, A History of Negro Americans* (1974); James M. McPherson, *The Struggle for Equality, Abolitionists and the Negro in the Civil War and Reconstruction* (1964) and *The Abolitionist Legacy, from Reconstruction to the NAACP* (1975); Robert C. Morris, "Reading 'Riting and Reconstruction" (unpublished Ph.D. dissertation, University of Chicago, 1976); Willie Lee Rose, *Rehearsal for Reconstruction, The Port Royal Experiment* (1964); Henry Lee Swint, *The Northern Teacher in the South, 1862–1870* (1941).

Chapters 7, 8, 9

Daniel J. Boorstin, *The Americans, The Democratic Experience* (1973); Daniel Dorchester, *Christianity in the United States from the First Settlement to the Present Time* (1888); Foster Rhea Dulles, *The American Red Cross* (1950); Joseph M. Hawes, *Children in Urban Society, Juvenile Delinquency in Nineteenth Century America* (1971); Morton Keller, *Affairs of State, Public Life in Late Nineteenth Century America* (1977); Verl S. Lewis, "The Development of the Charity Organization Movement in the United States, 1875–1900" (unpublished Ph.D. dissertation, Western Reserve University, 1954); Blake McKelvey, *American Prisons, A History of Good Intentions* (1977); Robert M. Mennel, *Thorns and Thistles, Juvenile Delinquents in the United States, 1825–1940* (1973); Samuel Rezneck, "Distress, Relief, and Discontent in the United States During the Depression of 1873–78," *The Journal of Political Economy*, vol. LVIII (1950), pp. 494–512; Peter Romanofsky, ed.: *Social Service Organizations* (2 vols., 1978); Sheila M. Rothman, *Woman's Proper Place, A History of Changing Ideals and Practices, 1870 to the Present* (1978); William Rhinelander Stewart, *The Philanthropic Work of Josephine Shaw Lowell* (1911); Walter I. Trattner, "Louisa Lee Schuyler and the Founding of the State Charities Aid Association," *New-York Historical Association Quarterly*, vol. LI (1967), pp. 233–48; Joseph Frazer Wall, *Andrew Carnegie* (1970).

Index

Abbott, Edith, 192
Abbott, Lyman, 126, 127, 130, 204
abolitionists and antislavery societies, xi, xiv, 4, 15, 16, 17, 20, 129
Adams, Herbert Baxter, 203–4
Addams, Jane, 223
Agnew, Cornelius, 40, 43
Alcott, Abigail, 33
Allen, Julian, 96
almshouses, *see* poorhouses and almshouses
Alvord, John W., 110, 127, 129, 137, 140, 141
American Bible Society, 16, 80
American Board of Commissioners for Foreign Missions, 16, 22, 80
American Colonization Society, 17, 209
American Freedmen's Friend Society, 103
American Freedmen's Union Commission, 129, 130, 131, 133, 180, 212
American Home Missionary Society, 16
American Missionary Association, 16, 100–1, 102, 105, 107, 110, 127–33 *passim*, 211, 212 and *n.*
American National Red Cross, 197–8; *see also* Barton, Clara
American Social Science Association, 200, 205
American Society for Improvement of Penal and Reformatory Institutions, 28
American Sunday School Union, 16
American Tract Society, 16, 17, 131, 183
American Union Commission, 94, 129
Anderson, Martin B., 160

Andrew, John A., 152–3, 154
Anthony, Susan B., 180, 181 *n.*
antislavery societies, *see* abolitionists and antislavery societies
Armstrong, Samuel C., 213
Arnold, R. D., 96
Astor, William B., 22
Augustus, John, 29–30, 223
Austro-French War, 36–7

Bache, Alexander Dallas, 40, 50
Bacon, Leonard Woolsey, 208–9
Banks, Nathaniel, 91–2, 109
Barnes, Joseph K., 117
Barnum, P. T., 14–15, 65, 145, 215–16
Barton, Clara, 65–9 *passim*, 145, 197–8
Bates, Joshua, 218
Beecher, Henry Ward, 32
Bellows, Henry W., xii, 33, 36, 37, 38, 182, 198, 204; and Freedmen's Bureau, 113, 118; and Sanitary Commission, 38–9, 39–40, 42–51 *passim*, 56, 60–1, 70, 146, 148–9
Benezet, Anthony, xi
Bennett, James Gordon, 199, 201
Bentley, George R., 141
Bergh, Henry, 183–4
Bickerdyke, Mary Ann, 148
Binney, Horace, Jr., 40
Bishop, Nathan, 123
blacks, *see* Negroes
blind, care and education of, 24, 27, 168–71
Blondin, Charles, 11
Boardman, W. E., 57
Bonner, Robert, 64
Booth, William A., 110

229

Robert H. Bremner was born in Brunswick, Ohio, in 1917. He took his B.A. from Baldwin-Wallace College in 1938 and his M.A. and Ph.D. from Ohio State University in 1939 and 1943, respectively. Since 1946 he has been on the faculty of Ohio State University, where he is now Professor of History. He is the author of *From the Depths, The Discovery of Poverty in the United States* (1956), and *American Philanthropy* (1960), and the editor of *Children and Youth in America, A Documentary History* (2 vols., 1970, 1974). He lives with his wife and children in Worthington, Ohio.

A NOTE ON THE TYPE

The text of this book was set on the Linotype in a new face
called Primer, designed by Rudolph Ruzicka, earlier responsible for the design of Fairfield and Fairfield Medium,
Linotype faces whose virtues have for some time now been
accorded wide recognition.

This book was composed by The Maryland Linotype Com-
position Company, Inc., Baltimore, Maryland, and printed
and bound by American Book–Stratford Press, Saddle
Brook, New Jersey.

Typography and binding based on designs by

WARREN CHAPPELL